The Right to Bear Arms

FORTHCOMING BOOKS IN AMERICA'S FREEDOMS
Donald Grier Stephenson Jr., Series Editor

Equal Protection of the Laws, Francis Graham Lee
Freedom of Association, Robert J. Bresler
Freedom of Speech, Ken I. Kersch
Protection against Cruel and Unusual Punishment, Joseph A. Melusky and Keith A. Pesto
Religious Freedom, Melvin I. Urofsky
Right to Counsel and Protection against Self-Incrimination, John B. Taylor
Right to Privacy, Richard A. Glenn
Right to Property, Polly J. Price

The Right to Bear Arms

Rights and Liberties under the Law

Robert J. Spitzer

ABC·CLIO

Santa Barbara, California • Denver, Colorado • Oxford, England

Copyright © 2001 by Robert J. Spitzer

All rights reserved. No part of this publication may be reproduced, stored in a retrieval system, or transmitted, in any form or by any means, electronic, mechanical, photocopying, recording, or otherwise, except for the inclusion of brief quotations in a review, without prior permission in writing from the publishers.

Library of Congress Cataloging-in-Publication Data
Spitzer, Robert J., 1953–
  The right to bear arms : rights and liberties under the law / Robert J. Spitzer.
      p.   cm. — (America's freedoms)
  Includes bibliographical references.
  ISBN 1-57607-347-5 (hardcover : alk. paper)
   1. Firearms—Law and legislation—United States.   2. Constitutional history—United States.   I. Title.   II. Series.
KF3941 .S68 2001
344.73'0533—dc21

2001005143

This book is also available on the World Wide Web as an e-book. Visit www.abc-clio.com for details.

07 06 05 04 03 02 01 10 9 8 7 6 5 4 3 2 1

ABC-CLIO, Inc.
130 Cremona Drive, P.O. Box 1911
Santa Barbara, California 93116-1911
This book is printed on acid-free paper.
Manufactured in the United States of America

To Jinny, Teresa, Skye, and Alexis

Contents

Series Foreword ... ix
Preface and Acknowledgments ... xix

1 **Introduction** ... 1
   What the Second Amendment Says, 6
   Outline of the Book, 9
   References and Further Reading, 12

2 **Origins** ... 13
   The British Heritage, 13
   The Colonial Experience, 15
   The Constitution, 20
   The Federalist-Antifederalist Debate, 23
   The Bill of Rights, 24
   The Decline of the Old Militia System, 28
   Supreme Court Rulings, 32
   Other Court Rulings, 38
   The Textbook View, 42
   Conclusion, 42
   References and Further Reading, 43

3 **Twentieth-Century Issues** ... 49
   Alternate Views, 51
   The "Right of Revolution," 59

Spreading Arguments in the Media, 62
Seeking Shelter under the Fourteenth Amendment, 64
The Second Amendment and Politics, 71
Rights Talk, 81
Conclusion, 84
References and Further Reading, 85

4   **The Twenty-first Century**   89

The Brady Law, the Assault Weapons Ban, and Beyond, 90
The New Militia Movement, 102
Recent Court Actions, 110
Escalating Second Amendment Rhetoric, 115
Conclusion, 126
References and Further Reading, 127

5   **Key People, Cases, and Events**   131

6   **Documents**   155

The Calling Forth Act of 1792, 156
The Uniform Militia Act of 1792, 159
United States v. Cruikshank (1876), 165
Presser v. Illinois (1886), 189
United States v. Miller (1939), 200
Quilici v. Village of Morton Grove (1982), 206
State Right-to-Bear-Arms Provisions, 218
Major Party Platforms on Gun Control, 227

Chronology   235
Table of Cases   243
Annotated Bibliography   247
Index   257
About the Author   263

Series Foreword

America's Freedoms promises a series of books that address the origin, development, meaning, and future of the nation's fundamental liberties, as well as the individuals, circumstances, and events that have shaped them. These freedoms are chiefly enshrined explicitly or implicitly in the Bill of Rights and other amendments to the Constitution of the United States and have much to do with the quality of life Americans enjoy. Without them, America would be a far different place in which to live. Oddly enough, however, the Constitution was drafted and signed in Philadelphia in 1787 without a bill of rights. That was an afterthought, emerging only after a debate among the foremost political minds of the day.

At the time, Thomas Jefferson was in France on a diplomatic mission. Upon receiving a copy of the proposed Constitution from his friend James Madison, who had helped write the document, Jefferson let him know as fast as the slow sailing-ship mails of the day allowed that the new plan of government suffered one major defect—it lacked a bill of rights. This, Jefferson argued, "is what the people are entitled to against every government on earth." Madison should not have been surprised at Jefferson's reaction. The Declaration of Independence of 1776 had largely been Jefferson's handiwork, including its core statement of principle:

> We hold these truths to be self-evident, that all men are created equal, that they are endowed by their Creator with certain unalienable

Rights, that among these are Life, Liberty, and the pursuit of Happiness. That to secure these rights, Governments are instituted among Men, deriving their just powers from the consent of the governed.

Jefferson rejected the conclusion of many of the framers that the Constitution's design—a system of both separation of powers among the legislative, executive, and judicial branches, and a federal division of powers between national and state governments—would safeguard liberty. Even when combined with elections, he believed strongly that such structural checks would fall short.

Jefferson and other critics of the proposed Constitution ultimately had their way. In one of the first items of business in the First Congress in 1789, Madison, as a member of the House of Representatives from Virginia, introduced amendments to protect liberty. Ten were ratified by 1791 and have become known as the Bill of Rights.

America's Bill of Rights reflects the founding generation's understanding of the necessary link between personal freedom and representative government, as well as their experience with threats to liberty. The First Amendment protects expression—in speech, press, assembly, petition, and religion—and guards against a union of church and state. The Second Amendment secures liberty against national tyranny by affirming the self-defense of the states. Members of state-authorized local militia—citizens primarily, soldiers occasionally—retained a right to bear arms. The ban in the Third Amendment on forcibly quartering troops in houses reflects the emphasis the framers placed on the integrity and sanctity of the home.

Other provisions in the Fourth, Fifth, Sixth, Seventh, and Eighth amendments safeguard freedom by setting forth standards that government must follow in administering the law, especially regarding persons accused of crimes. The framers knew firsthand the dangers that government-as-prosecutor could pose to liberty.

Even today, authoritarian regimes in other lands routinely use the tools of law enforcement—arrests, searches, detentions, as well as trials—to squelch peaceful political opposition. Limits in the Bill of Rights on crime-fighting powers thus help maintain democracy by demanding a high level of legal scrutiny of the government's practices.

In addition, one clause in the Fifth Amendment forbids the taking of private property for public use without paying the owner just compensation and thereby limits the power of eminent domain, the authority to seize a person's property. Along with taxation and conscription, eminent domain is one of the most awesome powers any government can possess.

The Ninth Amendment makes sure that the listing of some rights does not imply that others necessarily have been abandoned. If the Ninth offered reassurances to the people, the Tenth Amendment was designed to reassure the states that they or the people retained those powers not delegated to the national government. Today, the Tenth is a remainder of the integral role states play in the federal plan of union that the Constitution ordained.

Despite this legacy of freedom, however, we Americans today sometimes wonder about the origin, development, meaning, and future of our liberties. This concern is entirely understandable, because liberty is central to the idea of what it means *to be American*. In this way, the United States stands apart from virtually every other nation on earth. Other countries typically define their national identities through a common ethnicity, origin, ancestral bond, religion, or history. But none of these accounts for the American identity. In terms of ethnicity, ancestry, and religion, the United States is the most diverse place on earth. From the beginning, America has been a land of immigrants. Neither is there a single historical experience to which all current citizens can directly relate: someone who arrived a decade ago from, say, southeast Asia and was naturalized as a citizen only last year is just as much an American as someone whose forebears served in General George Washington's army at Valley Forge during the American War of Independence (1776–1783). In religious as in political affairs, the United States has been a beacon to those suffering oppression abroad: "the last, best hope of earth," Abraham Lincoln said. So, the American identity is ideological. It consists of faith in the value and importance of liberty for each individual.

Nonetheless, a longstanding consensus among Americans on the *principle* that individual liberty is essential, highly prized, and widely shared hardly assures agreement about liberty *in practice*. This is because the concept of liberty, as it has developed in the United States, has several dimensions.

First, there is an unavoidable tension between liberty and restraint. Liberty means freedom: we say that a person has a "right" to do this or that. But that *right* is meaningless unless there is a corresponding *duty* on the part of others (such as police officers and elected officials) not to interfere. Thus, protection of the liberty of one person necessarily involves restraints imposed on someone else. This is why we speak of a *civil* right or a *civil* liberty: it is a claim on the behavior of another that is enforceable through the legal process. Moreover, some degree of order (restrictions on the behavior of all) is necessary if everyone's liberties are to be protected. Just as too much order crushes freedom, too little invites social chaos that also threatens freedom. Determining the proper balance between freedom and order, however, is more easily sought than found. "To make a government requires no great prudence," declared English statesman and political philosopher Edmund Burke in 1790. "Settle the seat of power; teach obedience; and the work is done. To give freedom is still more easy. It is not necessary to guide; it only requires to let go the rein. But to form a *free government;* that is, to temper together these opposite elements of liberty and restraint in one consistent work, requires much thought; deep reflection; a sagacious, powerful, and combining mind."

Second, the Constitution does not define the freedoms that it protects. Chief Justice John Marshall once acknowledged that the Constitution was a document "of enumeration, and not of definition." There are, for example, lists of the powers of Congress in Article I, or the rights of individuals in the Bill of Rights, but those powers and limitations are not explained. What is the "freedom of speech" that the First Amendment guarantees? What are "unreasonable searches and seizures" that are proscribed by the Fourth Amendment? What is the "due process of law" secured by both the Fifth and Fourteenth Amendments? Reasonable people, all of whom favor individual liberty, can arrive at very different answers to these questions.

A third dimension—breadth—is closely related to the second. How widely shared is a particular freedom? Consider voting, for example. One could write a political history of the United States by cataloging the efforts to extend the vote or franchise to groups such as women and nonwhites that had been previously excluded. Or, consider the First Amendment's freedom of speech. Does it include the expression of *all* points of view or merely *some?* Does the same amendment's protection of the "free exercise of religion" include all faiths, even obscure ones that may seem weird or even irritating? At different times questions like these have yielded different answers.

Similarly, the historical record contains notorious lapses. Despite all the safeguards that are supposed to shore up freedom's foundations, constitutional protections have sometimes been worth the least when they have been desperately needed. In our history the most frequent and often the most serious threats to freedom have come not from people intent on throwing the Bill of Rights away outright, but from well-meaning people who find the Bill of Rights a temporary bother, standing in the way of some objective they want to reach.

There is also a question that dates to the very beginning of American government under the Constitution. Does the Constitution protect rights not spelled out in, or fairly implied by, the words of the document? The answer to that question largely depends on what a person concludes about the source of rights. One tradition, reflected in the Declaration of Independence, asserts that rights predate government and that government's chief duty is to protect the rights that everyone naturally possesses. Thus, if the Constitution is read as a document designed, among other things, to protect liberty, then protected liberties are not limited to those in the text of the Constitution but may also be derived from experience, for example, or from one's assessment of the requirements of a free society. This tradition places a lot of discretion in the hands of judges, because in the American political system, it is largely the judiciary that decides what the Constitution means. Partly due to this dynamic, a competing tradition looks to the text of the Constitution, as well as to statutes passed consistent with the Constitution, as a *complete* code of law containing *all* the liberties that Americans possess. Judges, therefore, are not free to go outside the text to "discover" rights that the people, through the process of lawmaking and constitutional amendment, have not declared. Doing so is undemocratic because it bypasses "rule by the people." The tension between these two ways of thinking explains the ongoing debate about a right to privacy, itself nowhere mentioned in the words of the Constitution. "I like my privacy as well as the next one," once admitted Justice Hugo Black, "but I am nevertheless compelled to admit that government has a right to invade it unless prohibited by some specific constitutional provision." Otherwise, he said, judges are forced "to determine what is or is not constitutional on the basis of their own appraisal of what laws are unwise or unnecessary." Black thought that was the job of elected legislators who would answer to the people.

Fifth, it is often forgotten that at the outset, and for many years afterward, the Bill of Rights applied only to the national government, not to the states. Except for a very few restrictions, such as those in section 10 of Article I in the main body of the Constitution, which expressly limited state power, states were restrained only by their individual constitutions and state laws, not by the U.S. Bill of Rights. So, Pennsylvania or any other state, for example, could shut down a newspaper or barricade the doors of a church without violating the First Amendment. For many in the founding generation, the new central government loomed as a colossus that might threaten liberty. Few at that time thought that individual freedom needed *national* protection against *state* invasions of the rights of the people.

The first step in removing this double standard came with ratification of the Fourteenth Amendment after the Civil War in 1868. Section one contained majestic, but undefined, checks on states: "*No State* shall make or enforce any law which shall abridge the privileges or immunities of citizens of the United States; nor shall any *State* deprive any person of life, liberty, or property, without due process of law; nor deny to any person within in its jurisdiction the equal protections of the laws" (emphasis added). Such vague language begged for interpretation. In a series of cases mainly between 1920 and 1968, the Supreme Court construed the Fourteenth Amendment to include within its meaning almost every provision of the Bill of Rights. This process of "incorporation" (applying the Bill of Rights to the states by way of the Fourteenth Amendment) was the second step in eliminating the double standard of 1791. State and local governments became bound by the same restrictions that had applied all along to the national government. The consequences of this development scarcely can be exaggerated because most governmental action in the United States is the work of state and local governments. For instance, ordinary citizens are far more likely to encounter a local police officer than an agent of the Federal Bureau of Investigation or the Secret Service.

A sixth dimension reflects an irony. A society premised on individual freedom assumes not only the worth of each person but citizens capable of rational thought, considered judgment, and measured actions. Otherwise democratic government would be futile. Yet, we lodge the most important freedoms in the

Constitution precisely because we want to give those freedoms extra protection. "The very purpose of a Bill of Rights was to ... place [certain subjects] beyond the reach of majorities and officials and to establish them as legal principles to be applied by the courts," explained Justice Robert H. Jackson. "One's right to life, liberty, and property, to free speech, a free press, freedom of worship and assembly, and other fundamental rights may not be submitted to vote; they depend on the outcome of no elections." Jackson referred to a hard lesson learned from experience: basic rights require extra protection because they are fragile. On occasion, people have been willing to violate the freedoms of others. That reality demanded a written constitution.

This irony reflects the changing nature of a bill of rights in history. Americans did not invent the idea of a bill of rights in 1791. Instead it draws from and was inspired by colonial documents such as the Pennsylvania colony's Charter of Liberties (1701) and the English Bill of Rights (1689), Petition of Right (1628), and Magna Carta (1215). However, these early and often unsuccessful attempts to limit government power were devices to protect the many (the people) from the few (the English Crown). With the emergence of democratic political systems in the eighteenth century, however, political power shifted from the few to the many. The right to rule belonged to the person who received the most votes in an election, not necessarily to the first-born, the wealthiest, or the most physically powerful. So the focus of a bill of rights had to shift too. No longer was it designed to shelter the majority from the minority, but to shelter the minority from the majority. "Wherever the real power in a Government lies, there is the danger of oppression," commented Madison in his exchange of letters with Jefferson in 1788. "In our Government, the real power lies in the majority of the Community, and the invasion of private rights is *chiefly* to be apprehended, not from acts of government contrary to the sense of its constituents, but from acts in which the Government is the mere instrument of the major number of the Constituents."

Americans, however, do deserve credit for having discovered a way to enforce a bill of rights. Without an enforcement mechanism, a bill of rights is no more than a list of aspirations: standards to aim for, but with no redress other than violent protest or revolution. Indeed this had been the experience in England with which the framers were thoroughly familiar. Thanks to judicial review—the authority courts in the United States possess to invalidate actions taken by the other branches of government, which, in the judges' view, conflict with the Constitution—the provisions in the Bill of Rights and other constitutionally protected liberties became judicially enforceable.

Judicial review was a tradition that was beginning to emerge in the states on a small scale in the 1780s and 1790s and that would blossom in the U.S. Supreme Court in the nineteenth and twentieth centuries. "In the arguments in favor of a declaration of rights," Jefferson presciently told Madison in the late winter of 1789 after the Constitution had been ratified, "you omit one which has great weight with me, the legal check which it puts into the hands of the judiciary." This is the reason why each of the volumes in this series focuses extensively on judicial decisions. Liberties have largely been defined by judges in the context of deciding cases in situations where individuals thought the power of government extended too far.

Designed to help democracy protect itself, the Constitution ultimately needs the support of those—the majority—who endure its restraints. Without sufficient support among the people, its freedoms rest on a weak foundation. My earnest hope is that this series will offer Americans a renewed appreciation and understanding of their heritage of liberty.

Donald Grier Stephenson Jr.

Preface and Acknowledgments

This book will examine what many would consider to be the most politically charged of all the constitutional amendments—the Second Amendment. Added to the Constitution in 1791 as part of the package of ten amendments composing the Bill of Rights, the Second Amendment says: "A well regulated Militia, being necessary to the security of a free State, the right of the people to keep and bear Arms, shall not be infringed."

The political controversy surrounding this amendment is, ironically, not the product of thousands, or even hundreds, of lawsuits or other legal challenges percolating through the courts. This contrasts sharply with other parts of the Bill of Rights, such as free speech, religious freedom, and right to counsel, which have generated literally thousands of court cases and a huge body of constitutional interpretation and writing. By comparison, relatively few Second Amendment–based court cases have made their way through the courts. A handful of key court cases have set out the meaning of this amendment, and they are of course discussed in this book. But, to add to the irony surrounding the constitutional law of the Second Amendment, these few cases are usually ignored in the intense political struggle over gun control, or, if mentioned at all, their meaning is distorted. Despite this fact, the amendment is often cited, mostly by opponents of gun control, as a kind of political talisman or symbol of what is vaguely but vehemently labeled *gun rights*. The frequent invocation of Second Amendment rights in the ongoing U.S. political debate over gun control usually bears no relationship to the actual rights established in this amendment and by the courts. Furthermore, the actual constitutional and legal rights established by the Second Amendment have virtually no connection with the continuing political and policy debate over the extent to which guns should or should not be regulated in the United States. Why, then, is the Second Amendment banner so often raised in the U.S. gun debate?

One purpose of this book will be to answer this paradoxical, but important, question. A second purpose is to provide a useful and specific example of how one determines the meaning of a provision of the Constitution. This is done by drawing on history, the opinions and intentions of those who shaped and wrote the Second Amendment, the application and evolution of this right from the beginnings of the United States up to the present time, and the views expressed by the courts. A third purpose of this book is to compare the intended and applied meaning of the Second Amendment with the many, varied views of this amendment that have been expressed in the last few decades. The temptation to use, and even distort, the Constitution for political purposes, is great. It is thus very important in a book such as this to distinguish between that which is true and that which is myth.

In addition, the gun issue is one that provokes no minor hysteria. Exaggerated claims and heated debate are as likely to be observed in the gun control debate as in few other political subjects. Unfortunately, some of the writings on this subject are overtaken by this hysteria, a fact that makes it more difficult to identify what is true, what is plausible, and what is simply false. It also causes confusion between the empirical (what is) and the normative (what ought to be). The concern of this book is with the former, not the latter. I also note that, as of this writing, the U.S. Fifth Circuit Court of Appeals is still considering the case of *U.S. v. Emerson*, in which a lower court judge ruled, contrary to every federal court ruling from 1876 to the present, in support of an individualist interpretation of the Second Amendment. One cannot predict what the fifth Circuit will do, nor whether the case will make its way to the Supreme Court.

My own interest in constitutional interpretation, the Second Amendment, and the broader issue of gun control extends back nearly twenty years. After completing a book chapter on the gun control issue for an edited book on controversial social issues (Tatalovich and Daynes 1988), I continued to study and write on various aspects of the gun control debate. This eventually led to my own book on the subject (Spitzer 1998), first published in 1995, which included a brief analysis of the Second Amendment. In addition, I have studied and written on other elements of constitutional law and meaning, primarily in the area of presidential power. This research has helped me place writings on the Second Amendment into the broader context of how one goes about understanding the meaning of the Constitution. As for the Second Amerendment, I have contemplated the idea of writing a book devoted solely to this subject for several years but did not follow through with that idea until now.

For this reason, I am very grateful to ABC-CLIO for the opportunity to contribute to its substantial and respected body of writings on law-related subjects. In particular, I am indebted to ABC-CLIO's America's Freedoms series editor, Donald Grier Stephenson, to senior acquisitions editor Alicia Merritt, and to senior production editor Melanie Stafford. They have provided thoughtful and productive guidance, advice, and help on this project.

In addition, I would like to thank and acknowledge Jerry O'Callaghan, Michael Dorf, Deb Dintino, Jinny Spitzer, Skye Wilson, Jason Popa, Melissa and Aaron Mitchell, Shannon Long, and Alexis Long. And to Teresa Wilson, I extend all of my love, devotion, and admiration.

Robert J. Spitzer
SUNY Cortland

1

INTRODUCTION

On April 20, 1999, two high school boys shattered the relative security and placidity of their public school, Columbine High, located in Littleton, Colorado, when they brought four guns to school and began shooting. When they were done, twelve students had been killed in the space of less than fifteen minutes, and one teacher was mortally wounded (he bled to death in the library while waiting for help to arrive). Twenty-three others were wounded. Eighteen-year-old Eric Harris and seventeen-year-old Dylan Klebold then turned the guns on themselves.

The guns had been purchased on their behalf in 1998 by Klebold's eighteen-year-old senior prom date and friend, Robyn Anderson, who purchased two shotguns and a 9-mm Hi-Point carbine for them at the Tanner Gun Show in nearby Denver. They supplied the money; she supplied the identification. At the time of Anderson's purchases, neither boy was old enough to buy the guns (Harris was still seventeen at the time). The fourth gun, a TEC-DC9 semiautomatic pistol, was provided to them later by a friend, twenty-two-year-old Mark Edward Manes, who bought the gun at a different gun show and then resold it to the boys for $500 (Olinger 2000). All four of the gun show purchases were conducted by private sellers exempted from background check requirements—the so-called gun show loophole that allows sales at gun shows by nonlicensed dealers to be conducted without checks or waiting periods. When Anderson purchased the guns on behalf of the boys, she was acting as a "straw buyer," a practice outlawed in some states, but not in Colorado. Repeated efforts to close the gun show loophole were defeated in the Colorado legislature, although a statewide referendum on the measure won approval by a wide margin in November 2000. (Oregon also adopted by referendum a measure to close the gun show loophole in the 2000 election.) A similar bill, along with other measures to strengthen federal gun laws, passed in the U.S. Senate in 1999 but failed in the House of Representatives, and the measure then died in conference committee, despite widespread public support for the changes and public outrage over these and other school killings.

The familiar national gun debate underscores the uniquely strong attachment of the United States to the gun, and the unique stigma related to that attachment. As critics here and abroad often note, the United States consistently maintains the highest per capita rate of gun deaths of any industrialized nation. A United Nations study comparing firearms deaths in forty-nine nations for 1997 found that the United States led the way with 13.7 gun deaths per 100,000 people, followed by Canada at 4.08 per 100,000; Australia at 3.05; Sweden at 2.31; Germany at 1.47; Spain at 1.01; the United Kingdom at 0.57; Vietnam at 0.18; and Japan at 0.07 ("Primer" 1999). Gun control supporters cite such comparisons to buttress their belief that the strict gun laws in these nations help drive down gun deaths, whereas relatively weak gun laws in the United States open the door to the high death rate. Control opponents counter that the higher gun death rate has mostly to do with cultural differences that cannot be legislated away and that these simple comparisons do not take into account the positive reasons for lawful gun possession.

People on all sides of the national gun control debate have deplored the Columbine massacre and other senseless killings. No one suggested that Harris and Klebold were exercising their Second Amendment rights—the oft-quoted right to bear arms. Yet public debate over what, if anything, to do about the nation's uneven gun laws is laced with references to this part of the Bill of Rights. A brief article by National Rifle Association Vice President Wayne LaPierre (2000), written in defense of gun ownership and against stronger gun laws and printed on the first anniversary of the Columbine massacre, raised the Second Amendment succinctly: "Second Amendment freedoms don't cause criminal behavior."

The purpose of this book is to explain the so-called Second Amendment freedoms to which LaPierre, and many other Americans, so often refer. To judge by public debate, one would think that the Second Amendment was one of the most active and heavily litigated portions of the Bill of Rights. Yet the opposite is true. Relatively few court cases have addressed the Second Amendment, and legal claims by individuals to Second Amendment protections have arisen in only a relative handful of cases. This modest legal record compares starkly to that of other Bill of Rights freedoms, such as free speech, freedom of religion, protection from improper searches and seizures, and right to counsel, each of which has generated literally hundreds, if not thousands, of rights claims in the courts.

This does not mean that the Second Amendment has somehow been ignored by the law and the courts or that its meaning is somehow unfathomable. The amendment was proposed, debated, amended, and passed by the First Congress as part of what became the Bill of Rights. Congress has enacted several important laws, beginning shortly after the adoption of the Bill of Rights in the 1790s, that were designed to carry out the purposes of the Second Amendment. Further, the Supreme Court, and lower federal courts, have also interpreted the meaning of the amendment in several important, if little-known, cases. Yet these legal actions are few in number when compared to the intense attention given by Congress and the courts to other Bill of Rights freedoms. In short, the political significance of the Second Amendment is great; the legal significance of the Second Amendment is small.

In order to understand what the Second Amendment means, why the "right to bear arms" and a "well regulated militia" were inserted in the Bill of Rights, how the courts have interpreted this right, and what all this means for citizens, gun control, and the law, we will examine the history, law, and politics of this talisman of the gun control debate. In doing so, it is important to point out what this book does not do. It does not offer analysis or opinion on whether more or fewer gun control laws are needed or whether guns are good or bad. Nor is this book concerned with the effects of guns on crime or the political impact of U.S. institutions, such as Congress, the presidency, the bureaucracy, or state actions on gun habits. These are, of course, vitally important matters, but they are analyzed elsewhere (e.g., Bruce and Wilcox 1998; Spitzer 1998; Windlesham 1998; Vizzard 2000). Some congressional enactments are also examined because they help shed light on how Congress sought to implement the terms of the Second Amendment early in the country's history and because congressional enactments contribute to the meaning of constitutional law (a fact little known to most) along with court rulings. In addition, this book is not about the legality of gun ownership. The U.S. Constitution need not enshrine every action, act, or practice of American life in order for such actions to be accepted or to be considered legal. Much of that which occurs in everyday life is legal, acceptable, and honorable, yet also has no direct connection with the Constitution or with the body of law referred to as constitutional law.

Some political considerations as they relate to our understanding of the Second Amendment will be examined, especially as they affect what Americans think the Second Amendment means. Such public perceptions of the law matter to the extent that Americans define their nation, and their relationship to it, according to the way they interpret rights. But fundamental rights are not determined by majority vote or by public perceptions. U.S. courts were designed to be insulated from public pressure precisely so that they could make determinations concerning basic rights and the meaning of law without suffering political retribution. The fact that most Americans would like to have regular, organized prayer in public schools, for example, is irrelevant to the Supreme Court's verdict that organized prayer in public schools violates the First Amendment's prohibition against the establishment of a state religion. (Individuals may, of course, pray in school on their own at any time.) Likewise, the courts' interpretation of the Second Amendment overrides popular perceptions and misperceptions.

Patterns of gun ownership and use in the United States have historically operated mostly separate and apart from the Second Amendment. Although gun ownership was relatively rare in America from colonial times until the Civil War, gun ownership certainly predated the Second Amendment. After the amendment's adoption in 1791, along with the rest of the first ten amendments constituting the Bill of Rights, the government tried repeatedly, but unsuccessfully, to encourage gun ownership so that militia-eligible men would be prepared to meet military emergencies if called into militia service. Yet the effort to arm early Americans failed mostly because guns were relatively rare, expensive, difficult to maintain, and not all that necessary to, or useful for, the everyday lives of most Americans. Technological advances in the 1850s, combined with the demand for more and better firearms during the Civil War, prompted the spurt in gun ownership that led to the proliferation of firearms so familiar to modern Americans (Bellesiles 2000).

Even though gun ownership was somewhat rare until the second half of the nineteenth century, two habits accounted for gun ownership patterns that did exist. One was the just-described militia tradition, which will be discussed in greater detail in chapter 2. The other was the hunting-sporting tradition, which, unlike the militia tradition, survives to the present. It was this second tradition that did and does account for most gun ownership in the United States. Of the roughly 200 million guns in the nation, about two-thirds of them are long guns—rifles and shotguns—that are owned or used primarily for hunting and sporting purposes. Handguns account for the remainder; surveys reveal that, unlike long guns, most people who own handguns do so for self-protection (Spitzer 1998). Whether one approves or disapproves of hunting, target shooting, and other such recreational uses of guns, it is a tradition entirely unrelated to the rights set out in the Second Amendment.

What the Second Amendment Says

In order to understand the Second Amendment, we begin with the plain text. The Second Amendment says, "A well regulated Militia, being necessary to the security of a free State, the right of the people to keep and bear Arms, shall not be infringed." As the sentence makes clear, the right to bear arms is prefaced by the necessity for the government to maintain a militia in order to ensure security for the nation. As former Supreme Court Chief Justice Warren Burger noted, the Second Amendment "must be read as though the word 'because' was the opening word" of the sentence, as in "[Because] a well-regulated militia [is] necessary to the security of a free state, the right of the people to keep and bear arms shall not be infringed" (1990, 5). That is, the keeping and bearing of arms stems from and is connected to the maintenance of a government-organized and regulated militia.

In addition, the phrase "bear arms" is one that has long been understood to mean having weapons or arms for a military, as opposed to a personal, purpose. For example, the *Oxford English*

Dictionary defines "arms" as "Defensive and offensive outfit for war," and to "bear arms" is defined as "to serve as a soldier, do military service, fight." The *OED* traces the military basis of "bearing arms" back to the Middle Ages. A nineteenth-century state court ruling echoed the military basis of bearing arms when it ruled in 1840 that "the phrase, 'bear arms,'.... has a military sense, and no other" (*Aymette v. State,* 21 Tenn. 154, 161). The Tennessee Supreme Court also said that "a man in the pursuit of deer, elk, and buffaloes, might carry his rifle every day, for forty years, and, yet, it would never be said of him, that he had borne arms." An 1874 Georgia Supreme Court ruling noted that "the language of the constitution of this state as well as that of the United States guarantees only the right to keep and bear the 'arms' necessary for a militiaman" (*Hill v. Georgia,* 53 Ga. 472, 475).

Sometimes confusion arises when only a part of the Second Amendment is quoted. For example, the National Rifle Association (NRA) often refers to the "right to bear arms" in its publications and in the speeches of its leaders. If the Second Amendment consisted of only the second half of the sentence, one might well conclude that citizens have a constitutional right to own guns for any and all purposes. But the second half of the sentence does not stand alone, and those who wrote the amendment obviously meant that the bearing of arms be joined with service in "a well regulated militia" that was considered "necessary to the security of a free state."

Still, the Constitution's plain text can be confusing or ambiguous. Any student who has read documents or other writings of the eighteenth century knows that the language seems arcane and that it often refers to ideas or concepts that are no longer a part of American life.

To pick an example from another part of the Constitution, in Article I, Section 8, Congress is given the power to "grant Letters of Marque and Reprisal." No modern reader of the Constitution could know what this refers to without engaging in some historical research. That research would show that this phrase gave Congress the now outdated power to authorize private individuals to prey on an enemy nation's shipping and property without being labeled pirates. This practice was outlawed by the Declaration of Paris in 1856 and is no longer considered a legitimate tool of U.S. military policy (Spitzer 1993).

In the case of the Second Amendment, the reference in the first half of the sentence to a "well regulated militia" often prompts similar confusion, because the old-style militia concept is no longer a part of U.S. military organization and because many who quote the amendment simply omit the phrase, focusing instead on the second part of the sentence referring to "the right of the people to keep and bear arms" not being "infringed." Obviously, the two parts of the Second Amendment discussed here—well regulated militias and the right to keep and bear arms—are directly linked within the single sentence that makes up the amendment. The confusion over the meaning of this sentence is enhanced because, by comparison, other sentences in the Bill of Rights were constructed differently. The First Amendment, for example, is also made up of a single sentence, but here, the construction was quite different. The First Amendment begins by saying that "Congress shall make no law respecting . . .," and then listing six different freedoms, including a prohibition against the establishment of a state religion, the free exercise of religion, free speech, free press, the right to peaceably assemble, and the right to petition the government to redress grievances. Other amendments composing the Bill of Rights address a variety of other freedoms, powers, and rights.

The reason for the lack of consistency in the Bill of Rights as a whole is that the first ten amendments were the product of many different political forces and opinions that arose from the thirteen states and that were subject to extensive debate and bargaining during the First Congress (1789–1790). In fact, the original Bill of Rights sent to the states for ratification consisted of twelve amendments, not ten. Two of the twelve failed to win approval from three-quarters of the states. (One of those two, which barred Congress from increasing its pay until after an election, was revived in the 1980s and was eventually added to the Constitution as the Twenty-seventh Amendment in 1992.) This short list of twelve began as a catalogue of nearly 200 amendments, arising mostly from the states and their respective constitutional ratifying conventions. Like the modern legislative process, the bills produced by Congress often addressed unrelated subjects in ways that now seem inconsistent or even illogical. This incongruency resulted because, then as now, legislation was the product of many hands and reflected compromises that were necessary to produce legislation capable of winning the support of a majority of members of Congress. For these reasons, the rather plain language of the Second Amendment has become vulnerable to misinterpretation.

Outline of the Book

In order to understand the Second Amendment, we must examine its beginnings, meaning, and heritage. Chapter 2 explores the origins and early development of the Second Amendment, beginning with its roots in seventeenth-century Great Britain, where the bearing of arms was considered important to the ability of militias to effectively resist opposing armed forces. American colonial experiences reflected two important beliefs drawn from the British: mistrust of standing armies, which often suppressed democratic impulses in European nations; and the popularity of militias, a more democratic, if less effective, fighting force. These beliefs converged on the American Revolution, where a combination of a small professional army, the Continental Army, supplemented by state militias, eventually won the United States its independence. The Constitution of 1787 created a national government that, for the first time, possessed the power to establish and maintain a professional standing army. The document also gave power over the militias to the new national government. This vast new power prompted opposition to the new Constitution from Antifederalists, who sought reassurances for state power that eventually found expression in the Second Amendment and in other parts of what became the Bill of Rights. Although it continued to be popular, the old militia system proved to be inefficient, unreliable, and ultimately unworkable. And as the government adopted the practice of providing the necessary arms and equipment for national and state military forces, the need for citizens to "keep and bear arms" was eclipsed. When we look at the Bill of Rights today, some of the rights are considered vital to modern life, such as free speech or right to counsel. Other rights, such as the Third Amendment protection against the quartering of troops in people's homes in peacetime, have proven to be irrelevant to modern life.

In several key Supreme Court cases, the meaning of the Second Amendment—that the right of citizens to keep and bear arms described in the amendment came into play only in connection with citizen service in a government-organized and -regulated militia—was ratified. In order to provide a smooth narrative concerning court rulings on the Second Amendment, both nineteenth- and twentieth-century cases are discussed in this chapter.

Chapter 3 examines the twentieth-century legal and political view of the Second Amendment. In the last few decades, some writers have sought to impose new meanings on this amendment, in order to argue that it protects a private or individual right to own firearms, aside or apart from militia service. Some have gone even further, arguing that the amendment authorizes a right of private citizens to make war against the U.S. government (a so-called right of revolution) if the citizens believe that the government has become tyrannical. A few have also turned to the Fourteenth Amendment in an attempt to argue that this post–Civil War amendment somehow extended or expanded the right to bear arms. These recent writings have, in turn, fueled the effort by various political gun-rights groups to argue that the Second Amendment does, or should, bar various gun control laws. Thus, even though only a few court cases have raised Second Amendment issues, the amendment has become an important political symbol for those opposing stronger gun laws.

Chapter 4 examines four recent manifestations of renewed interest in gun control and the Second Amendment. The first is the flurry of national legislative action witnessed in the 1990s, including the Brady Law, the assault weapons ban, and an effort to tighten national gun laws at the end of the 1990s following several school shootings. These actions did much to spur the other events discussed in this chapter. The second is the rise of private extremist groups calling themselves "militias," formed by disaffected individuals who believe that the U.S. government has already become tyrannical and that armed resistance is a proper or necessary response. These individuals believe, contrary to the Second Amendment's authors and court rulings, that the Second Amendment provides them with a right to form so-called militias free from government regulation or control. The third element of the modern Second Amendment debate revolves around recent efforts to win a reinterpretation of the Second Amendment in the courts that would establish a private, individual right to own firearms. The fourth element of the modern debate over gun rights involves the escalating political rhetoric surrounding the right to bear arms. In its most extreme form, this rhetoric argues that, contrary to past history and law, the Second Amendment is actually the most important of all the amendments. At a time when gun control is more hotly debated than ever, such "rights talk" underscores the importance of the Constitution as a patriotic symbol.

Chapter 5 offers an alphabetically organized reference section that provides brief definitions of pertinent terms and concepts. Chapter 6 compiles a variety of source materials, including some early legislation that implemented the Second Amendment, court cases, state arms-bearing provisions, and party platform excerpts pertaining to gun control and the Second Amendment. The book includes a brief chronology of pertinent events related to gun control and the Second Amendment and an annotated bibliography of useful works on the subject.

References and Further Reading

Bellesiles, Michael. 2000. *Arming America: The Origins of a National Gun Culture.* New York: Alfred A. Knopf.
Bruce, John M., and Clyde Wilcox, eds. 1998. *The Changing Politics of Gun Control.* Lanham, MD: Rowman and Littlefield.
Burger, Warren. 1990. "The Right to Bear Arms." *Parade Magazine,* (14 January): 4–6.
LaPierre, Wayne. 2000. "Advancing Agendas." *USA Today* (20 April).
Olinger, David. 2000. "Massacre Energizes Gun Debate but Not Lawmakers." *Denver Post* (19 April).
"Primer." 1999. *Washington Post* (2 May).
Spitzer, Robert J. 1993. *President and Congress.* New York: McGraw-Hill.
———. 1998. *The Politics of Gun Control.* New York: Chatham House.
Vizzard, William J. 2000. *Shots in the Dark: The Policy, Politics, and Symbolism of Gun Control.* Lanham, MD: Rowman and Littlefield.
Windlesham, Lord. 1998. *Politics, Punishment, and Populism.* New York: Oxford University Press.

2

Origins

*T*HE WORDS THAT COMPOSE the Second Amendment trace their lineage back through early U.S. governance. The issues raised in the amendment were discussed not only in the First Congress but in the Constitutional Convention of 1787 and in state governments as they arose in colonial society, as well as in the British heritage. We thus turn to historical and constitutional background, the intent of those who framed the Second Amendment, and the courts.

The British Heritage

Military threats to the American colonies were numerous in the seventeenth and eighteenth centuries. The most effective and reliable protection against such threats, whether from the French, the Spanish, or from Native Americans, was a professional standing army. But early Americans maintained a strong suspicion of standing armies. Much of this American suspicion came from their acquaintance with European history, in which professional armies had often overthrown civilian governments and deprived people of their rights and liberties. Europeans who came to the colonies in America did so in part to enjoy greater freedom and avoid government oppression. In fact, Great Britain had recently experienced such oppression and turmoil. For thirteen years in the middle of the seventeenth century, professional military forces under the control of Oliver Cromwell ruled England. The country was, in the words of British historian Thomas Macaulay, "governed by the sword" in that "the civil power" was "subjected to military dictation." Under Cromwell's standing army, "the King had been murdered, the nobility degraded, the landed gentry plundered, the Church persecuted"(1879, I, 117, 269).

Only a few years after Cromwell, King James II, a devout Catholic, attempted to transform Britain into a Catholic nation, referred to as promoting "papism," by barring Protestants and appointing Catholics to the top posts in government and in the army. Contrary to existing law, James attempted to disarm Protestants in this mostly Protestant country. James's oppressive practices in the cause of advancing Catholicism, including the threat of a swelling Catholic-led army that might overwhelm local Protestant militias (controlled by local landed gentry), eventually led to his overthrow and replacement by William of Orange and Mary II, an event dubbed the Glorious Revolution of 1688.

Thereafter, Parliament enacted the British Bill of Rights, also known as the Declaration of Rights, in 1689, in which various grievances against James II were listed, including that he "did endeavor to subvert and extirpate the Protestant Religion and the Laws and Liberties of this Kingdom. . . . By causing several good Subjects, being Protestants, to be disarmed at the same Time when Papists were both armed and employed contrary to Law" (quoted in Weatherup 1975, 973). The right defined in Article VII of this document was "that the subjects which are protestants, may have arms for their defence suitable to their conditions, and as allowed by law." The law to which this sentence referred stipulated that firearms could be owned only by the nobility, wealthy landowners, and members of the militia executing their duty to defend the country. These restrictions were consistent with a wide variety of government restrictions on gun ownership imposed by the British government extending back more than a century before 1689 (Bogus 1998, 377–378; Malcolm 1994, 26–36). As historian Lois Schwoerer noted of Article VII, "Englishmen did not secure to 'ordinary citizens' the right to possess weapons" (2000, 59). This provision from the British Bill of Rights is that cited as the forerunner of the Second Amendment in the U.S. Bill of Rights, although there is no direct evidence that the founders treated it as the source of what became the Second Amendment.

Foreshadowing the U.S. experience, the British recognized the superior fighting capabilities of standing armies, but for political and historical reasons they found it necessary to maintain a militia system as well because, in Macaulay's words, "the militia was an institution eminently popular" (1879, I, 269). These important episodes in British history revealed the actual and feared mischief of standing armies of which British subjects in the American colonies were keenly aware. They also underscored the connection of firearms ownership and regulation with militia/military service.

THE COLONIAL EXPERIENCE

The mistrust of standing armies was a common sentiment in America during the colonial period and was directly related to the bearing of arms by citizens. In 1776, Samuel Adams wrote that a "standing army, however necessary it may be at sometimes, is always dangerous to the liberties of the people" (quoted in Jensen 1965, 29). George Washington observed that "mercenary [professional] armies . . . have at one time or another subverted the liberties of almost all the Countries they have been raised to defend . . ." (quoted in Feller and Gotting 1966, 51). In this way, the reliance on the militia's citizen-soldier became synonymous with the revolutionary spirit. The Virginia Bill of Rights, written in 1776, said that "standing armies, in time of peace, should be avoided, as dangerous to liberty." The other states copied Virginia's wording.

Sentiments favoring the militia as more compatible with democratic values were supported by the prevailing public myth of the time concerning the military effectiveness of militias. "The Cincinnatus complex" embodied the belief of the time that no professional army could fight as effectively as a citizen militia (Rossiter 1953, 386–387). This and related sentiments were also reflected in the political thought of such philosophers as Francois-Marie Voltaire, Anne-Robert-Jacques Turgot, Francois Quesnay, and Jean-Jacques Rousseau (Kennett and Anderson 1975, 61). As was the case with Britain, military reality would prove this politically popular myth to be false.

Militiamen were defined as adult males of fighting age (roughly between eighteen and forty-five) who were obligated to enroll with the government for military service. They received limited training, served for a few months out of the year, were covered only partially by military law, and were generally under state command. By comparison, professional soldiers were usually volunteers who enlisted for several years, received extensive military training and pay, served even in peacetime, and were under federal control and full military discipline (Mahon 1960; Spitzer 1998).

From colonial times on, militia forces were composed of two parts: the unorganized or general militias, and the organized or select militias. The first was defined as the entire body of eligible males that participated in the minimum required service. The select militias were volunteer units that organized and trained more rigorously, often with their own equipment, uniforms, and unit loyalty. These more professionalized militias were subject to periodic criticism from those who feared that they bore too close a resemblance to a professional army. Despite these doubts, the select militias continued to exist and played an increasingly important role in national defense.

In actual operation, colonial militias' size and organization fluctuated according to military necessity. Moreover, those who actually served "were not the men who bore a military obligation as part of their freedom" (Shy 1990, 37–38). That is, freed slaves and property owners would often opt out of their militia duties, while vagrants, vagabonds, and the unemployed more often filled the ranks. Thus, while militia service was often assumed to be universal, in fact the greatest burden of actual service fell on men of lower status and few resources. Although the unorganized militias withered in the early nineteenth century, the organized militias survived, and eventually were recognized by federal law as the National Guard (Cooper 1997; Millett and Maslowski 1984).

Throughout the colonial and early federal periods in America, firearms possession was closely regulated in two primary ways. One type of regulation required eligible males to own guns to support the local militia. The other type of regulation barred various groups from owning guns, including Catholics, indentured servants, slaves, and those who refused to swear allegiance to the government. The colonies also retained the right to confiscate firearms if they were needed for military purposes (Bellesiles 1998; Cornell 1999, 2000).

Not only had Americans inherited the mistrust of standing armies from the British, but that mistrust was magnified by the behavior of British troops on American soil. American outrage over the excesses of British troops was expressed in the Declaration of Independence of 1776 when Thomas Jefferson complained that "He [the King] has kept among us, in Times of Peace, Standing Armies, without the consent of our Legislatures. He has affected to render the Military independent of and superior to the Civil Power." The Declaration also complained that the British were "quartering large Bodies of Armed Troops among us" and "protecting them, by a mock Trial, from Punishment for any Murders which they should commit on the Inhabitants of these States." The British only compounded these grievances and suspicions by "transporting large armies of foreign mercenaries [Hessians] to compleat the works of death, desolation, and tyranny. . . ." Not surprisingly, the British also took any and every opportunity to seize American weapons and ammunition.

The most famous instance of the British army's effort to curtail rebellion by seizure of arms and supplies was its famous, or infamous, march from Boston to Lexington and Concord in April of 1775, where the latter in particular had become "an arsenal of revolution" (Fischer 1994, 84). The members of the Massachusetts militia who resisted the British advance were among the colony's best trained and most experienced. Fighting as they were on their home territory, they acquitted themselves for the most part admirably, a fact that helped lend credence to the popularity of, and mythology surrounding, the militiaman as soldier.

As a consequence, America fought the Revolutionary War with a combination of the Continental Army and state militias. The army, operating as a more-or-less professional fighting force, served as the core fighting unit, supplemented by various state militias. Although the reliance on militias was politically satisfying, it proved to be an administrative and military nightmare. State detachments could not be easily combined into larger fighting units; soldiers could not be relied on to serve for extended periods, and desertions were common; militia detachments would often enter the army encampment, consume food and supplies, and then leave before battle; officers were elected based on popularity rather than experience or training; discipline and uniformity were almost nonexistent (Boorstin 1964, 355–356). Owing to the militias' popularity, Commander-in-Chief George Washington defended the militia in public but made his real sentiments brutally clear in correspondence with Congress:

To place any dependence upon Militia, is, assuredly, resting upon a broken staff. Men just dragged from the tender Scenes of domestick life; unaccustomed to the din of Arms; totally unacquainted with every kind of military skill, which being followed by a want of confidence in themselves, when opposed to Troops regularly train'd, disciplined, and appointed, superior in knowledge and superior in Arms, makes them timid, and ready to fly from their own shadows.... if I was called upon to declare upon Oath, whether the Militia have been most serviceable or hurtful upon the whole; I should subscribe to the latter (quoted in Weatherup 1975, 979–980).

Despite the militia handicap, the United States did of course win its independence, owing to the size of its force (over 400,000 men participated during the course of the war), the protracted nature of the conflict, the adoption of tactics appropriate to North American terrain and the army's irregular nature, the assistance of the French, British difficulties related to distance and supply, and the Americans' "home court advantage." This last fact was particularly important to the militias—they generally fought best when they were fighting near their homes.

During the Revolutionary period, states maintained various requirements concerning gun ownership, as had been the case since the early days of the colonies. They retained the right to order individuals to surrender their firearms to the government should they be needed for military purposes. Some states, such as Pennsylvania, required citizens to swear loyalty oaths. Those refusing could be disarmed by the state. Others, such as non-Protestants, slaves, indentured servants, and other whites who did not own property, were typically barred from gun ownership. And the government had the power to conduct gun censuses—that is, to literally count and note the location and condition of guns owned throughout the country. This practice continued into the nineteenth century (Bellesiles 1998; Cornell 1999).

The Constitution

The first constitution of the United States, the Articles of Confederation (1777–1789), reflected suspicion of standing armies and of a strong national government. Formulated and adopted during the Revolution, the Articles gave most power to the states, including the primary burden of national defense. The Articles stipulated specifically that "every state shall always keep up a well regulated and disciplined militia, sufficiently armed and accoutered" (Article VI) and that Congress's military powers could be exercised only by a vote of nine of thirteen states (Article IX). No specific provision was made for a national standing army.

These and other shortcomings of the Articles eventually led to the Federal Constitutional Convention of 1787 and the adoption of the modern Constitution. The military issue was resolved in the new Constitution by recognition of both the militia and a standing army, and it split powers between the national government and the states (the principle of federalism). In Article I, section 8, Congress was given the power to "raise and support armies," "provide and maintain a Navy," and to finance and regulate both. In an important departure from the Articles, Congress would now have key authority over the state militias, as it could "provide for calling forth the Militia" in order "to execute the Laws of the Union, suppress Insurrections and repel Invasions"; and it could "provide for organizing, arming, and disciplining, the Militia, and for governing such Part of them as may be employed in the Service of the United States." In addition, the president would serve as commander-in-chief of the military forces, including the militia (Article II, section 2). On the other hand, the states retained some limited control, as the Constitution reserved "to the States respectively, the Appointment of the Officers, and the Authority of training the Militia according to the discipline prescribed by Congress" (Article I, section 8).

The founders recognized the longstanding mistrust of standing armies, but accepted the reality that the militia was no substitute for a trained professional force controlled by the national government. Those at the Constitutional Convention of 1787 who feared too much federal control over the military won two key concessions: first, control over the militias was divided between the states and the federal government (although state control of the militias was dwarfed by the federal powers given to Congress and the president); second, militia mobilization by Congress could only occur under the three circumstances listed in Article I.

The overriding necessity for an effective fighting force was keenly felt in the country's early history. The United States faced not only hostile European and Native American forces on all sides but threats from internal rebellion. As constitutional scholar Max Farrand noted, "Shays' rebellion [January 1787] had taught a much needed lesson. It was not sufficient to place the state militia under some central control. The central government must be empowered to maintain an efficient army and navy to protect the states against internal disorders, as well as against external dangers" (1913, 49).

Reflecting the prevailing political view of the time, Constitutional Convention delegate James Madison said that "as the greatest danger to liberty is from large standing armies, it is best to prevent them by an effectual provision for a good Militia" (Farrand 1966, II, 388). At the same time, Madison recognized that the states had often neglected their militias, making them unreliable unless the federal government could impose uniformity and discipline. Delegate George Mason attempted to insert into the Constitution the warning against the liberty-eroding tendencies of standing armies when he proposed (unsuccessfully) an amendment to Article I, section 8 to add the phrase "That the Liberties of the People may be the better secured against the Danger of regular Troops or standing Armys in time of Peace," preceding "To provide for organizing, arming & disciplining the Militia" (Farrand 1966, IV, 59).

Many of the issues and controversies raised during the Constitutional Convention also arose in state ratifying conventions. During the Virginia ratifying convention in 1788, Edmund Randolph (who had also been a delegate to the federal convention) said, "With respect to a standing army, I believe there was not a member in the federal convention who did not feel indignation at such an institution" (Farrand 1966, III, 319). From a distance of two decades, founder Gouverneur Morris reflected the underlying reality of the militia-army debate in a singularly blunt fashion when he wrote in 1815: "An overweening vanity leads the fond many . . . to believe or affect to believe, that militia can beat veteran troops in the open field and even play of battle. This idle notion, fed by vaunting demagogues, alarmed us [the founders] for our country, when in the course of that time and chance . . . she should be at war with a great power. . . . to rely on militia was to lean on a broken reed" (Farrand 1966, III, 420).

Defenders of the new Constitution sought to calm fears and counter criticisms in the *Federalist Papers* (Hamilton, Madison, and Jay 1961). In *Federalist Paper* 24, Alexander Hamilton, who served as George Washington's aide during the Revolution, argued that it would be a mistake to restrict or ban standing armies in times of peace, citing constant threats the young nation faced along its vast frontiers and the necessity of allowing Congress appropriate latitude to meet variable but persistent military threats. In 25, Hamilton argued forcefully that standing armies were naturally superior on the battlefield, the Revolutionary War notwithstanding, and were similarly superior in dealing with civil unrest (28). Further, Hamilton noted in 29 that the federal government must have the power to impose uniformity on the militias in order for them to be effective and efficient. Both he and Madison dismissed the fear that a standing army would deprive the states of their sovereignty or citizens of their liberties. To critics who predicted that a standing army would produce the downfall of state governments, Madison in 46 computed that the United States could at the time raise at best an army of 30,000 men—a force that could be opposed by state militias totaling one-half million men.

The Federalist-Antifederalist Debate

No dispute during the nation's formative years was more important than that between the Federalists, who embraced a stronger national government as established in the new Constitution, and the Antifederalists, who opposed the new Constitution and who supported a more decentralized governing system. This debate was the root of concerns that gave rise to the Second Amendment. More generally, however, Federalists and Antifederalists disagreed about three fundamental issues.

The first of these was representation. Antifederalists believed that the best government was that closest to the people. Federalists believed that better representation occurred when the government's officials were somewhat removed from the people. Second, both were concerned about tyranny but believed it to come from different sources. Antifederalists feared the tyranny of governing aristocrats, or what would today be labeled *elites*—those with money, position, and status. The Federalists feared that the greatest potential for tyranny would arise from majorities—citizen mobs who would deprive others of their rights and liberties. Third, Antifederalists feared centralized governmental power, preferring a more limited system of the kind the nation had endured under the Articles of Confederation. Federalists were also concerned about national governmental power but believed that the new, stronger national government could be effectively checked and limited by the separation of powers, as well as by the division of powers between the national and state governments. This debate led directly to the adoption of the Bill of Rights.

The Bill of Rights

The adoption of the Constitution enshrined within it the dual militia–standing army military system, but it did not resolve the nagging question of federalism; that is, the new Constitution not only created a national standing army but gave the federal government vast new power over the militia. Antifederalists were extremely concerned that this power might be used not only to undercut the effectiveness and independence of state militias (for example, by federal government refusal to organize, arm, or train them, although Federalists asserted that the states would retain such powers if the federal government failed to act) but to gut state power entirely. Constitutional Convention delegate and Antifederalist Luther Martin predicted nothing less than the demise of the states if the Constitution were adopted with federal control of militias included.

These fears found voice in several state ratifying conventions, most particularly that of Virginia, where the Antifederalist cause found no more eloquent champion than revolutionary firebrand Patrick Henry. Profoundly suspicious of the concentrated federal governmental power provided in the new Constitution, Henry spoke for many who preferred a weak national government and strong states when he asked, "Have we [in Virginia] the means of resisting disciplined armies, when our only defence, the militia, is put into the hands of Congress" (Schwartz 1971, II, 773). Henry sought assurance that Virginia, and other states, could arm their own militias if the federal government failed to do so. George Mason pressed the Virginia convention "to obtain 'an express declaration, that the State Governments might arm and discipline' the militia should Congress fail to do so" (quoted in Rakove 2000, 138). This, in a nutshell, was the purpose of what became the Second Amendment. The Virginia convention passed this wording when it ratified the Constitution:

That the people have a right to keep and bear arms; that a well regulated Militia composed of the body of the people trained to arms is the proper, natural and safe defence of a free State. That standing armies in time of peace are dangerous to liberty, and therefore ought to be avoided, as far as the circumstances and protection of the Community will admit; and that in all cases the military should be under strict subordination to and governed by the Civil power. (Cogan 1997, 182–183)

Following Virginia's lead, four other states—New Hampshire, New York, North Carolina, and Rhode Island—adopted similar resolutions. In short, Antifederalists sought greater protections for state militias. The central question giving rise to the Second Amendment was whether congressional authority over state militias could surpass that of the state governments and whether this new federal military power (over both the militia and the federally controlled professional army) might be used to limit state sovereignty and power. In particular, southern states were anxious to make sure that they would have the ability to mobilize adequately armed state militias to suppress slave revolts, since they were suspicious that a national government dominated by northern interests would not be willing to commit federal troops and supplies to keep African Americans in the bondage of slavery (Bogus 1998). Although the Federalist-Antifederalist dispute might seem like a quaint or irrelevant issue to modern Americans, it went to the very core of the dispute over the new Constitution of 1787.

Federalists resisted the idea of a Bill of Rights on two main grounds. First, they argued that such a document was unnecessary because the national government was already limited in what it could do; it could exercise only the powers delegated to it, therefore rendering any listing of individual rights to be unnecessary. Second, opponents argued that the Constitution was itself a Bill of

Rights, because it included the enumeration of specific rights (such as in Article I, section 9).

Nevertheless, the pressure for a Bill of Rights to limit federal authority and retain states' rights became all but irresistible. On June 8, 1789, Madison (who had initially opposed the addition of a Bill of Rights) introduced in the House of Representatives of the First Congress a proposed list of rights to be added to the Constitution. Drawn heavily from Virginia's 1776 Declaration of Rights, the list included the wording that follows, originally to be inserted in Article 1, section 9 (a section of the Constitution that lists several limits on the federal government and that followed the section dealing with military matters). The fact that this wording, along with the rest of what became the Bill of Rights, was listed separately and at the end of the seven articles of the Constitution itself, instead of integrated into the text, occurred because of a political compromise that Madison had to accept in order to win key Federalist support for the Bill of Rights in the House. Delegate Roger Sherman and others insisted that the amendments not be integrated into the original Constitution, but listed separately at the end, so as not to tamper with the actual text of the Constitution. As Representative George Clymer said, "I wish Sir that the Constitution may forever remain in its original form, as a monument of the wisdom and patriotism of those who framed it" (Veit, Bowling, and Bickford 1991, 110). The initial text of what became the Second Amendment read:

> The right of the people to keep and bear arms shall not be infringed; a well armed, and well regulated militia being the best security of a free country: but no person religiously scrupulous of bearing arms, shall be compelled to render military service in person.

As reported out of House committee on July 28, the amendment said:

A well regulated militia, composed of the body of the people, being the best security of a free State, the right of the people to keep and bear arms shall not be infringed, but no person religiously scrupulous shall be compelled to bear arms.

On August 24, the House passed this wording:

A well regulated militia, composed of the body of the People, being the best security of a free State, the right of the People to keep and bear arms, shall not be infringed, but no one religiously scrupulous of bearing arms, shall be compelled to render military service in person.

This and the other amendments then went to the Senate, where the final wording of what became the Second Amendment emerged:

A well regulated militia, being necessary to the security of a free State, the right of the people to keep and bear arms, shall not be infringed.

The limited debate in the First Congress surrounding the Second Amendment dealt with a few familiar questions, all dealing with military matters: whether the amendment wording should codify the right of conscientious objectors to opt out of military service for religious reasons; the relationship between militias, standing armies, and liberty; the need to subordinate the military to civilian authority; and the military unreliability of the militia as compared with a professional army. To judge by the brief debate about and modest wording changes in the amendment's four versions quoted here, the basic sentiment was held throughout—that citizens have a constitutionally protected right to serve in militias when called into service by, and in defense of, state and country. The aim was to ensure the continued existence of state militias as a military and political supplement and counterbalance to the national army and more broadly to national power (Wills 1999). This was the basic federalism question that repeatedly concerned the nation's leaders. Indeed, all of the debate dealt with military questions.

Thus, the Second Amendment is founded on federalism, balancing powers between the federal government and the states, and on military necessity, developing a political compromise between politically popular and state-controlled militias and a politically unpopular but militarily necessary national professional army. Many believed that the nation's very survival might well have required massive mobilization of the eligible adult male population. Missing from this extended history is any connection between the Second Amendment and any personal, private, or individual use of weapons, for purposes including hunting, sporting, recreation, or even personal protection, which was already covered by the eighteenth century in common law (Samaha 1993, ch. 6; Herz 1995, 65–67). The Second Amendment's purpose, like the Bill of Rights as a whole, was to place limits on the federal government and strike a balance between national power and state power. Its only connection to what might be termed an *individual right* was that individuals would need to retain the ability to respond to a call from the government. As the next section discusses, in early U.S. history such a call-up necessitated that citizens bring their own weapons.

The Decline of the Old Militia System

Soon after the ratification of the Bill of Rights in 1791, Congress moved ahead to establish rules and procedures governing the militias. Titled "An Act more effectively to provide for the National Defence by establishing an Uniform Militia throughout the United States," the Uniform Militia Act of 1792 (see chapter 6) defined the nation's militia (in keeping with U.S. militia tradition) as "every free able-bodied white male citizen of the respective states" between the ages of eighteen and forty-five.

Also in keeping with the militia tradition, the militia members were legally obligated to provide their own weapons, ammunition, and accoutrements: "That every citizen so enrolled... shall... provide himself with a good musket or firelock, a sufficient bayonet and belt, two spare flints, and a knapsack, a pouch with a box therein to contain not less than twenty-four cartridges... each cartridge to contain a proper quantity of powder and ball..." (1 U.S. Stat. 271; 1792). It is not hard to understand why the Second Amendment was so careful to protect the right to keep and bear arms when those called to the militia, by law and tradition, bore the burden of arming themselves. Indeed, even though the Constitution said that Congress bore responsibility for arming the militia (Article I, section 8), Madison "observed that *arming* as explained did not extend to furnishing arms." Rufus King elaborated that arming meant providing "for uniformity of arms," including "authority to regulate the modes of furnishing" them (Farrand 1966, II, 385). The government could, of course, provide arms if it chose to do so, and from the mid-nineteenth century on, it invariably did.

In the two years following the passage of the Uniform Militia Act, all fifteen states passed their own laws to bring their militia systems into line with federal guidelines. Both the wisdom of and fears prompting the militia system seemed borne out in the country's first few years. Some key battles with Native Americans were successfully won with militia forces in 1794, and the Whiskey Rebellion of the same year was suppressed with a militia force of 15,000. Also in 1794, the Georgia militia literally faced federal troops with weapons loaded and aimed in a dispute over the treatment of Creek and Cherokee Indians. A dispute over the Alien and Sedition Acts of 1798 nearly precipitated a similar encounter between federal troops and the Virginia militia in 1798 (Mahon 1960, 21–22, 25, 55).

Despite these events, it was already clear by the close of the eighteenth century that the militias were impractical, if not obsolete. Almost without exception, the states failed to implement the terms of the Uniform Militia Act. The system of fines imposed to impel men to arm and uniform themselves and to ensure that they showed up for drill failed to achieve these objectives and were almost never enforced. Part of the reason for this was the scarcity of firearms. Contrary to popular belief, firearms ownership was rare in America from the colonial period up to the time of the Civil War, when no more than 10 percent of the population owned working weapons. The reasons for this were obvious: firearms were difficult to produce, expensive, and required regular maintenance to prevent rusting and malfunction. Up until 1790, all of the guns made in the United States were handmade. Records of U.S. military activity during this period verified that relatively few in the militia owned working firearms and that most were poor shots (Bellesiles 2000).

The reputation of the citizen militias suffered a final, crippling blow as the result of their terrible performance in the War of 1812 (Cress 1982; Wiener 1940). The conflict was "the closest thing to a decisive military defeat the United States has ever suffered" (Snow and Drew 1994, 261). Even as a supplement to the regular army, the general militia system was considered useless. Neither the federal government nor the states took much interest in continuing universal militia training and service, although the social structure of the militia system continued for decades. Local militias continued to gather for "musters" throughout much of the nineteenth century, but such gatherings were primarily social occasions that often occurred at local taverns (Riker 1979; Millett and Maslowski 1984). As historian James McPherson noted, those militia outfits that continued to meet "spent more time drinking than drilling" (1988, 317). Indeed, the "history of the state militias between 1800 and the 1870s is one of total abandonment, disorganization, and degeneration" (Ehrman and Henigan

1989, 36). Instead, the government relied on its professional army and elite corps of volunteers, the select or organized militias (Higginbotham 1998). As political historian Stephen Skowronek noted: "By the 1840s the militia system envisioned in the early days of the republic was a dead letter. Universal military training fell victim to a general lack of interest and administrative incompetence at both the federal and state levels" (1982, 315). Thus, subsequent references to the militia pertained to the select militia, which in turn became the National Guard (Cooper 1997), not to the system of universal male service. The idea of universal militia service would persist, however, since Congress retained the theoretical power to mobilize such a force; more importantly, however, it persisted as part of the political symbolism surrounding the Second Amendment.

No significant legal changes occurred until the start of the twentieth century. In a 1901 message to Congress, President Theodore Roosevelt called for a long-overdue legal change, saying that "our militia law is obsolete and worthless." (Richardson 1913, IX, 6670) In 1903, Congress passed the Militia Act, which legally separated the "organized militia, to be known as the National Guard," from the "reserve militia," also called the unorganized militia, even though the unorganized militia had by now been discarded as a viable military entity, for the simple reason that fighting could no longer be given over to untrained amateurs. The balance of the act provided for federal arming, training, and drilling of the National Guard. It made no provision whatsoever for the unorganized militia (32 Stat. 775; 1903).

In 1916, Congress passed the National Defense Act, which mandated that the National Guard would be organized in the same method as the "Regular Army." It also placed state Guards under federal guidelines (39 Stat. 166; 1916).

Thus, from 1903 forward, the active militia in law was the National Guard which, though now under federal regulation, is still trained by the respective states (32 U.S.C. 7014–7016; 1959).

Congress retained for itself the theoretical option of calling up the reserve militia—all able-bodied men from age seventeen to forty-five (10 U.S.C. 311; 1983)—but the now-substantial regular army, plus National Guard, constituted formidable and ample military forces to meet national needs. Any gaps in those needs have been met in modern times by the selective service system— the military draft—rather than activation of the old-style militias. This history and interpretation of militias is described and ratified in the Supreme Court cases of *Maryland v. United States* (381 U.S. 41; 1965) and *Perpich v. Department of Defense* (496 U.S. 334; 1990).

In sum, the possession of firearms referred to in the Second Amendment comes into play only when (1) the unorganized militia is activated by a state or the federal government, a practice effectively abandoned before the Civil War, and (2) the government fails to provide weapons for that force. Thus, the Second Amendment has been rendered essentially irrelevant to modern American life, as is the prospect of, say, National Guard troops from New York and Pennsylvania squaring off against each other, weapons at the ready, along state borders.

Supreme Court Rulings

The Second Amendment has generated relatively little constitutional law. In a few instances, however, the Supreme Court has ruled directly on the meaning of this amendment. Most of these cases came in the nineteenth century, but some twentieth century cases are also included in this discussion so that the reader can more easily follow the progression of Court thinking. Chapter 3 will discuss other, more recent cases.

In the first case, *United States v. Cruikshank* (92 U.S. 542; 1876), Cruikshank and two other defendants were charged with thirty-two counts of depriving blacks of their constitutional rights, including two counts claiming that the defendants had deprived blacks of firearms possession, in violation of the Force Act of 1870. Speaking for the Court, Chief Justice Waite wrote:

> The second and tenth counts are equally defective. The right there specified is that of "bearing arms for a lawful purpose." This is not a right granted by the Constitution. Neither is it in any manner dependent upon that instrument for its existence. The Second Amendment declares that it shall not be infringed; but this ... means no more than that it shall not be infringed by Congress. This is one of the amendments that has no other effect than to restrict the powers of the National Government. ...

The Court in this case established two principles, which it and lower federal courts have consistently upheld: first, that the Second Amendment poses no obstacle to at least some regulation of firearms; and second, that the Second Amendment is not incorporated, meaning that it pertains only to federal power, not state power. (This is what the Court meant when it referred to the Second Amendment not being "infringed by Congress.") Admittedly, the Supreme Court did not begin to incorporate parts of the first ten amendments (that is, using the wording of the due process and equal protection clauses of the Fourteenth Amendment to extend parts of the Bill of Rights to the states) until 1897. But the Court has never accepted the idea of incorporating the entire Bill of Rights (Farber, Eskridge, and Frickey 1993), and it has never incorporated the Second Amendment, despite numerous opportunities to do so. In other words, the courts have continued to treat the Second Amendment differently from most of the rest of the Bill of Rights (this is discussed in more detail in Chapter 3).

Ten years later, the Court ruled in *Presser v. Illinois* (116 U.S. 252, 265; 1886) that an Illinois law that barred paramilitary organizations from drilling or parading in cities or towns without a license from the governor was constitutional and did not violate the Second Amendment. Herman Presser challenged the law after he was arrested for marching and drilling his armed fringe group through Chicago streets. In upholding the Illinois law, the Court reaffirmed that the Second Amendment did not apply to the states, citing *Cruikshank*. Speaking for a unanimous Court, Justice Woods also discussed the relationship between the citizen, the militia, and the government:

> It is undoubtedly true that all citizens capable of bearing arms constitute the reserved military force or reserved militia of the United States as well as of the States; and, in view of this prerogative... the States cannot, even laying the constitutional provision in question out of view, prohibit the people from keeping and bearing arms, so as to deprive the United States of their rightful resource for maintaining the public security, and disable the people from performing their duty to the General Government. But, as already stated, we think it clear that the sections under consideration do not have this effect.

The Court then went on to consider whether Presser and his associates had a right to organize with others as a self-proclaimed and armed military organization, against state law. No, the Court decided, since such activity "is not an attribute of national citizenship. Military organization and military drill and parade under arms are subjects especially under the control of the government of every country. They cannot be claimed as a right independent of law." In other words, militias exist only as defined and regulated by the state or federal government, which in Illinois at the time was the 8,000-member Illinois National Guard (as the Court noted in its decision). To deny the government the power to define and regulate militias would, according to the court, "be to deny the right of the State to disperse assemblages organized for sedition and treason, and the right to suppress armed mobs bent on riot and rapine [pillaging]." Thus, the *Presser* case confirmed the understanding that the right to bear arms came into play only in connection with the formation and conduct of the militia, as formed and regulated by the government. The Court emphatically rejected the idea that citizens could create their own militias, much less that the Second Amendment protected citizens' rights to own weapons for their own purposes.

In 1894, the Supreme Court ruled in *Miller v. Texas* (153 U.S. 535; 1894) that a Texas law "prohibiting the carrying of dangerous weapons" did not violate the Second Amendment. Again, the Court said that the right to bear arms did not apply to the states. The Court ruled similarly in *Robertson v. Baldwin* (165 U.S. 275; 1897), saying that a law barring the carrying of concealed weapons did not violate the Second Amendment. In *Patsone v. Commonwealth* (232 U.S. 138; 1914) the Court ruled that a Pennsylvania law prohibiting unnaturalized, foreign-born persons from possessing firearms was constitutional.

The most important Supreme Court case in this sequence is *United States v. Miller* (307 U.S. 174; 1939). (Even though this case came in the twentieth century, which is the subject of Chapter 3, it fits most logically with discussion of the three earlier Supreme Court cases.) The *Miller* case was founded on a challenge to the National Firearms Act of 1934, which regulated the interstate transport of various weapons. Jack Miller and Frank Layton were convicted of transporting an unregistered 12-gauge sawed-off shotgun (having a barrel less than eighteen inches long) across state lines in violation of the 1934 act. They challenged the act's constitutionality by claiming that it was a violation of the Second Amendment and that it represented an improper use of the commerce power.

A federal district court sided with Miller and Layton, saying that the law was indeed a violation of the amendment, although Judge Heartsill Ragon provided no explanation or justification for this conclusion in his very brief opinion.

On appeal to the Supreme Court, the lower court ruling was reversed (thereby wiping away its legal effect), and the claims of the defendants were turned aside. The unanimous Court ruled that the federal taxing power could be used to regulate firearms and that firearm registration was constitutional, as was the 1934 law. Beyond this, the Court was unequivocal in saying that the Second Amendment must be interpreted by its "obvious purpose" of ensuring an effective militia as described in Article I, section 8 of the Constitution (to which the Court referred in its decision). Speaking for the Court, Justice McReynolds wrote:

> In the absence of any evidence tending to show that possession or use of a "shotgun having a barrel of less than eighteen inches in length" at this time has some reasonable relationship to the preservation or efficiency of a well regulated militia, we cannot say that the Second Amendment guarantees the right to keep and bear such an instrument. Certainly it is not within judicial notice that this weapon is any part of the ordinary military equipment or that its use could contribute to the common defense.

Thus, the Court stated that citizens could only possess a constitutional right to bear arms in connection with service in a militia. In addition, it affirmed the constitutional right of the Congress, as well as the states, to regulate firearms. Most of the rest of the decision is an extended discussion of the antecedents of the Second Amendment. Justice McReynolds cited various classic works, colonial practices, and early state laws and constitutions to demonstrate the importance of militias and citizen-armies to the early United States as the explanation for the presence and meaning of the Second Amendment.

Critics of this case have on occasion taken the wording quoted above to mean that the Court would protect under the Second Amendment the private ownership of guns that do bear some connection with national defense. Such an interpretation is mistaken for two reasons. First, the Court is saying that possession of a weapon like a sawed-off shotgun could only be allowed by the

Court under existing law if that possession were connected with militia service. Since the two men charged with violating the 1934 law obviously did not have the gun while serving in the military, the government was justified in prosecuting them without running afoul of the Second Amendment. And as the *Presser* case established, citizens may not create their own militias; militia service can only occur through government-organized and regulated militias. (The Court cited *Presser* in the *Miller* case.)

Second, to protect the ownership of weapons based on their military utility alone (ignoring the question of whether individuals who owned firearms were doing so as part of their militia service) would justify the private ownership of a vast array of militarily useful weapons manageable by an individual, from bazookas and howitzers to tactical nuclear weapons, all of which are subject to extremely tight government restrictions. No serious argument can be made that the Second Amendment, or the *Miller* decision, protects the right of citizens to possess such weapons when they are not in actual military service. Ironically, sawed-off shotguns can and do have military value, as they were used in trench warfare during World War I (Lund 1987, 109). Presumably, the Court was unaware of this. Remembering that the Court's judgment in this case arose from the challenge to the National Firearms Act (the source from which it drew and quoted the definition of a sawed-off shotgun), its remedy lay in the failure of Miller and Layton to claim any credible connection to Second Amendment-based militia activities.

The Second Amendment has received brief mention in two other, more recent Supreme Court cases. In *Adams v. Williams* (407 U.S. 143; 1972) Justice Douglas, along with Justice Marshall, commented in a dissenting opinion of a case dealing with a search and seizure of a suspect that the Second Amendment posed no obstacle whatsoever to extremely strict gun regulations, even including the banning of weapons possession entirely. The Douglas-Marshall comments here were *dicta,* however, meaning that they did not pertain to the legal questions of the case at hand. In *Lewis v. United States* (445 U.S. 90; 1980), the Court upheld the constitutionality of a 1968 law that barred felons from owning guns, saying that the law did not violate the Second Amendment, citing *United States v. Miller*. In a challenge to the Gun Control Act of 1968, the Court said that gun regulations were allowable as long as there was some "rational basis" for them, meaning that the regulations merely had to serve some legitimate purpose, which, the Court said, the 1968 law served. This standard is significant because it is one that is easily met, especially as compared with the higher standard the Court has set for laws that might conflict with other Bill of Rights freedoms, such as free speech or free press. Thus, the *Lewis* case made clear that the Second Amendment was not accorded the same importance as other parts of the Bill of Rights.

None of this means that gun ownership is somehow illegal or unrecognized by the law. As the Supreme Court noted in the case of *Staples v. United States* (511 U.S. 600, 608; 1994), "there is a long tradition of widespread lawful gun ownership by private individuals in this country." This does not mean, nor did the Court say, that private firearms ownership is protected by the Second Amendment. All of the Court cases make clear that the Second Amendment comes into play only in connection with citizen service in a government organized and regulated militia. None of these Court cases endorses or protects any Second Amendment–based individual right of citizens to own firearms for their own uses or purposes.

OTHER COURT RULINGS

These Supreme Court cases represent an unbroken line to current Court thinking. Some critics have argued that the nineteenth-century cases, especially *Cruikshank* and *Presser,* are no longer pertinent to interpreting the Second Amendment because they were handed down over 100 years ago, rendering them somehow obsolete or irrelevant (Levinson 1989). This assertion is false, not only because court cases are not discarded merely because they are old, but because the courts continue to cite them as good law pertinent to understanding and interpreting the Second Amendment. For example, these two cases were cited as good law on the Second Amendment, consistent with the fact that the Supreme Court has held with its refusal to incorporate the Second Amendment from the nineteenth century to the present, in a 1964 Supreme Court case (*Malloy v. Hogan*, 378 U.S. 1, 5).

Lower federal courts have followed the Supreme Court's reasoning on the meaning of the Second Amendment in a variety of cases. Challenges to gun regulations and related efforts to win a broader interpretation of the Second Amendment (including efforts to incorporate the Second Amendment) have been uniformly turned aside. In more than twenty cases since *United States v. Miller*, federal courts of appeal "have analyzed the Second Amendment purely in terms of protecting state militias, rather than individual rights" (*United States v. Nelson*, 859 F.2d 1318 [8th Cir. 1988], at 1320).[1]

In a case appealed to the Supreme Court from New Jersey in 1969, *Burton v. Sills* (394 U.S. 812), a challenge to a gun law alleging a violation of the Second Amendment was "dismissed for want of a substantial federal question." The Supreme Court has declined to hear appeals in the several instances when such appeals were made (referred to as denying certiorari, or "cert. denied"), thus letting the lower court rulings stand. The inescapable conclusion is that the Supreme Court has settled this matter (Burger 1990) and has no interest in crowding its docket with cases that merely repeat what has already been decided.

In the most famous of these federal appeals court cases, the Supreme Court declined to hear an appeal of two lower federal court rulings upholding the constitutionality of a strict gun control law passed in Morton Grove, Illinois, in 1981. The ordinance banned the ownership of working handguns, except for peace officers, prison officials, members of the armed forces and National Guard, and security guards, as long as such possession was in accordance with their official duties. The ordinance also exempted licensed gun collectors and owners of antique firearms. Residents who owned handguns could actually continue to own them, but they were required to keep them at a local gun club instead of in the home (*Quilici v. Village of Morton Grove*, 532 F. Supp. 1169; 1981; 695 F.2d 261; 1982). Brushing aside arguments of those opposing the law, the court of appeals confirmed that possession of handguns by individuals is not part of the right to keep and bear arms; that this right pertains only to militia service; that the local law was a reasonable exercise of police power; and that the Second Amendment does not apply to the states, "even if opponents to gun control find it illogical." Stating the matter succinctly, the federal appeals court concluded: "Construing the [Second Amendment] according to its plain meaning, it seems clear that the right to bear arms is inextricably connected to the preservation of a militia...." These rulings from the federal courts are consistent with the little-known fact that in the twentieth century, no gun law was ever declared unconstitutional as a violation of the Second Amendment. (The same was true in the nineteenth century, including dozens of state court rulings, with the exception of a case from a Georgia state court, *Nunn v. State* [1 Kelly 243; 1846], when the court did void part of a state gun law partly on Second Amendment grounds.)

Beyond this, we can summarize several observations about the Second Amendment. First, the amendment reflected a vital concern of the country's founders pertaining to the type of military force that would defend the country from manifold threats within and outside of the country, the desire to protect state power and sovereignty as distinct from that of the federal government, and the expectation that eligible members of the militia would have to bring their own weapons, given the uncertainty about whether the government could or would supply adequate arms. Second, like some other elements of the Constitution, such as the Third Amendment prohibition against the quartering of troops in people's homes during peacetime, the concerns that gave rise to the Second Amendment evaporated as reality changed—that is, as the country turned away from unorganized or general citizen militias, the Second Amendment was rendered obsolete. The surviving element of the old militia system, the organized or volunteer militia, was brought mostly under federal government control through a series of federal laws enacted in the early twentieth century. Therefore, government control of what remained of the old militia system shifted mostly to the national government. Although this arrangement was a departure from the militia system contemplated by the Constitution's founders and the authors of the Bill of Rights, it reflected the nation's shifting military priorities and was ruled constitutional in several Supreme Court cases (in particular, the *Maryland* and *Perpich* cases discussed earlier in this chapter).

Third, the Supreme Court and federal courts have consistently recognized these new military and political realities, and thus have not incorporated the Second Amendment, as the courts have most of the rest of the Bill of Rights (also not incorporated is the Third Amendment, the grand jury clause of the Fifth Amendment, the Seventh Amendment, the excessive fines and bail clause of the Eighth Amendment, and the Ninth and Tenth Amendments). The consensus of constitutional law scholars is that the incorporation process is at an end (since the last incorporation decision in 1969), with the possible exception of the fines and bail clause (Cortner 1981, 279). Thus, even if the Second Amendment did protect an individual right to bear arms outside of service in a militia, it would still not apply to the states because it has not been incorporated and so would not be a right citizens could claim in their daily lives. Conversely, even if the Court reversed itself and incorporated the Second Amendment, it would apply only to the old concept of universal militia service, a practice abandoned before the Civil War.

THE TEXTBOOK VIEW

Added confirmation of the courts' understanding is found in most standard texts on the Bill of Rights. From classic analyses such as those of Joseph Story (1987) and Thomas Cooley (1931) to modern treatments, the verdict is the same. In his standard text on the Bill of Rights, Irving Brant says: "The Second Amendment, popularly misread, comes to life chiefly on the parade floats of rifle associations and in the propaganda of mail-order houses selling pistols to teenage gangsters..." (1965, 486). Similar, if less sarcastic sentiments are found in other standard works. For example, Peltason noted that the Second Amendment "was designed to prevent Congress from disarming the state militias, not to prevent it from regulating private ownership of firearms" (1988, 168). (See also Dumbauld 1957; Sexton and Brandt 1986.) According to Robert A. Rutland, the Second Amendment (along with the Third) has become "obsolete" (1955, 229). Moreover, standard legal reference works used by lawyers and judges reflect this perspective (*American Law Reports* 1983).

CONCLUSION

Based on the intentions of the Constitution's framers, the authors of the Second Amendment, historical practices, and court interpretation, the Second Amendment protects citizen service in a government-organized and regulated militia. It was not designed to provide any set of individual rights distinct or apart from that service. Even if the old-style militia system were reactivated, these restrictions would apply. Although some may view this conclusion as a threat to liberty, or as an entree to undesirable gun regulations, neither concern is supported by this analysis.

The United States has a long and sentimental attachment to legitimate gun uses, referred to as the gun culture, that continues to preserve and protect the proper place of guns in the modern United States, primarily as they are used for hunting and sporting purposes (Spitzer 1998). Even though the actual frequency of gun use and ownership during the colonial and early U.S. periods has been exaggerated, it is nevertheless a long and honorable tradition. The presence or absence of gun laws in the United States rests with the political process involving Congress, the presidency, and state and local governments, not with the Second Amendment. However, the amendment will continue to receive great attention.

This discussion leads to an important question: if the Second Amendment is essentially an artifact of a bygone era, why is it so often invoked, and why does it provoke so much discussion? This two-part question has a two-part answer: because anything mentioned in the Constitution evokes special reverence and awe, a fact that encourages those who debate gun control to cite the amendment to support their political arguments; and because some writers in recent years have sought to prod the courts to reinterpret the Second Amendment as protecting an individual right to own firearms for personal (that is, other than militia) uses. In the next chapter, we will examine these elements of the gun debate.

NOTE

1. The other federal court of appeals cases include: *Cases v. U.S.*, 131 F.2d 916, 922-23 (1st Cir. 1942), cert. denied sub nom *Velazquez v. U.S.*, 319 U.S. 770 (1943); *U.S. v. Tot*, 131 F.2d 261, 266 (3d Cir. 1942), reversed on other grounds, 319 U.S. 463 (1943); *U.S. v. Johnson*, 441 F.2d 1134, 1136 (5th Cir. 1971); *U.S. v. McCutcheon*, 446 F.2d 133, 135-36 (7th Cir. 1971); *Stevens v. U.S.*, 440 F.2d 144, 149 (6th Cir. 1971); *Cody v. U.S.*, 460 F.2d 34, 36-37 (8th Cir. 1972), cert. denied, 409 U.S. 1010 (1972); *Eckert v. City of Philadelphia*, 477 F.2d 610 (3d Cir. 1973); *U.S. v. Day*, 476 F.2d 562, 568 (6th Cir. 1973);

U.S. v. Johnson, 497 F.2d 548, 550 (4th Cir. 1974); *U.S. v. Warin*, 530 F.2d 103, 106 (6th Cir. 1976), cert. denied, 426 U.S. 948 (1976); *U.S. v. Graves*, 554 F.2d 65, 66-67 (3d Cir. 1977); *U.S. v. Oakes*, 564 F.2d 384, 387 (10th Cir. 1977), cert. denied, 435 U.S. 926 (1978); *Quilici v. Village of Morton Grove*, 695 F.2d 261, 270 (7th Cir. 1982), cert. denied, 464 U.S. 863 (1983); *Thomas v. Members of City Council of Portland*, 730 F.2d 41 (1st Cir. 1984); *Farmer v. Higgins*, 907 F.2d 1041 (11th Cir. 1990), cert. denied, 111 S.Ct. 753 (1991); and *Fresno Rifle & Pistol Club v. Van de Camp*, 965 F.2d 723 (9th Cir. 1992); *Love v. Pepersack*, 47 F.3d 120, 124 (4th Cir. 1995); *Hickman v. Block*, 81 F.3d 168 (9th Cir. 1996); *U.S. v. Wright*, 117 F.3d 1265, 1273 (11th Cir. 1997); *Peoples Rights Organization, Inc. v. City of Columbus*, 152 F.3d 522, 539 (6th Cir. 1998); *U.S. v. Napier*, 233 F.3d 394 (6th Cir. 2000); *U.S. v. Metcalf*, 221 F.3d 1336 (6th Cir. 2000), cert. denied; *U.S. v. Finitz*, 2000 WL 1171139 (9th Cir. Aug. 17, 2000); *U.S. v. Hancock*, 231 F.3d 557 (9th Cir. 2000).

References and Further Reading

American Law Reports, Federal. 1983. Rochester, NY: The Lawyers Co-Operative Pub. Co.

Bellesiles, Michael A. 1998. "Gun Laws in Early America." *Law and History Review* 16 (Fall): 567–589.

———. 2000. *Arming America: The Origins of a National Gun Culture.* New York: Alfred A. Knopf.

Bogus, Carl T. 1998. "The Hidden History of the Second Amendment." *U.C. Davis Law Review* 31 (Winter): 309–408.

Boorstin, Daniel J. 1964. *The Americans: The Colonial Experience.* New York: Vintage.

Brant, Irving. 1965. *The Bill of Rights.* Indianapolis, IN: Bobbs-Merrill Co.

Burger, Warren. 1990. "The Right to Bear Arms." *Parade Magazine* (14 January): 4–6.

Cogan, Neil H., ed. 1997. *The Complete Bill of Rights.* New York: Oxford University Press.

Cooley, Thomas M. 1931. *General Principles of Constitutional Law.* Boston: Little, Brown. First pub. 1880.

Cooper, Jerry. 1997. *The Rise of the National Guard.* Lincoln, NE: University of Nebraska Press.

Cornell, Saul. 1999. "Commonplace or Anachronism." *Constitutional Commentary* 16 (Summer): 221–246.

Cornell, Saul, ed. 2000. *Whose Right to Bear Arms Did the Second Amendment Protect?* Boston: Bedford/St. Martin's.

Cortner, Richard C. 1981. *The Supreme Court and the Second Bill of Rights.* Madison: University of Wisconsin Press.

Cress, Lawrence D. 1982. *Citizens in Arms: The Army and the Militia in American Society to the War of 1812.* Chapel Hill: University of North Carolina Press.

Dumbauld, Edward. 1957. *The Bill of Rights.* Norman: University of Oklahoma Press.

Ehrman, Keith A., and Dennis A. Henigan. 1989. "The Second Amendment in the Twentieth Century." *University of Dayton Law Review* 15 (Fall): 5–58.

Farber, Daniel A., William N. Eskridge Jr., and Philip P. Frickey. 1993. *Constitutional Law.* St. Paul, MN: West Pub. Co.

Farrand, Max. 1913. *The Framing of the Constitution of the United States.* New Haven, CT: Yale University Press.

Farrand, Max, ed. 1966. *The Records of the Federal Convention of 1787.* 4 vols. New Haven, CT: Yale University Press.

Feller, Peter Buck, and Karl L. Gotting. 1966. "The Second Amendment: A Second Look." *Northwestern University Law Review* 61 (March/April): 46–70.

Fischer, David Hackett. 1994. *Paul Revere's Ride.* New York: Oxford University Press.

Hamilton, Alexander, James Madison, and John Jay. 1788. *The Federalist Papers.* Reprint 1961, New York: New American Library.

Herz, Andrew D. 1995. "Gun Crazy: Constitutional False Consciousness and Dereliction of Dialogic Responsibility." *Boston University Law Review* 75 (January): 57–153.

Higginbotham, Don. 1998. "The Federalized Militia Debate." *William and Mary Quarterly* 55 (January): 39–57.

Jensen, Merrill. 1965. *The New Nation.* New York: Vintage.

Kennett, Lee, and James LaVerne Anderson. 1975. *The Gun in America.* Westport, CT: Greenwood.

Levinson, Sanford. 1989. "The Embarrassing Second Amendment." *Yale Law Journal* 99 (December): 637–659.

Lund, Nelson. 1987. "The Second Amendment, Political Liberty, and the Right to Self-Preservation." *Alabama Law Review* 39 (Fall): 103–130.

Macaulay, Thomas Babington. 1879. *The History of England from the Accession of James II.* 5 vols. New York: T. Y. Crowell.

Mahon, John K. 1960. *The American Militia: Decade of Decision, 1789–1800.* Gainesville: University of Florida Press.

Malcolm, Joyce Lee. 1994. *To Keep and Bear Arms.* Cambridge, MA: Harvard University Press.

McPherson, James M. 1988. *Battle Cry of Freedom.* New York: Oxford University Press.

Millett, Allan R., and Peter Maslowski. 1984. *For the Common Defense.* New York: Free Press.

Peltason, Jack W. 1988. *Corwin and Peltason's Understanding the Constitution.* New York: Holt, Rinehart, and Winston.

Rakove, Jack N. 2000. "The Second Amendment: The Highest Stage of Originalism." *Chicago-Kent Law Review* 76: 103–166.

Richardson, James D., ed. 1913. *Messages and Papers of the Presidents.* 11 vols. Washington, DC: Bureau of National Literature.

Riker, William. 1979. *Soldiers of the States: The Role of the National Guard in American Democracy.* Salem, NH: Ayer Co.

Rossiter, Clinton. 1953. *Seedtime of the Republic.* New York: Harcourt, Brace, and World.

Rutland, Robert A. 1955. *The Birth of the Bill of Rights.* Chapel Hill: University of North Carolina Press.

Samaha, Joel. 1993. *Criminal Law.* Minneapolis/St. Paul: West Pub. Co.

Schwartz, Bernard. 1971. *The Bill of Rights: A Documentary History.* 2 vols. New York: Chelsea House.

Schwoerer, Lois G. 2000. "To Hold and Bear Arms: The English Perspective." *Chicago-Kent Law Review* 76: 27–60.

Sexton, John, and Nat Brandt. 1986. *How Free Are We?* New York: M. Evans and Co.

Shy, John. 1990. *A People Numerous and Armed.* Ann Arbor: University of Michigan Press.

Skowronek, Stephen. 1982. *Building a New American State.* New York: Cambridge University Press.

Snow, Donald M., and Dennis M. Drew. 1994. *From Lexington to Desert Storm.* Armonk, NY: M. E. Sharpe.

Spitzer, Robert J. 1998. *The Politics of Gun Control.* New York: Chatham House.

Story, Joseph. 1987. *Commentaries on the Constitution.* Durham, NC: Carolina Academic Press. First published 1833.

Veit, Helen E., Kenneth R. Bowling, and Charlene Bangs Bickford, eds. 1991. *Creating the Bill of Rights.* Baltimore: The Johns Hopkins University Press.

Weatherup, Roy G. 1975. "Standing Armies and Armed Citizens: An Historical Analysis of the Second Amendment." *Hastings Constitutional Law Quarterly* 2 (Fall): 961–1001.

Wiener, Frederick B. 1940. "The Militia Clause of the Constitution." *Harvard Law Review* 54 (December): 181–220.

Wills, Garry. 1999. *A Necessary Evil.* New York: Simon and Schuster.

3

Twentieth-Century Issues

*T*HE TWO MOST IMPORTANT powers exercised by any government are the power of the purse (that is, over the raising and spending of revenue) and the power of the sword (that is, over the use of force, including police power and military power). Under the nation's first constitution, the Articles of Confederation, these key powers rested primarily with the states, a fact that explained why national governance was ineffectual under the Articles. Not surprisingly, two key national crises in the 1780s, arising directly from the purse and the sword, provided the critical impetus for calling a national convention to revise the nation's system of governance: economic woes and political instability (McLaughlin 1962).

Over the objections of Antifederalists, the new system of governance created under the modern Constitution vested the powers of the purse and the sword squarely, although not exclusively, with the new federal government. The Second Amendment pertained to the second of these as it arose from concerns in the eighteenth century about maintaining the proper balance of military power between the states and the national government, through the states' instrument of military authority—the militias. Yet the old-style universal militia system, always unstable in the eighteenth century, declined rapidly during the nation's formative years. The needs and concerns that gave rise to the Second Amendment disappeared, as did those that prompted the inclusion of the Third Amendment in the Bill of Rights pertaining to the quartering of troops in people's homes during peacetime.

As the old militia system died out, so, too, did the vagaries of the law behind it. The outstanding fact of the constitutional law of the Second Amendment in the twentieth century is that there is so little of it, as compared with other Bill of Rights freedoms. Only occasionally in the twentieth century were legal challenges to gun control laws based on the Second Amendment filed. In no instance were these relatively few challenges successful (see chapter 2); that is, no gun control law was ever declared unconstitutional as a violation of the Second Amendment (of several dozen state court decisions in the nineteenth century, one did strike down a state gun law; that case is discussed later). As former Harvard Law School Dean and Nixon administration Solicitor General Erwin Griswold noted, "Never in history has a federal court invalidated a law regulating the private ownership of firearms on Second Amendment grounds" (1990). Thus, while gun control was one of the most enduringly controversial issues in the second half of the twentieth century, and into the twenty-first, court actions concerning the Second Amendment have played virtually no legal role in the political firestorm of gun politics—although the amendment has played an important symbolic role in the political debates concerning this issue, a factor discussed later in this chapter. In recent decades, however, some writers and advocates of gun use and gun rights have sought to resurrect the Second Amendment as law by trying to vest it with new meanings, in order to reinject the amendment into contemporary law and politics.

ALTERNATE VIEWS

Some argue that the Second Amendment really bestows upon every U.S. citizen a right to have guns, aside from or in addition to militia service. This argument first appeared in a law journal article published in 1960 (Hays). Up until that time, law journal articles published as early as 1874 ("The Right to Keep and Bear Arms") interpreted the Second Amendment as did the courts—as one pertaining only to citizen service in a government-organized and regulated militia (Spitzer 2000).

Hays admitted that the courts had adopted the collective view in interpreting the Second Amendment, saying that there was no individual right to bear arms to be derived from the amendment, as the courts had read it. He also referred to the bearing of arms as a privilege, not a right. But Hays went on to raise two new Second Amendment arguments that would appear often in subsequent publications. One argument asserted that the Second Amendment supported an individual or personal right to have firearms, in particular for personal self-defense, separate and apart from citizen service in a government militia. The second argument was that the amendment created a citizen "right of revolution" or "insurrection," meaning that citizens had a right to engage in armed revolt against their government if they felt that the government was behaving in an unjust manner. Consistent with this second argument, Hays offered the startling proposition that the Civil War was a "lawful effort" by the South to secede from the United States. These two arguments have been the basis for modern controversy concerning the meaning of the Second Amendment. Both views have been strongly promoted by political groups opposed to stronger gun laws, such as the National Rifle Association, as a way to win support for their arguments against new gun laws. This phenomenon is discussed in greater detail in this and the next chapter.

The Individualist Argument

The individualist interpretation is usually supported by citing selected quotations from colonial or federal documents or debate that emphasize the right of all Americans, or individual citizens, to carry guns, aside or apart from their service in a militia. The main problem with this analysis is that none of the available direct evidence that explains the purpose of the Second Amendment supports the individualist view. As historian Jack Rakove concluded, "No coherent intention or understanding of the existence and scope of a private, individual right to keep and bear arms could accordingly be derived" from this evidence (2000, 112), including the debates at the Constitutional Convention and those of the First Congress.

Information that is cited to support the individualist view is usually far removed from direct debates on the amendment or often relies on isolated supporting quotes pulled out of context. For example, Halbrook (1982, 25) supports the individualist point of view by quoting Antifederalist leader Patrick Henry during the Virginia convention convened in 1788 to ratify the new Constitution. Henry said: "The great object is, that every man be armed.... Every one who is able may have a gun." This quote would seem to support the view that at least some early leaders advocated general popular armament aside from militia purposes. Yet here is the full quote of Henry from the original debates:

> May we not discipline and arm them [the states], as well as Congress, if the power be concurrent? so that our militia shall have two sets of arms, double sets of regimentals, &c.; and thus, at a very great cost, we shall be doubly armed. *The great object is, that every man be armed.* But can the people afford to pay for double sets of arms, &c.? *Every one who is able may have a gun.* But we have learned, by experience, that, necessary as it is to have arms, and though our Assembly has, by a succession of laws for many

years, endeavored to have the militia completely armed, it is still far from being the case. (Elliot 1836, III, 386; emphasis added)

When one reads the full quotation, it is obvious that Henry's comments are about citizens having guns to serve in the militia and the impact this might have on the balance of power between the states and Congress.

To take another example, Kates argues that the phrase "bear arms" in the Second Amendment means to carry them and must refer to personal weapons and therefore to a personal or individual right (1983). A person cannot, for example, bear or literally carry an artillery piece or a cannon. But as historian Garry Wills notes, the phrase "bear arms" has a long historical lineage that refers specifically to the equipment used by soldiers in war. As Wills says, "One does not bear arms against a rabbit" (1999, 257).

Some also cite debate from Pennsylvania during its consideration of the new Constitution. In a motion that was defeated, but supported by a minority of convention members, the following wording was offered:

> That the people have a right to bear arms for the purpose of defense of themselves and their own state, or the United States, or for the purpose of killing game; and no law shall be passed for disarming the people or any of them, unless for crimes committed, or real danger of public injury from individuals; and as standing armies in the time of peace are dangerous to liberty, they ought not to be kept up; and that the military shall be kept under strict subordination to and governed by the civil power. (Cogan 1997, 182)

The fact that this motion was defeated means, obviously, that it did not represent the views of the majority of Pennsylvania delegates (nor the views of ratifiers in the other states, nor the views of the authors of the Second Amendment, since no such wording was offered, or debated, in these instances). One can thus conclude, for example, that killing game was not covered under the Second Amendment. But even if we accept for a moment the idea that these opinions did have some bearing on the Second Amendment, we note that the paragraph provides for governmental authority to disarm citizens in the cases of "crimes committed" and "danger of public injury." It therefore would have endorsed the government's power to regulate the ownership of firearms. In addition, the paragraph also has as its primary focus military concerns. As legal historian Paul Finkelman concluded, "The fact that Madison and Congress did not propose amendments along the lines demanded by the Pennsylvania minority leads to a prima facie conclusion that they did not intend to incorporate such protections into the Bill of Rights" (2000, 212).

In sum, the issue of the bearing of arms as it pertained to the U.S. Constitution and the Bill of Rights always came back to military service and the balance of power between the states and the federal government, as seen in the two most important historical sources, the records of the Constitutional Convention of 1787 and those of the First Congress when the Bill of Rights was formulated.

At the state level, a handful of court cases have been cited to lend some support to the individualist argument. For example, the early case of *Bliss v. Commonwealth* (2 Littell 90; Ky. 1822) struck down a state restriction on weapons carrying as a violation of "the right of the citizens to bear arms." Yet this law was found to be in violation of Kentucky's state right-to-bear-arms-type provision, not of the Second Amendment in the federal Bill of Rights. The wording of the state provision was different, and broader, than that found in the Second Amendment. The Kentucky provision said "the right of the citizens to bear arms in defence of themselves, and the State, shall not be questioned." The *Bliss* case did not rule on, nor did it discuss, the federal right to bear arms. Even so, the *Bliss* ruling was the exception among state court rulings. As another state court noted in 1907: "Nearly all the states have enacted laws prohibiting the carrying of concealed weapons, and the validity of such laws has often been assailed because of denying to the citizen the right to bear arms, but we are not aware that such a contention has ever prevailed, except in the courts of the state of Kentucky" (*State v. Gohl*, 46 Wash. 408).

In *Aymette v. State* (21 Tenn. 154; 1840), the Tennessee state court rejected *Bliss* and did discuss the Second Amendment in the federal Bill of Rights, saying that the purpose of keeping and bearing of arms was for "common defence," and that the phrase "bear arms" referred to military use, not to individuals who wish to carry weapons for their own private purposes. Most of the more than 100 state court cases that deal with the right to bear arms focus on their own state provisions of this right. (See chapter 6 for a listing of state right-to-bear-arms provisions, the wording of which varies widely from state to state.) Obviously, it would be a mistake to try and interpret the federal Second Amendment in the light of a differently worded state right-to-bear-arms-type provision—although some have attempted to do so to support the individualist argument. When the federal Second Amendment was discussed in state cases, it was almost always as a right connected only with citizen service in a government-organized and regulated militia. Indicative of this thinking was the Illinois state court's ruling in an 1879 case, *Dunne v. People* (94 Ill. 120, 135–136, 140). In an extended discussion of the Second Amendment, the court offered several propositions "which are so plain as to admit of no controversy," including this: "The citizen is not entitled under any law, State or Federal, to demand as a matter of right that arms shall be placed in his hands." The court concluded that "The right of the citizen to 'bear arms' for the defence of his person and property is not involved, even remotely, in this discussion. This section [the Second Amendment] has no bearing whatever on that right, whatever it may be...."

Standing almost alone among nineteenth century state cases is *Nunn v. State* (1 Kelly 243, 251). In this 1846 case, the Georgia court did void a portion of a state gun control law that prohibited the open carrying of arms, citing in part the U.S. Constitution's Second Amendment. Yet after proclaiming the comprehensive nature of the right to bear arms, the court said that "all this [is] for the important end to be attained: the rearing up and qualifying [of] a well-regulated militia, so vitally necessary to the security of a free State." Thus, the court embraced the militia-based meaning of the Second Amendment and voided a portion of the state law because it believed that the law impeded the ability to maintain state militias.

The Meaning of "The People"

Some have argued that the reference to "the people" in the Second Amendment has the same meaning as it does in other parts of the Bill of Rights, as in "the right of the people [to] peaceably assemble" in the First Amendment, or the "right of the people to be secure in their persons, houses, papers and effects" from the Fourth Amendment. After all, all citizens are considered to have such First and Fourth Amendment protections, so why shouldn't the Second Amendment be read as meaning that all citizens have an individual right to bear arms? In support of this claim, some have pointed to a 1990 Supreme Court case, *United States v. Verdugo-Urquidez* (494 U.S. 259) for support.

This claim is mistaken on four grounds. First, as discussed in chapter 2, militia service, from colonial times on, always pertained only to those capable and eligible to serve in a militia—that is, healthy young-to-middle-aged men from eighteen to forty-five (excluding the infirm, older men, and nearly all women).

Second, the courts (especially in the *Presser* case) and federal law have clearly defined and interpreted the Second Amendment as having this specific meaning. Thus, the meaning of "the people" in the Second Amendment is indeed different than its meaning elsewhere in the Bill of Rights or Constitution.

Third, there is no reason to believe that the authors of the Bill of Rights attempted, or succeeded, in imposing a single, uniform definition of "the people" in the document, any more than the Bill of Rights was the product of a single person. The Bill of Rights did have the general purpose of enshrining various rights, freedoms, privileges, and protections. But some were very broad, whereas others were very specific. Some, even at the time of their formulation, were considered more important than others, as Bill of Rights author James Madison noted (Brant 1965). Further, like any important bill produced by Congress, legislation is the product of many hands, reflecting many goals, interests, and purposes that interact through legislative bargaining and compromise. The ten amendments composing the Bill of Rights cover many different subjects and concerns, and one cannot assume that the amendments were all constructed the same way. This fact becomes even more clear when one realizes that what became the Bill of Rights began as nearly 200 different amendments when they were considered by the House of Representatives in committee. Of that original number, the House committee reported out seventeen (strongly reflecting Madison's influence). When the proposal went to the Senate, it reduced the number to twelve, omitting freedom of religion, speech, press, and jury trials. Final compromise negotiations resulted in the reinsertion of these rights. Of the twelve then sent to the states for ratification, only ten were adopted. (The two that failed pertained to House of Representatives reapportionment and congressional salary increases; this latter amendment was eventually ratified in 1992 as the Twenty-seventh Amendment.)

Fourth, the *Verdugo-Urquidez* case, sometimes cited to support the claim that the phrase "the people" in the Second Amendment has the same meaning as it does in the rest of the Bill of Rights and the Constitution, has nothing to do with interpreting the Second Amendment, nor does it make any such sweeping ruling. In fact, the case deals with the Fourth Amendment issue of whether an illegal alien from Mexico was entitled to constitutional protection regarding searches. In the majority decision, Chief Justice Rehnquist discussed what was meant by the phrase "the people," since the phrase appears not only in several parts of the Bill of Rights, but also in the Constitution's preamble, in order to determine how, if at all, it might apply to a noncitizen. Rehnquist speculated that the phrase "seems to have been a term of art" that probably pertains to people who have developed a connection with the national community. Rehnquist's speculations about whether the meaning of "the people" could be extended to a noncitizen and his two passing mentions of the Second Amendment in that discussion shed no light, much less legal meaning, on this amendment.

Self-defense

Related to the individualist view is the argument pertaining to personal self-defense. Some argue that the principle of personal self-protection or self-defense (aside from collective defense of one's community from, say, foreign invaders) is, or ought to be, covered by the Second Amendment (Dowlut 1983; Kates 1992). In doing so, some of this analysis intermixes the defense needs of early Americans (against Indians, or predators, for example) with modern personal self-defense against robberies, assaults, rapes, intrusions into people's homes, or other life-threatening circumstances. The fear of crime is a very real modern-day threat, and guns are one potentially useful means to defend one's self or one's home. But as this and the previous chapter show, the Second Amendment pertains to the threats confronted by armies and militias, not to individuals seeking to defend their persons or property from robbery or mayhem.

This does not mean that the law affords no legal protection to individuals who engage in personal self-defense—far from it. American and British common law has recognized and legally sanctioned personal self-defense for hundreds of years, prior to and independent of the Second Amendment. But this right arises from the area of criminal law, not constitutional law. A standard, long accepted definition of self-defense from common law says:

> A man may repel force by force in the defense of his person, habitation, or property, against one or many who manifestly intend and endeavor, by violence or surprise, to commit a known felony on either. In such a case he is not obliged to retreat, but may pursue his adversary until he find himself out of danger; and if, in a conflict between them, he happens to kill, such killing is justifiable. The right of self-defense in cases of this kind is founded on the law of nature; and is not, nor can be, superseded by any law of society.... (American Law Institute 1985, I, pt. 1, 380–381)

The Second Amendment is simply unnecessary as a legal protection for personal defense or defense of the home today, just as it was two centuries ago. Indeed, as defined in the common law tradition, the self-defense principle supersedes even constitutional guidelines. In addition, guns make up only part of the self-defense principle, as they are only one of many methods by which individuals may defend themselves, their families, or their homes.

The "Right of Revolution"

An additional challenge to the standard view that takes an extreme individualist point of view argues that the Second Amendment does or should encompass the right for everyone to have arms because of an innate right of revolution, also referred to as a right of insurrection. This argument says that an armed citizenry is an effective way to keep the government from trampling citizens' rights and liberties because the threat of citizen violence against the government could deter the government from becoming tyrannical. Critics point to the American Revolution as a concrete example of Americans rising up to overthrow the tyrannical British government rulers (Gottlieb 1982; Kopel and Little 1997; LaPierre 1994; Reynolds 1994).

The American Revolution did indeed eliminate British rule through violence. However, that revolution, while fought against one government (the British), was also fought on behalf of another government—the new U.S. government. The Revolution was, in fact, organized by the U.S. national and state governments. And as soon as the United States began its revolution, it established its own new governing system under the Articles of Confederation, followed by the Constitution of 1787. The purpose of these documents was to establish democratic means by which citizens could shape, influence, and even alter their government, through the peaceful means of elections, juries, constitutional amendment, and other modes of democratic expression, so that violence would not be necessary. In any case, for the country's founders, the right of revolution was a "natural right" that was not dependent on the government or its laws for its existence. Violent revolution was the means used to establish self-government. Once that goal was achieved, violence was readily and rapidly set aside as a basis for political change. A constitution was installed in its place.

Most citizens recognize the importance of influencing the actions of the U.S. government by the expression of peaceful democratic values through elections, public opinion, the interest group process, political parties, and the jury box, rather than by pointing guns (whether by threat or deed) at governmental leaders, such as members of Congress, the justices of the Supreme Court, or the president. Few Americans approve of those radical elements in the United States that actively pursue something resembling a right of revolution—the Ku Klux Klan, the skinheads, John Wilkes Booth, Lee Harvey Oswald, the Branch Davidians, convicted Oklahoma City bomber Timothy McVeigh, or Los Angeles rioters (see chapter 4 for further discussion). The clearest instance of Americans attempting to exercise a right of revolution was the Civil War, when the southern states attempted to end rule by the government in Washington, D.C. Virtually no one would argue today that the South had a right under the Constitution to use violence. As legal scholar Roscoe Pound noted, a "legal right of the citizen to wage war on the government is something that cannot be admitted.... In the urban industrial society of today a general right to bear efficient arms so as to be enabled to resist oppression by the government would mean that gangs could exercise an extralegal rule which would defeat the whole Bill of Rights" (1957, 90–91). In other words, the greatest threats to people's rights and liberties have come from individuals who have decided to use force on their own, either against other citizens or against the government.

Further, to carry out any so-called right of revolution is to carry out violence against the government, which means against that government's constitution as well, including the Bill of Rights and the Second Amendment. In short, one cannot carry out a right of revolution against the government while at the same time claiming protections within it.

The Constitution itself makes this point forcefully, as Congress is given the powers "to provide for calling forth the Militia to execute the Laws of the Union, *suppress Insurrections* and repel Invasions" (emphasis added) in Article I, section 8; to suspend habeas corpus "in Cases of Rebellion or Invasion" in section 9; and to protect individual states "against domestic Violence" if requested to do so by a state legislature or governor in Article IV, section 4. Furthermore, the Constitution defines treason in Article III, section 3, this way: "Treason against the United States, shall consist only in levying War against them [the United States was originally referred to in the plural]...." In other words, the Constitution specifically and explicitly gives the national government the power to suppress, by use of force, anything even vaguely resembling revolution. Such revolt or revolution is by constitutional definition an act of treason against the United States. As the Constitution says, the militias are to be used to suppress, not cause, revolution or insurrection. These governmental powers were further detailed and expanded in the Calling Forth Act of 1792 (1 U.S. Stat. 264; see chapter 6), which give the president broad powers to use state militias to enforce both state and federal laws in instances where the law is ignored or in cases of open insurrection. This act was passed by the Second Congress shortly after the passage of the Bill of Rights. In current law, these powers are further elaborated in the *U.S. Code* (10 U.S.C. 331–334) sections on "Insurrection." No government could survive with a provision in its constitution saying that, in effect, if the citizens of the country do not like their government, they could overthrow it by force.

Spreading Arguments in the Media

These new arguments concerning the meaning of the Second Amendment have been aggressively pushed into the popular media. When this happens, minor distortions can be depicted as major findings.

For example, an article in a prominent national newspaper reported in 1999 that one of the key factors leading to new academic interest in the Second Amendment was "a recently unearthed series of clues to the Framers' intentions." Two examples were cited in the article. One is an allegedly recently discovered "early draft" of the Second Amendment authored by James Madison where "he made 'The right of the people' the first clause [of the Second Amendment]. . . ." The second is a letter written by Thomas Jefferson to an English scholar, John Cartwright, in which "Jefferson wrote that 'the constitutions of most of our states assert, that all power is inherent in the people; . . . that it is their right and duty to be at all times armed'" (Levey 1999). Despite the article's claim to the contrary, neither of these quotes is recently unearthed, nor are they clues to the meaning of the Second Amendment. The first of these quotes has been known to scholars of the Constitution for decades, as it was part of Madison's original Bill of Rights resolution, offered in the House of Representatives on June 7, 1789, and has been a part of publicly available congressional records from that day to the present. It has also been cited in past writings on the Second Amendment and the Bill of Rights. It is thus no new discovery, nor does it alter what is already known about the Second Amendment.

The Jefferson letter to Cartwright was reprinted in *The Writings of Thomas Jefferson*, published in 1904. Leaving aside the facts that Jefferson did not attend the Constitutional Convention of 1787, was not a member of the First Congress, and penned the letter in question in 1824, the full quotation from which the brief excerpt above was drawn makes clear what Jefferson was writing about:

> The constitutions of most of our States assert, that all power is inherent in the people; that they may exercise it by themselves, in all cases to which they think themselves competent (as in electing functionaries executive and legislative, and deciding by a jury of themselves, in all judiciary cases in which any fact is involved,) or they may act by representatives, freely and equally chosen; that it is their right and duty to be at all times armed; that they are entitled to freedom of person, freedom of religion, freedom of property, and freedom of the press. (Lipscomb 1904, XVI, 45)

Jefferson was referring to state constitutions and offering a seat-of-the-pants listing of Bill of Rights freedoms, therefore including the reference to being armed as a right and duty (remembering that federal and state laws then required men of militia age to be so armed for militia service). Nothing Jefferson said in this letter amounts to a new contribution to the understanding of the Second Amendment, nor does it contradict existing meaning. Yet newspaper readers, and other reporters, might reasonably conclude that these so-called new clues to understanding the Second Amendment are both, when in fact they are neither.

Seeking Shelter under the Fourteenth Amendment

As discussed in chapter 2, the Supreme Court has declined to incorporate the Second Amendment—that is, to apply it to the states through the due process and equal protection clause of the Fourteenth Amendment, which says that "No State shall ... deprive any person of life, liberty, or property, without due process of law; nor deny any person within its jurisdiction the equal protection of the laws." The most important civil liberties described in the Bill of Rights, such as freedom of speech, press, religion, protection from unlawful searches and seizures, and the right to counsel, were applied to the states by the Supreme Court from the 1930s through the 1960s (the last incorporation case, applying the protection against double jeopardy in the Fifth Amendment to the states, was in 1969). There is general agreement that the incorporation process is at an end, with the possible exception of the excessive fines and bails clause of the Eighth Amendment. Those portions of the Bill of Rights that have not been incorporated, in addition to the Second Amendment, include the Third Amendment (quartering of troops in people's homes in peacetime), the grand jury clause of the Fifth Amendment, the Seventh Amendment (pertaining to the right to a jury trial in civil cases), the fines and bails clause of the Eighth Amendment, and the Ninth and Tenth Amendments.

The reasons for the Supreme Court's refusal to incorporate these are twofold: first, most of these unincorporated enumerated rights are simply not considered vital or essential for the administration of due process in the states; second, they already establish rights for the states or the people, making incorporation unnecessary (Abraham 1972). Thus, the Ninth Amendment simply says that "The enumeration in the Constitution of certain rights shall not be construed to deny or disparage others retained by the people." That is, the fact that certain specific rights are protected in the Constitution does not mean that other rights cannot be possessed by the people. The Tenth Amendment says that "The powers not delegated to the United States by the Constitution, nor prohibited by it to the States, are reserved to the States respectively, or to the people." The whole point of this amendment was to reassure the states that they could retain powers not otherwise barred to them, or specifically given to the national government. Here again, the incorporation of this amendment would be unnecessary, as its purpose was to assure state power (Chase and Ducat 1973).

In the case of the Second Amendment, both of these circumstances apply. Like the Tenth Amendment, the Second provided a reassurance to the states—specifically, that they would maintain the right to form militias. The abandonment of the old militia system, and the subsequent nationalization of defense responsibilities, had the effect of removing the Second Amendment far from any vital or fundamental due process right. It is conceivable, of course, that the courts might someday decide to incorporate the Second Amendment. If they were to do so, it would mean that the states could be held subject to the amendment's terms and protections, meaning that the keeping and bearing of arms by citizens in connection with service in a government-organized and regulated militia could not be infringed. In short, it would signal a new affirmation of the states' right to renew militia activities of old. Yet the actual effect on the states of incorporating the Second Amendment would be little to none, because virtually every state already has a Second-Amendment–type provision in its state constitution (see chapter 6 for a list of these provisions), and most of those state provisions are broader and more sweeping in their wording than the Second Amendment. (Six states have no right-to-bear-arms–type provision in their state constitution: California, Iowa, Maryland, Minnesota, New Jersey, and New York.) One of the most sweeping provisions is that in the West Virginia Constitution. It says that "a person has the right to keep and bear arms for the defense of self, family, home, and state, and for lawful hunting and recreational use." Yet even under these more expansive state right-to-bear-arms provisions, gun regulations have generally been upheld in state and federal courts as a constitutional and proper exercise of state powers to regulate firearms.

This discussion of incorporation raises an additional, related argument offered by a few—namely, that the Fourteenth Amendment somehow created, enhanced, or validated a constitutionally based individual right to bear arms aside or apart from citizen militia service. To support this claim, advocates generally cite post–Civil War debate in Congress that referenced the Second Amendment or the bearing of arms. Typical of these claims is that of Halbrook (1984, 112), who quotes Senator Jacob M. Howard's (R-MI) comments during debate over the Fourteenth Amendment in 1866. "When he introduced the Fourteenth Amendment in Congress, Senator Jacob M. Howard . . . referred to 'the personal rights guaranteed and secured by the first eight amendments of the Constitution; such as freedom of speech and of the press; . . . *the right to keep and bear arms*. . . . [emphasis added by Halbrook]'" Halbrook makes two claims from this and related quotes. One is that the reference to "personal rights," apparently offered in the same context as mention of the right to bear arms, means that this "personal right" is an "individual right." The second claim is to argue for total incorporation—that is, application of all of the Bill of Rights to the states. Although even this abbreviated quote suggests that Senator Howard was merely listing the parts of the Bill of Rights, the full quote from Senate debate clarifies the point further:

> To these privileges and immunities [spoken of in Article IV of the Constitution], whatever they may be—for they are not and cannot be fully defined in their entire extent and precise nature—to these should be added the personal rights guaranteed and secured by the

first eight amendments of the Constitution; such as the freedom of speech and of the press [First Amendment]; the right of the people peaceably to assemble and petition the Government for redress of grievances, a right appertaining to each and all the people [First Amendment]; the right to keep and bear arms [Second Amendment]; the right to be exempted from the quartering of soldiers in a house without the consent of the owner [Third Amendment]; the right to be exempt from unreasonable searches and seizures, and from any search or seizure except by virtue of a warrant issued upon formal oath or affidavit [Fourth Amendment]; the right of an accused person to be informed of the nature of the accusation against him, and his right to be tried by an impartial jury of the vicinage [Sixth Amendment]; and also the right to be secure against excessive bail and against cruel and unusual punishments [Eighth Amendment]. (Avins 1967, 219)

It is clear from the full quote that the senator's reference to "personal rights" was simply a synonym for all of the rights of the Bill of Rights. There is no reason to believe that this reference articulates, or implies, an individual right to bear arms aside or apart from the conventional understanding of citizen participation in a government-organized and regulated militia. As for the question of full incorporation of the Bill of Rights under the Fourteenth Amendment, one may argue that this quote supports such an idea. Although the argument that the Fourteenth Amendment was designed to provide for total incorporation is a minority viewpoint among constitutional scholars (and it has been rejected by the courts), it is at least a bona fide argument. The claim that the Fourteenth Amendment somehow created, elevated, or ratified an individual right to bear arms, either as part of the Second or Fourteenth Amendments, is not. In any case, to make such an argument about the Fourteenth Amendment is also to argue implicitly that the Second Amendment, as originally drafted, did not create such an individual right in the first place (otherwise, there would be no reason to resort to the Fourteenth to support such a line of reasoning).

Halbrook (1998, viii) expands this Fourteenth Amendment analysis when he attempts to link together the Fourteenth Amendment with two pieces of regular legislation enacted by Congress at about the same time—the Freedman's Bureau Act of 1866 and the Civil Rights Act of 1866—so he can draw on the debate and text of these bills to argue that, when taken together, they provide "the rights of personal security and personal liberty [and] include the 'constitutional right to bear arms.'" Again, Halbrook culls congressional and state debate for any and all references to firearms, the bearing of arms, and the like. Not only is Halbrook seeking to argue that "the Fourteenth Amendment was intended to incorporate the Second Amendment," but further to argue that the "Fourteenth Amendment protects the rights to personal security and personal liberty, which its authors declared in the Freedmen's Bureau Act to include 'the constitutional right to bear arms.' To the members of the Thirty-Ninth Congress, possession of arms was a fundamental, individual right worthy of protection from both federal and state violation" (43). In other words, beyond arguing for total incorporation, Halbrook argues that the Fourteenth Amendment itself protects the bearing of arms.

This line of reasoning has several obvious problems. First and foremost, while it is true that the same congress sought to extend similar, basic rights through the trio of enactments, including the Fourteenth Amendment, the Fourteenth Amendment simply does not provide for anything like a right to bear arms. No court or historian has ever found, or suggested, that the Second Amendment was somehow repeated, amplified, or elevated by the Fourteenth. And while similar, each of these three enactments is, as a matter of law, different, and to attempt to draw out legislative intent behind one enactment (the Fourteenth Amendment) by bringing in others (the Civil Rights Act and the Freedmen's

Bureau Act, both of which were regular pieces of legislation) is erroneous. In fact, when this same argument was presented to the U.S. Court of Appeals for the Ninth Circuit in a 1992 case raising Second Amendment issues, the court also said that these other legislative enactments and the Fourteenth Amendment had no relevance to interpreting the Second Amendment (*Fresno Rifle and Pistol Club v. Van De Kamp*, 965 F.2d 723 (9th Cir. 1992)).

Second, the discussion of arms, personal security, and militias in Congress during this time is by no means a discussion that revolves solely around the Second Amendment. Remember that the U.S. South was in a state of near-total destruction and utter chaos after the end of the Civil War, a fact heightened by the race hatred found in the region in the aftermath of the freeing of millions of slaves and the presence of thousands of former Confederate soldiers who were allowed to keep their arms. Little wonder that there was so much discussion in Congress of security and safety issues.

Third, as an interpretation of the Second Amendment, the congressional debates of the 1860s deserve no special, if any, consideration. These debates were not debates over the meaning of that amendment per se, occurring as they did over seventy years after adoption of the Bill of Rights. They were political debates over how best to extend hard-won rights, restore order, and reconstruct new governments in the South.

Fourth, the yearning for total incorporation, or any kind of elevation of the Second Amendment, was rejected by political leaders of the time. Eight years after adoption of the Fourteenth Amendment, the Supreme Court explicitly rejected the idea in *United States v. Cruikshank* (discussed in chapter 2). Three years before *Cruikshank*, in 1873, the Supreme Court dealt total incorporation what constitutional scholar Henry J. Abraham has called "a crushing defeat" (1972, 43) in *The Slaughterhouse Cases* (16 Wallace 36; 1873). The thinking of most constitutional scholars on this subject is summarized by Andrea L. Bonnicksen this way: "A look at the debates surrounding the framing of the Fourteenth Amendment reveals some evidence that the members of Congress did intend the amendment's due process clause to incorporate the Bill of Rights, but the more compelling evidence shows otherwise" (1982, 13). As discussed earlier, the Court did not incorporate any part of the Bill of Rights until 1897. This fact alone puts to rest the idea that total incorporation was somehow the consensus of opinion of the time.

In Supreme Court history, three justices have, at one point or another, advanced the idea that the Bill of Rights should be incorporated in its totality: John M. Harlan, William O. Douglas, and Hugo Black. Justice John M. Harlan served around the turn of the twentieth century (not to be confused with his grandson of the same name, Justice John Marshall Harlan who served on the court from the 1950s to the 1970s); Douglas and Black served from the 1930s to the 1970s. Justice Black made the case for total incorporation most strongly in his dissent in *Adamson v. California* (332 U.S. 46; 1947). He made no specific mention of the Second Amendment in his opinion. In an article he published later, Black defended his total incorporation thesis (1960, 873). In that article, he offered this brief comment on the Second Amendment: "Although the Supreme Court has held this Amendment to include only arms necessary to a well-regulated militia, as so construed, its prohibition is absolute." Black thus endorsed the militia-based view of the amendment laid out in the 1939 *Miller* case. His further comment concerning its absolute nature referred to the fact that the amendment was not modified as, say, the way the Fourth Amendment barred only "unreasonable" searches and seizures (allowing reasonable searches and seizures to proceed). Black's efforts notwithstanding, support for total incorporation died with these justices, and no Court member has advanced the idea since.

The research tactic applied to attempting to find a connection between the Fourteenth and Second Amendments follows that described by historian Garry Wills (1999, 257–258) in his analysis of individualist research on the Second Amendment. "The tactic . . . is to ransack any document, no matter how distant from the . . . debates, in the hope that someone, somewhere, ever used 'bear arms' in a non-military way. . . ." In the case of incorporation, this search extends, fruitlessly, to eight decades after the writing of the Second Amendment.

The Second Amendment and Politics

Despite the problems with the individualist and right of revolution theories, they have received considerable attention in recent years, because some well-known writers have published articles advancing these ideas in prominent legal publications (e.g., Amar 1992; Levinson 1989; Williams 1991). These articles have, in turn, received attention in newspapers and magazines. To take one example, Sanford Levinson's often-cited article (1989) advances several familiar, but mistaken, arguments. He asserts that: the Second Amendment has been largely ignored in standard legal publications like law reviews; that the three nineteenth-century Supreme Court cases interpreting the Second Amendment are of no use in interpreting the Second Amendment now because they came before the Court began the process of incorporating parts of the Bill of Rights; that the Second Amendment invites ordinary citizens to use firearms to both threaten their own government and to engage in vigilantism (citizens taking the law into their own hands rather than relying on the police or other law enforcement agencies); and that the Second Amendment protects an individual right of citizens to use firearms for personal self-defense. Levinson supports these propositions by arguing that the wording of the Second Amendment is sufficiently vague so as to allow for the individualist interpretation, that the definition of militias can be taken broadly enough to encompass all citizens and to lead to a blending of both collective and individual interpretations, and that the wording of other amendments supports his reading of the Second Amendment.

To discuss each of the arguments in turn, while it is true that the amount of writing on the Second Amendment in legal publications has not matched in volume that of other Bill of Rights subjects, Levinson ignores the thirty-nine articles published in law reviews from 1912 to 1979 that discuss the meaning of the Second Amendment (more accurately, forty-one with articles published in 1874 and 1917 that were omitted from legal indexes), as well as most of more than two dozen articles written and published in the 1980s on this subject before the publication of his article (Spitzer 2000). The subject thus has not been ignored in legal writings. The nineteenth-century Supreme Court cases interpreting the Second Amendment, discussed in detail in chapter 2, are not somehow invalid or irrelevant because they came before the Supreme Court began to incorporate the Bill of Rights, because the Court has had numerous opportunities to hear Second Amendment cases in recent years and could have accepted any of them for review. That it chose not to do so simply means that it was content to leave the Second Amendment unincorporated, as it has done with other parts of the Bill of Rights. As the courts themselves have noted, these nineteenth-century cases continue to be valid for interpreting the meaning of the Second Amendment.

As discussed earlier in this and the previous chapter, the idea that the Second Amendment provides a legal basis for citizens to make violent revolution against the U.S. government was specifically rejected by the Court in the *Presser* case, and it is flatly contradicted by the Constitution itself, which specifies that militias are to be used to suppress, not cause, insurrection. And there is no basis for the assertion that the Second Amendment gives citizens the right to take the law into their own hands, instead of leaving law enforcement to police agencies. As for personal self-defense, this is indeed a right of citizens, but the Second Amendment is both irrelevant and unnecessary to this right, as it is protected in state criminal laws and the common law tradition.

The ideas advanced by Levinson and other writers have received wider attention partly because they are novel. They have also been promoted aggressively by interest groups that oppose stronger gun laws.

Raising the Second Amendment Banner

Most importantly, the National Rifle Association (NRA) has devoted ever more of its efforts and resources toward advancing its political agenda of opposing the enactment of additional gun control laws, repealing existing restrictions, and protecting the rights and practices of gun users and gun owners. In its political campaigns, the NRA has come to rely heavily on an individualist view of the Second Amendment in order to argue that any effort to restrict citizen access to guns is an infringement on the Second Amendment, even though the law has never supported such a claim. More importantly, the NRA has thrown its considerable resources behind efforts to generate publications that support this point of view. Although the NRA has referred to the right to bear arms for decades in its publications, it intensified its efforts to argue that the Second Amendment specifically protected the right of individuals to own guns when the organization became more politically active, and more unflinchingly conservative, in the 1970s (Spitzer 1998).

For example, here is an excerpt from a typical NRA membership letter that demonstrates its now-frequent invocation of the Second Amendment (note also that it refers to the second portion of the Second Amendment—the "right to bear arms"—but makes no mention of the first half of the amendment—"a well regulated militia"):

> They [the government] try to take away our right to bear arms. . . . The gun banners simply don't like you. . . . They don't want you to

own a gun. And they'll stop at nothing until they've forced you to turn over your guns to the government.... *if the NRA fails to restore our Second Amendment freedoms, the attacks will begin on freedom of religion, freedom of speech, freedom from unreasonable search and seizure* (quoted in Anderson 1996, 14; emphasis in original).

As in so much of the NRA's political rhetoric in recent decades, any and every gun regulation is described as an infringement on the Second Amendment. The right to bear arms is also placed like a domino against other Bill of Rights freedoms, as seen in the warning that gun regulations will somehow lead to the destruction of other Bill of Rights protections, including freedom of religion, speech, and from unreasonable search and seizure. No law, court case, or credible legal doctrine supports any of these assertions. Their significance, rather, is the politically scary message that gun laws somehow represent improper tampering with the Second Amendment, which in turn will allegedly lead to improper tampering with other Bill of Rights freedoms. As journalist Jack Anderson concluded, "The version of the Second Amendment endlessly propagandized by the NRA is a myth and nothing but a myth, pure and simple" (1996, 60). The NRA's use of Second Amendment rhetoric extends back many decades (at least to the 1930s), as seen in its publications, such as the *American Rifleman.* But as the organization became more politicized in the 1970s and 1980s, it accelerated this rhetoric. The NRA has also encouraged outside writing in support of its views, as, for example, when it began an annual "Stand Up for the Second Amendment" essay contest in 1994, giving out $25,000 as a first prize. Chapter 4 will detail recent efforts by the NRA to inject the Constitution, and specifically the Second Amendment, into the gun debate to an even greater degree. It will also discuss the modern militia movement, which has also drawn heavily on the views of the Second Amendment espoused by the NRA and other organizations.

Other political organizations have formed, usually with direct or indirect assistance from the NRA, to promote the individualist view of the Second Amendment. The earliest of these groups is the Citizens Committee for the Right to Keep and Bear Arms, formed in 1971 by gun enthusiasts who felt that the NRA was not being tough enough on gun issues. The research arm of the organization is the Second Amendment Foundation (SAF), a nonprofit, tax-exempt organization formed in 1974. Both organizations were founded by Alan M. Gottlieb, who has also promoted his views, and those of the organization, though his writings (1981; 1982). The SAF Web site says that it is "dedicated to promoting a better understanding about our Constitutional heritage to privately own and possess firearms."

The Gun Owners of America (GOA) is another gun-related group formed to promote gun ownership and gun rights. Formed in 1975, the organization has been headed since 1976 by Larry Pratt. Although small by comparison with the NRA, the GOA takes an even harder line against gun control than the NRA. It also aggressively promotes the Second Amendment as both a basis for an individual right to own firearms and as a basis for arming citizens to make war on their government if, in their view, the government becomes tyrannical. Pratt was active in Republican presidential candidate Pat Buchanan's 1996 campaign, until it was learned that Pratt had associations with extremists in the militia movement. Pratt has also alienated some by arguing that public school teachers should be armed to ward off gun violence in schools (Bruni 1999).

A group formed in 1992 by individuals seeking to promote the individualist interpretation of the Second Amendment, called Academics for the Second Amendment (ASA), asserted in an open letter first published as an advertisement in several national publications that "the Second Amendment does not guarantee merely a 'right of the states,' but also a 'right of the people,' a term which ... is widely understood to encompass a personal right of citizens." The organization further stated: "Our primary goal is to give the 'right to bear arms' enshrined in the Bill of Rights its proper, prominent place in Constitutional discourse and analysis." Thirty-three of the forty-eight individuals who signed the letter were lawyers or had law school affiliations. This group has received funding for its activities, including academic conferences, research, advertisements, the filing of "friend of the court" briefs in gun control cases, and money awards for publications from the NRA and from member contributions. The ASA's president, Joseph Olson, has served on the NRA's governing board (Heller 1995; Hoffman 1996).

Another group, formed in 1994 and called the Lawyer's Second Amendment Society, similarly seeks to advance the individualist view through its activities and publications, including a newsletter called "The Liberty Pole." This organization also maintains a legal defense fund to finance legal actions against gun control laws. It should be noted, however, that these lawyers represent a minority view within their profession, as the American Bar Association has repeatedly endorsed the collective-militia view of the Second Amendment for several decades.

Finally, a number of individualist writers have direct ties to the NRA or other gun groups. Seven such writers, who alone are responsible for over two dozen law journal articles on the Second Amendment, have been employed by the NRA or served on its governing board, or have served as officials of state gun groups. Most prominently, Stephen Halbrook, whose writings are discussed in this chapter at some length, has served as the NRA's chief legal counsel in court (for example, he argued before the Supreme Court in *Printz v. United States* (521 U.S. 898) and during congressional hearings) (Spitzer 2000).

According to one critic, these organizations' activities have a very specific public policy purpose—namely, they are "part of a concerted campaign to persuade the courts to reconsider the Second Amendment, to reject what has long been a judicial consensus, and to adopt a different interpretation—one that would give the Amendment judicial as well as political vitality and would erect constitutional barriers to gun control legislation" (Bogus 1998, 316). Aside from the articles that have been published in recent years advancing the individualist point of view, there is reason to believe that these efforts have had other effects, which will be discussed in chapter 4.

Gun control groups have not matched the NRA and its allied groups in promoting and financing writing, although Dennis Henigan, who directs the Legal Action Project for the Center to Prevent Handgun Violence (a pro–gun control group), has published several articles on the meaning of the Second Amendment. And in 2000, the Chicago-Kent Law School joined with the Joyce Foundation to underwrite a conference on the Second Amendment, in which I participated, designed to provide a fresh scholarly look at the Second Amendment debate that proved to be mostly critical of the individualist view ("Symposium on the Second Amendment" 2000).

The 1920s Gun Debate

The irony of this ever-greater reliance on Second Amendment rhetoric on the part of the NRA and its allies, and the related effort to attach dire warnings of destruction of the amendment to any and every gun control proposal, is that this rhetoric is a relatively recent phenomenon. Before the 1960s, the Second Amendment was rarely mentioned in connection with the political debate over attempts to strengthen gun laws. This fact is starkly apparent in an examination of the national gun control debate in the 1920s.

Although it may seem strange today, there was much national discussion and debate in the 1920s over the enactment of gun laws that, by contemporary standards, would be considered very strict. The gun control debate of the 1920s was brought on by growing public dismay at the apparently rising toll of handgun-related deaths and mayhem (witnessed especially in urban areas), dating back to the late 1800s, and by the rise of gangster-related violence witnessed after Prohibition took effect in 1919. Chief among the reforms proposed was licensing of gun owners and the outright banning of pistols. This latter proposal is especially interesting, because it represents the most extreme and dramatic proposed gun regulation raised in the public forum from the 1920s to the present. Many books, articles, and countless editorials discussed the many facets of a ban on pistols and other gun control measures (Hoffman 1925). For example, an entire book of essays and arguments, pro and con, on the virtues and problems with a pistol ban was published in 1926. The book consists of a detailed summary of the arguments on both sides, followed by a bibliography of over ninety articles, mostly from newspapers and magazines, and eleven articles reprinted in full. The book begins with the following "Resolved," offered in classic debate style: "That the manufacture, sale, importation, transportation, and possession of pistols and cartridges to fit them should be prohibited except as needed for army, navy, police, and other official purposes" (Beman 1926, 7). This proposition had already won the support of prosecutors, police chiefs, judges, many lawmakers around the country, and the American Bar Association through its Special Committee on Law Enforcement.

In the detailed summary of arguments against the pistol ban proposal, no mention was made of the Second Amendment, even though the arguments against such a law included the assertion of rights violations—specifically, that a pistol ban would be an "interference with personal liberty" and that it would infringe on "the inalienable right of self-defense" (12). Opponents of a pistol ban in the 1920s clearly understood that the right of self-defense was not dependent on the Second Amendment, a fact that escapes many contemporary writers.

To take another example from the era, a magazine article published in 1922 titled "The Right to Bear Arms" offers vigorous criticism of a pistol ban, arguing that murders would occur with or without pistols present. As Kephart says, it is "silly to blame the instrument for the deed" (1922, 70). "If we must pass a nation-wide law about pistols," he concludes, "let it be a law that encourages reputable citizens to get the best ones and train themselves to use them right, and that makes it as difficult as possible for disreputable citizens to get arms equally good" (71). Even though the article's title might lead the modern reader to believe that the author relies on the Second Amendment to support his belief that law-abiding citizens should have access to pistols and other firearms, the author makes no mention of the amendment. Even law-related objections to such restrictive gun law proposals also generally ignored the Second Amendment. For example, when Arizona's governor vetoed a more strict pistol law in 1927, his objection to the bill was framed as "a serious invasion of personal liberties" (Imlay 1930, 800).

An even more startling fact of the gun debate in the 1920s was the active and affirmative role played by gun groups. A leading and pioneering force in the construction of uniform firearms legislation was the United States Revolver Association, "a non-commercial organization of amateur experts in the use of revolvers" (Imlay 1926, 767). Although it worked to ensure that responsible gun owners could continue to obtain access to firearms, including pistols, it also supported tough gun regulations to keep guns out of the wrong hands. In 1923 alone, California, North Dakota, and New Hampshire all adopted firearms legislation copied from the Revolver Association's recommendations.

This description of the gun control debate in the 1920s does not mean that commentators from the era were somehow unaware of, or insensitive to, the Second Amendment or constitutional considerations. For example, a 1925 article in the popular magazine the *Literary Digest* ("Closing the Mails", 33) discussed debate in the House of Representatives concerning a bill to bar mail order sale of pistols, a measure eventually enacted in 1927. Summarizing that debate, the article noted that "one congressman is reported to have thought it an abridgement of the citizen's constitutional right to bear arms. . . ." To take another example, Imlay's discussion of a uniform firearms law concluded that "the provisions of the Uniform Firearms Act present no constitutional objections . . ." (769). A 1927 editorial from a New York newspaper commented on the meaning of the amendment, after quoting its text, by saying:

> . . . the framers of the [Second] amendment were thinking of a State or National Guard and not of putting deadly weapons into the hands of any murderous bandit in the streets who chose to call himself a "citizen." Moreover, the courts have held that the Second Amendment of the Federal Constitution refers to the National Government and does not restrict the State in its right to exercise its police powers in matters that concern the regulation of the manufacture, sale and possession of firearms. ("The Battle" 1927, 9)

Even though strict pistol regulations were widely discussed and debated in the press, in state capitals, and in Congress in the 1920s, the federal government failed to act except for a 1927 law that barred the sale of handguns to private individuals through the mail. This failure was attributable in large measure to opposition by President Calvin Coolidge, the general belief of the time that the federal government should be little involved in such policy matters, and the belief that state action was the most appropriate venue for policy change (Leff and Leff 1981). This attitude changed in the depths of the Great Depression and as a consequence of Franklin D. Roosevelt's New Deal in the 1930s, when the national government assumed sweeping new powers and responsibilities formerly left to the states or to private individuals. Some state governments responded with tougher laws in the 1920s, but even then policymakers realized that sporadic state responses were likely to be ineffective without a uniform national standard (Leff and Leff 1981).

Dragging in the Bill of Rights

By the 1960s, groups opposing gun control had succeeded in infusing public discourse on gun control issues with Second Amendment rhetoric. Notably, debate over the Gun Control Act of 1968 included invocation of the Second Amendment by the NRA, although even by this time the argument played only a limited, supporting role ("Gun Controls" 1968; "The Gun" 1968). Historian Richard Hofstadter wrote with undisguised dismay at the end of the 1960s of the "supposed 'right' to bear arms . . ." to which "otherwise intelligent Americans cling with pathetic stubbornness . . ." (1970, 4).

The escalating Second Amendment rhetoric coincided with an opposing political trend—public fear and outrage over gun-related crime and escalating pressures to enact stronger gun laws. The unique political advantage to the invocation of the Second Amendment by gun law opponents in Congress and elsewhere is that it "can serve as a smokescreen to avoid taking up a position based on the facts" and that this position "owed more to a desire to enhance an elected representative's prospects of re-election than any devotion to the actuality of constitutional principle" (Windlesham 1998, 209). That is, members of Congress and other government decision-makers could explain their opposition to politically popular gun control measures by saying that they felt them to infringe on the Constitution's Second Amendment, rather than saying that they were bowing to political pressure from the NRA. In recent gun control efforts in Congress, such as the Brady Law of 1993 and the assault weapons ban of 1994, opponents of the bills often argued that they opposed these measures because they believed them to violate the Second Amendment (Nicholson 1995).

Rights Talk

The debates over the Second Amendment that have been described up until now in this chapter, including the individualist view, the "right" of revolution, and the relationship between the Second Amendment and the Fourteenth Amendment have been the subject of some heated debate among legal specialists. But with the exception of some recent controversies to be discussed in chapter 4, they have played virtually no role in the legal struggles concerning gun control in the twentieth century. Although there have been court challenges to gun control laws based on the argument that they violated the Second Amendment, no gun law has ever been declared unconstitutional as a violation of that amendment. Why, exactly, does the Second Amendment provide the kind of "political cover" just described for those who oppose stronger gun laws, and why does it arouse both passion and awe?

A key answer is provided by constitutional scholar Mary Ann Glendon, who argues that, in contemporary U.S. politics, there is an "increasing tendency to speak of what is most important to us in terms of rights, and to frame nearly every social controversy as a clash of rights" (1991, 4). For most of U.S. history, she notes, political debates were far less likely to be peppered with grand references to rights. Without doubt, contemporary Americans are quick to claim that their preferences and wants are based on rights, regardless of whether any actual, legal right stands behind such a claim or not. The advantage of rights claims is obvious. Any political goal or preference is advanced, elevated, and even enshrined, when the advocate can claim that the goal belongs to him or her as a matter of right rather than mere preference. In the case of gun control, if gun owners can persuade the country that gun ownership by individuals is somehow protected by the Second Amendment, then the debate over gun control is transformed from one focused on necessity or practicality to one focused on hallowed constitutional doctrine.

So, for example, gun enthusiasts who enjoy using assault weapons for target shooting will win little public sympathy if they argue for keeping such guns legal merely because they are fun to use. If, on the other hand, they argue for keeping such weapons available because they are protected under the Second Amendment, the argument acquires a dignity similar to that surrounding the Constitution as a whole. According to Glendon, rights talk makes political resolution of such disputes less likely because it "promotes unrealistic expectations, heightens social conflict, and inhibits dialogue that might lead toward consensus, accommodation, or at least the discovery of common ground" (14). This is an accurate description of the prevailing political gridlock that stifles the U.S. gun control debate (Spitzer 1998).

One other place where "rights talk" has become more evident is in the platforms of the political parties. Before 1968, no major party platform made any mention of gun control. That year both Republican and Democratic Party platforms addressed gun control for the first time. With great consistency, the Republican platforms emphasized crime control, whereas the Democratic platforms emphasized gun control, although the Democrats later included a greater emphasis on crime control and preserving legitimate gun use and ownership purposes, such as hunting and sporting. (See chapter 6 for a complete compilation of party platform statements on the gun issue.)

More strident references, ones pertinent to this discussion, began to seep in to the Republican Party platform as the issue became more prominent in the national consciousness. In 1968, the Republican platform supported legislation to control "indiscriminate availability of firearms," but also endorsed "the right of responsible citizens to collect, own and use firearms for legitimate purposes." The same "safeguard" language appeared in the Republicans' 1972 platform. In 1976 the party's platform said, "We support the right of citizens to keep and bear arms." This is the first time that this phrase from the Second Amendment appears. (The Democratic platforms never invoked the Second Amendment, although they did talk about protecting some gun rights.) In 1980, the Republican platform strengthened this wording, saying, "We believe the right of citizens to keep and bear arms must be preserved." This greater emphasis on the constitutional touchstone coincided with the NRA's increased political role and the party's nomination of Ronald Reagan, who strongly endorsed the NRA position (only after his presidency did Reagan publicly disagree with the NRA, when he reversed his previous positions to come out in favor of both the Brady Law and the assault weapons ban). In every subsequent Republican presidential platform through 2000, the phrase "defend the constitutional right to keep and bear arms" appears. This language is indicative of the political effort to offer opposition to stronger gun laws as a synonym for supporting the Second Amendment. If the history of gun control legislation and of court rulings reveal anything, it is that, as a matter of law, support for gun control does not contradict, emasculate, or compromise the Second Amendment. In political terms, however, Second Amendment rhetoric offers useful political shelter for opposition to stronger gun laws.

Conclusion

The Second Amendment would seem, to the average citizen, to lie at the very heart of the ongoing debate over gun control. As a matter of law, this is not true. For most of U.S. history, the law of the Second Amendment has been a settled matter, in that the amendment has been understood by the courts as pertaining only to citizen service in a government-organized and regulated militia—an activity that came to an end before the Civil War.

Law that is well settled normally receives very little attention. This was true for the Second Amendment. In the second half of the twentieth century, however, the amendment began receiving more attention from two interrelated sources: from political groups, like the NRA, that were trying to gather resources to oppose stronger gun laws; and from a few writers in legal publications who tried to come up with new ways of thinking about the right to bear arms. These two sources were at least partly interrelated, since groups like the NRA encouraged and even financed this new writing, which was produced in part by individuals who worked for such groups. Eventually, this writing was seen as a new interpretation of the Second Amendment, and it therefore began to receive notice by other legal writers and by the media. The effects of these efforts are discussed in chapter 4.

References and Further Reading

Abraham, Henry J. 1972. *Freedom and the Court.* New York: Oxford University Press.
Amar, Akhil. 1992. "The Bill of Rights and the Fourteenth Amendment." *Yale Law Journal* (April): 1193–1284.
American Law Institute. 1985. *Model Penal Code and Commentaries.* Philadelphia: American Law Institute.
Anderson, Jack. 1996. *Inside the NRA.* Beverly Hills, CA: Dove Books.
Ansell, S. T. 1917. "Legal and Historical Aspects of the Militia." *Yale Law Journal* 26 (April): 471–480.
Avins, Alfred. 1967. *The Reconstruction Amendments' Debates.* Richmond: Virginia Commission on Constitutional Government.
"The Battle to Disarm the Gunman." 1927. *The Literary Digest* (19 February): 9.
Beman, Lamar T., ed. 1926. *Outlawing the Pistol.* New York: H. W. Wilson Co.
Black, Hugo L. 1960. "The Bill of Rights." *New York University Law Review* 35: 865–881.
Bogus, Carl T. 1998. "The Hidden History of the Second Amendment." *U.C. Davis Law Review* 31 (Winter): 309–408.
Bonnicksen, Andrea L. 1982. *Civil Rights and Liberties.* Palo Alto, CA: Mayfield Pub.
Brant, Irving. 1965. *The Bill of Rights.* Indianapolis, IN: Bobbs-Merrill Co.
Bruni, Frank. 1999. "Speaking Up for Guns, Lots of Them, for Nearly Anyone." *New York Times* (26 April).
Chase, Harold W., and Craig R. Ducat. 1973. *Edward S. Corwin's The Constitution and What It Means Today.* Princeton, NJ: Princeton University Press.
"Closing the Mails to Murder." 1925. *Literary Digest* (10 January): 33–34.

Cogan, Neil H., ed. 1997. *The Complete Bill of Rights.* New York: Oxford University Press.

"Constitutional Rights in Jeopardy: The Push for 'Gun Control.'" 1998. National Rifle Association.

Dowlut, Robert. 1983. "The Right to Arms." *Oklahoma Law Review* 36 (Winter): 65–105.

Elliot, Jonathan, ed. 1836. *Debates in the Several State Conventions on the Adoption of the Federal Constitution.* 4 vols. Washington, DC: Clerk's Office of the District Court.

Finkelman, Paul. 2000. "'A Well Regulated Militia': The Second Amendment in Historical Perspective." *Chicago-Kent Law Review* 76: 195–236.

Glendon, Mary Ann. 1991. *Rights Talk.* New York: Free Press.

Gottlieb, Alan M. 1981. *The Rights of Gun Owners.* Ottawa, IL: Green Hill Pubs.

———. 1982. "Gun Ownership: A Constitutional Right." *Northern Kentucky Law Review* 10: 113–140.

Griswold, Erwin. 1990. "Phantom Second Amendment 'Rights.'" *Washington Post* (4 November).

"Gun Controls Extended to Long Guns, Ammunition." 1968. *CQ Almanac.* Washington, DC: Congressional Quarterly, Inc.: 549–566.

"The Gun Under Fire." 1968. *Time* (21 June): 13–18.

Halbrook, Stephen P. 1982. "To Keep and Bear Their Private Arms." *Northern Kentucky Law Review* 10: 13–39.

———. 1984. *That Every Man Be Armed.* Oakland, CA: The Independent Institute.

———. 1998. *Freedmen, the Fourteenth Amendment, and the Right to Bear Arms, 1866–1876.* Westport, CT: Praeger.

Hays, Stuart R. 1960. "The Right to Bear Arms: A Study in Judicial Misinterpretation." *William and Mary Law Review* 2: 381–406.

Heller, Scott. 1995. "The Right to Bear Arms." *The Chronicle of Higher Education,* (21 July): A8, A12.

Herz, Andrew D. 1995. "Gun Crazy: Constitutional False Consciousness and Dereliction of Dialogic Responsibility." *Boston University Law Review* 75 (January): 57–153.

Hoffman, Frederick L. 1925. *The Homicide Problem.* Newark, NJ: Prudential Press.

Hoffman, Jan. 1996. "Fund Linked to N.R.A. Gave $20,000 for Goetz's Defense." *The New York Times* (16 April).

Hofstadter, Richard. 1970. "America as a Gun Culture." *American Heritage* 21 (October): 4–11, 82–85.

Imlay, Charles V. 1926. "The Uniform Firearms Act." *American Bar Association Journal* 12 (November): 767–769.

———. 1930. "Uniform Firearms Act Reaffirmed." *American Bar Association Journal* 16 (December): 799–800.

Kates, Don B. 1983. "Handgun Prohibition and the Original Meaning of the Second Amendment." *Michigan Law Review* 82 (November): 204–273.

———. 1992. "The Second Amendment and the Ideology of Self-Protection." *Constitutional Commentary* 9 (Winter): 87–104.

Kephart, Horace. 1922. "The Right to Bear Arms." *Outing: A Journal of Recreation* 80 (May): 70–71.

Kopel, David B., and Christopher C. Little. "Communitarians, Neorepublicans, and Guns: Assessing the Case for Firearms Prohibition." *Maryland Law Review* 56 (1997): 438–554.

LaPierre, Wayne. 1994. *Guns, Crime, and Freedom.* Washington, DC: Regnery.

Leff, Carol Skalnik, and Mark H. Leff. 1981. "The Politics of Ineffectiveness: Federal Firearms Legislation, 1919–38." *Annals of the American Academy of Political and Social Science* 455 (May): 48–62.

Levey, Collin. 1999. "Liberals Have Second Thoughts On the Second Amendment." *Wall Street Journal* (22 November).

Levinson, Sanford. 1989. "The Embarrassing Second Amendment." *Yale Law Journal* 99 (December): 637–659.

Lipscomb, Andrew A., ed. 1904. *The Writings of Thomas Jefferson.* Washington, DC: The Thomas Jefferson Memorial Association.

McLaughlin, Andrew C. 1962. *The Confederation and the Constitution, 1783–1789.* New York: Collier.

Moncure, T. M. 1990. "Who is the Militia." *Lincoln Law Review* 19: 1–25.

Nicholson, E. Bruce. 1995. "Guns and the Congress." In Dennis A. Henigan et al., eds., *Guns and the Constitution.* Northampton, MA: Aletheia Press.

Pound, Roscoe. 1957. *The Development of Constitutional Guarantees of Liberty.* New Haven, CT: Yale University Press.

Rakove, Jack N. 2000. "The Second Amendment: The Highest Stage of Originalism." *Chicago-Kent Law Review* 76: 103–166.

Reynolds, Glenn H. 1994. "The Right to Keep and Bear Arms under the Tennessee Constitution." *Tennessee Law Review* 61 (Winter): 647–673.

"The Right to Keep and Bear Arms for Private and Public Defence." 1874. *The Central Law Journal* 1 (May 28, June 4, June 11, June 18): 259–261, 273–275, 285–287, 295–296.

Rovella, David E. 2000. "Circuit Sights Gun Right." *National Law Journal* (31 May).

Spitzer, Robert J. 1998. *The Politics of Gun Control.* New York: Chatham House.

———. 2000. "Lost and Found: Researching the Second Amendment." *Chicago-Kent Law Review* 76(1): 349–401.

Subcommittee on the Constitution, Judiciary Committee, U.S. Senate. 1982. "The Right to Keep and Bear Arms." 97th Cong., 2d sess. Washington, DC: Government Printing Office.

"Symposium on the Second Amendment: Fresh Looks." 2000. *Chicago-Kent Law Review* 76(1).

Tahmassebi, S. B. 1990. "Gun Control and Racism." *George Mason University Civil Rights Law Journal* 2 (Winter): 6–99.

Williams, David C. 1991. "Civic Republicanism and the Citizen Militia." *Yale Law Journal* 101 (December): 551–615.

Wills, Garry. 1999. *A Necessary Evil.* New York: Simon and Schuster.

Windlesham, Lord. 1998. *Politics, Punishment, and Populism.* New York: Oxford University Press.

4

THE TWENTY-FIRST CENTURY

*I*N THE 1990S, several new developments related to the Second Amendment spurred both renewed political attention and renewed legal action. These actions arose in four different areas. First, Congress grappled with the enactment of new gun control laws that, in turn, intensified public attention, opposition from gun groups, and increased invocation of the Second Amendment by these anticontrol groups. Second, an upsurge in hostility toward the national government helped spur the growth of new, self-styled "militia" groups around the country. These groups claimed the Second Amendment as one basis for their actions. Third, renewed court challenges to gun control laws based on alleged violations of Second Amendment rights persisted in the courts. Fourth, the political invocation of Second Amendment rhetoric in the national gun debate continued to escalate.

One sign of the mounting desire to impose an individualist spin on the Second Amendment arose in 1989 when Rep. Philip Crane (R-IL) introduced a concurrent resolution in the House of Representatives that read in part:

> Whereas the Framers of the second amendment to the Constitution and those who ratified the second amendment intended that the individual retain the right to keep and bear arms in order to protect life, liberty, and property and to protect our Nation from those who would attempt to destroy our freedom: Now, therefore, be it Resolved . . . That it is the sense of the Congress that the Constitution provides that all individual citizens have the right to keep and bear arms, which right supersedes the power and authority of any government. (Subcommittee on Crime 1989, 53–54)

The resolution never came to the floor of the House. Obviously, no such resolution would be necessary if the verdict of history, law, and the courts concerning the meaning of the Second Amendment supported this proposition to begin with. The political stage for the contemporary gun control debate, and for debate about the Second Amendment, was set by the three key national legislative struggles discussed in the next section.

THE BRADY LAW, THE ASSAULT WEAPONS BAN, AND BEYOND

From 1987 to 1993, gun control proponents, led by Handgun Control, Inc. (HCI), placed their primary political emphasis on the enactment of a national waiting period for handgun purchases. The purpose of such a rule was twofold: first, to provide authorities with the opportunity to conduct a background check on the prospective purchaser in order to void handgun purchases by felons, the mentally incompetent, or others who should not have handguns; and second, to provide a cooling off period for those who seek to buy and perhaps use a handgun impulsively, in a fit of temper or rage. The idea of waiting periods for prospective gun buyers dates back at least to the 1930s, when a 48-hour waiting period was applied in the District of Columbia; the drafting of that rule was assisted by the National Rifle Association (NRA), which continued to support the idea until the 1970s when it reversed its position.

On its face, such a procedure certainly represents a modest degree of government regulation, since it merely postpones a handgun purchase by a few days and denies handguns only to those who everyone agrees should not have them. Yet the struggle over enactment of a waiting period took on epic proportions as a bitter power struggle between regulation opponents and proponents, where the ground being fought over was far less important than the struggle itself.

The Brady bill was named after James Brady, the former White House press secretary and subsequent gun control advocate who was seriously injured in the assassination attempt against President Reagan in 1981. The bill was first introduced in Congress in 1987 in the U.S. Senate by Howard Metzenbaum (D-OH) and in the House of Representatives by Rep. Edward F. Feighan (D-OH). It quickly became the top priority of HCI and Sarah Brady, James Brady's wife and HCI leader. The NRA opposed the measure, saying that it would merely be a prelude to stronger regulation, that it would not stop criminals from getting guns, and that it merely inconvenienced those entitled to guns.

The Brady bill was put up to a chamberwide vote for the first time in the House in September 1988, when opponents led by the NRA succeeded in defeating the bill by substituting an NRA-backed amendment for the waiting period, despite a concerted effort by HCI and a coalition of police organizations called the Law Enforcement Steering Committee. By its own account, the NRA spent from $1.5 million to $3 million in the successful effort to kill the bill, mostly on a media campaign and grassroots efforts. Assessing the failed effort, Rep. Feighan noted that at least two dozen House members had privately spoken of their support for the bill but had refused to vote for it not because they feared losing their seats, but because of "the aggravation" that accompanied opposing the NRA.

Two years later, both chambers voted to approve the Brady bill. Initial House approval for a seven-day waiting period came in May 1991 (by a 239–186 vote), with Senate approval (by a 71–26 vote) following a month later. Before passing the Brady bill, the House defeated an NRA-backed substitute, sponsored by Rep. Harley O. Staggers (D-WV), that called instead for an instant computerized background check of prospective handgun purchasers. Such a system would, in theory, eliminate the need for waiting, yet still bar gun purchases by those not eligible.

The problem with such a proposal was that for such a system to work it would require that pertinent records from all the states be fully automated. Yet in 1991, only ten states had such automation; eight states still handled files manually, and nine states did not even maintain the necessary felony records. Moreover, according to an analysis by Congress's Office of Technology Assessment, the time lapse between the conclusion of a criminal case and its logging in state records runs from weeks to months. Thus, the actual development of a viable system would take years and would cost hundreds of millions of dollars. The political motive behind the Staggers proposal was based on the principle that a motion is easier to defeat if the opposition has something to offer in its place. By proposing an alternative of little or no immediate feasibility, the NRA and its allies were proposing a plan that seemed to offer a meaningful reform, yet posed no actual change in gun purchasing procedures for many years to come. The Staggers proposal would become Brady bill opponents' chief rallying point. The Senate version differed from that of the House in that it called for a five-day waiting period instead of seven days and also was attached to a controversial omnibus crime bill. A conference version was hammered out, but it was killed by filibuster in the Senate.

President Bush publicly opposed the Brady bill throughout 1991 and 1992, but linked it with the larger crime bill, saying that he would sign the measure even if Brady was included—but only if the larger crime bill was to his liking. Bush's veto threat hung over the bill, yet it also opened the door to presidential approval, since it provided a means whereby he could have signed the measure into law without seeming to entirely abandon his inclination to oppose most gun control measures. In the end, Bush's qualified veto threat had little effect on the outcome, except to the extent that it buttressed the cause of Senate Republicans who succeeded in blocking the measure.

The Brady bill struggle climaxed in 1993, when supporters promoted a five-business-day waiting period bill. The presence of gun control supporter and newly elected President Bill Clinton in the White House also buttressed Brady's supporters. House Judiciary Committee approval was won on November 4, despite the objections of committee chair and gun control opponent Jack Brooks (D-TX), who also boosted the bill's chances by consenting with reluctance to separate the measure (HR 1025) from a new crime bill. Six days later, the full House approved the Brady bill after fending off several amendments (sponsored by Republicans and Rep. Brooks) designed to weaken the bill. One such amendment, to phase out the waiting period after five years, was adopted. The final vote to pass the bill, HR 1025, was 238–189.

Following the lead of the House, the Senate separated the Brady bill (S. 414) from the larger crime package. The bill faced a Republican filibuster almost immediately, but this move was forestalled by an agreement between the political party leaders to allow floor consideration of a substitute version that included two NRA-backed provisions. The first called for all state waiting periods to be superseded by the federal five-day waiting period (24 states had waiting periods of varying lengths in 1993; 23 also had background checks). This was objectionable to Brady supporters because many states had waiting periods longer than five days, and the move was seen as a violation of states' rights. This amendment was stricken from the bill by a Senate floor vote. The second measure called for ending the five-day waiting period after five years. It survived a vote to kill it. The Senate then faced another filibuster, which looked as though it would be fatal to the bill. Brady supporters and congressional allies all conceded that the bill was dead for the year. The post mortems proved to be premature, however, as within a couple of days the Republicans decided to end their opposition on November 20, sensing a rising tide of impatience and no sense that they could win further concessions from Democratic leaders. The bill was passed that day by a 63–36 vote.

The bill then went to a contentious House-Senate conference on November 22. Opposing factions finally reached an accommodation, and the bill was approved in the Senate by voice vote on November 24, with a promise to consider several modifications in early 1994. President Clinton signed the bill into law on November 30.

As enacted, the Brady Handgun Violence Prevention Act of 1993 (PL 103–159; 107 Stat. 1536) codified a five-business-day waiting period for handgun purchases for the succeeding five years. According to the law, handgun purchases are to be rejected if the applicant has been convicted of a crime that carries a sentence of at least one year (not including misdemeanors); if there is a violence-based restraining order against the applicant; if the person has been convicted of domestic abuse, arrested for using or selling drugs, is a fugitive from justice, is certified as mentally unstable or is in a mental institution, or is an illegal alien or has renounced U.S. citizenship. The law also authorized $200 million per year to help states improve and upgrade their computerization of criminal records, increased federal firearms license fees from $30 to $200 for the first three years, plus $90 for renewals, made it a federal crime to steal firearms from licensed dealers, barred package labeling for guns being shipped to deter theft, required state and local police to be told of multiple handgun sales, and said that police must make a "reasonable effort" to check the backgrounds of gun buyers. In addition, it provided for ending the five-day wait after five years, to be replaced with an instant background check, which began in December 1998. Such checks are conducted through information provided by the FBI's National Instant Criminal Background Check System (NICS). The check must be completed within three days, but 95 percent of the background checks are completed within two hours, according to a U.S. Justice Department report. Even though waiting periods are no longer required by the national government, nineteen states have their own, ranging from a few days to several months. They include Alabama, California, Connecticut, Florida, Illinois, Indiana, Kansas, Maryland, Massachusetts, Minnesota, Missouri, New Jersey, New York, North Carolina, Ohio, Rhode Island, South Dakota, Washington, and Wisconsin.

Opponents of the law, including the NRA, challenged its constitutionality—not as a violation of the Second Amendment's right to bear arms, but as a violation of states' rights under the Tenth Amendment. In 1997, a sharply divided Supreme Court struck down the law's provision requiring local police to conduct background checks in the case of *Printz v. United States* (521 U.S. 898). The ruling did not challenge the propriety of restricting handgun sales (see discussion later in this chapter). Despite the ruling, handgun background checks generally continued on a voluntary basis. From the time of the law's enactment through 2000, nearly 600,000 handgun sales were blocked as the result of the law (about 2.5 percent of all handgun purchases). In addition, the increase in federal firearms license fees helped reduce the number of license holders (that is, gun dealers) from nearly 300,000 to about 74,000 by 2000, as most license holders were not storefront dealers, but private individuals who were willing to pay the low fee in order to save money on their own gun purchases. The Clinton administration issued regulations to monitor dealers more closely as well. Critics argued that the federal government failed to prosecute most Brady law violators. In response, the Clinton administration proposed hiring several hundred additional Bureau of Alcohol, Tobacco, and Firearms (ATF) agents and federal prosecutors to focus on gun law violators. Congress approved the proposal in 2000.

Brady law supporters also continued to note that the background check provision only applied to licensed dealers. At gun shows and flea markets in most states, guns can be bought and sold by unlicensed individuals. An estimated 40 percent of gun sales occur at gun shows, flea markets, and other unregulated secondary market venues (over 4,000 gun shows are held every year). National legislative efforts to close this so-called gun show loophole failed in 1999 and 2000.

The second major legislative enactment of the 1990s was the Assault Weapons Ban of 1994, enacted under Title XI as part of the Violent Crime Control and Law Enforcement Act of 1994 (PL 103–322; 108 Stat. 1796). This provision banned for ten years the possession of nineteen named assault weapons and several dozen copycat models (fully automatic weapons were already regulated under federal law). Under the terms of the law, semiautomatic assault weapons were defined under three categories: rifles, pistols, and shotguns. Semiautomatic rifles and pistols fell under the law if they had the ability to accept a detachable magazine, plus possessed at least two other characteristics of such weapons; shotguns were considered semiautomatic if they possessed at least two of the assault weapon features. The law also specifically exempted 661 named weapons. In addition, it banned large capacity ammunition feeding devices (those that could hold more than ten rounds). The ban did not apply to assault weapons already in circulation. Guns neither banned nor protected by the law were exempted from its regulations.

These weapons began to come into civilian hands in large numbers with the sale of U.S. Army surplus M1 carbines to civilians in the 1960s, Chinese-made semiautomatic rifles in the 1980s (modeled after the Russian AK-47), and semiautomatic pistols like the MAC-10 in the 1980s and the Tec–9 in the 1990s. In the

1980s, several factors converged to build support for some kind of legal restriction on assault weapons (meaning firearms designed for military use), including spiraling crime rates, the increasing availability of such weapons, and the belief that such weapons served no legitimate hunting or sporting purpose. The key event spurring control supporters was a senseless January 1989 schoolyard massacre in Stockton, California, when five children were killed and twenty-nine others were wounded in a shooting spree by drifter Patrick Purdy, who used a Chinese AK-47 assault rifle. Within weeks, thirty states and many localities were considering bans on these weapons. Two years later, the worst such massacre in U.S. history occurred in a cafeteria in Killeen, Texas, when George J. Hennard killed twenty-two people and himself and wounded twenty-three others. Several studies of guns used in crimes supported the concern that assault weapons were appealing to criminals. Although assault weapons accounted for only about 2–3 percent of all firearms owned in the United States, they accounted for 6–8 percent of gun crimes in the 1990s.

Aside from the fierce political opposition to the ban from the NRA, regulation of such weapons posed a practical problem, since the definition of a semiautomatic weapon is one that fires a round with each pull of the trigger, which would include wooden-stocked hunting rifles. By comparison, a fully automatic weapon is one that fires a continuous stream of bullets as long as the trigger is depressed. Assault-style semiautomatic weapons are distinguished from other semiautomatic weapons in that they have large clips holding twenty to thirty bullets, are more compact in design, have barrels under twenty inches in length, take intermediate-sized cartridges, include extensive use of stampings and plastics, are lighter weight (about six to ten pounds), and were designed for military use. In addition, they often have folding or telescoping stocks, heat-dispersing shrouds, pistol grips, grenade launchers, flash suppressors, and bayonet fittings.

President George Bush responded to public outcry in March 1989 by announcing a temporary ban on the import of certain assault rifles by executive order. The temporary ban became permanent and was later expanded to include a larger number of weapons, earning Bush the ire of the NRA. President Bill Clinton expanded the scope of the import ban in 1993, also by executive order, to include assault-style handguns, like the Uzi. Clinton expanded the order again in 1998.

In Congress, several bills aimed at curbing or banning assault weapons were introduced in 1989, but those bills languished in committee until 1990, when the Senate narrowly approved a provision to ban the production, sale, and possession of nine semiautomatic assault-type weapons. The provision was added to an omnibus crime bill. The House Judiciary Committee had approved a similar measure, but it never left committee. In conference committee, the assault weapons ban was removed from the bill that was enacted into law. In 1991, the Senate again included an assault weapons ban in a larger crime bill. A similar provision was included in the House version of the bill, but it was stripped out in a highly emotional floor vote that occurred one day after the massacre in Killeen, Texas.

In November 1993, the Senate passed a ban on the manufacture of nineteen assault weapons but also included a provision allowing gun dealers to sell guns that had already been produced. The measure, added to a crime bill, also exempted over 650 types of hunting weapons. In the spring of 1994, the House took up the assault weapons ban. From the start, ban supporters shared little optimism that the House would approve the measure. Although the majority of Democrats in Congress were more sympathetic to the measure, some of their leaders, such as Speaker Tom Foley (D-WA), were not. In April, President Clinton weighed in strongly for the ban, enlisting the help of several cabinet secretaries, most notably Treasury Secretary and gun owner Lloyd Bentsen. Ban supporters received unexpected help from Rep. Henry Hyde (R-

IL), a staunch conservative who had opposed gun measures in the past. Thanks in part to Hyde's support, the measure was approved by the Judiciary Committee on April 28, despite the opposition of Committee Chair Jack Brooks (D-TX).

Despite a final tally showing that the measure lacked the necessary votes for passage, the assault weapons ban managed to pass in the House in a stunning finale by a two-vote margin, 216–214, on May 5. The drama was heightened when Rep. Andrew Jacobs Jr. (D-IN), at the urging of several colleagues, switched his vote from against to for in the final seconds of the roll call vote. As with other gun control legislation, the political pressures were intense. A staff person for one freshman Republican representative who supported the bill commented, "You don't know the threats we received" (Spitzer 1998, 116).

Because the assault weapons ban was part of a larger crime bill that had passed in different versions in the two houses, a conference committee was called to iron out those differences. Typically, a bill that survives the legislative gauntlet up to the point of conference committee is all but assured final passage. Such was not the case for the assault weapons ban. Bill supporters initially predicted that the conference committee would complete its work by the end of May. Yet it did not report a bill back to the House and Senate until the end of July, during which time Rep. Brooks, a member of the House-Senate conference, attempted repeatedly to kill the assault weapons ban. Brooks's efforts failed, but he did succeed in inserting provisions that exempted pawnbrokers from the Brady law, and that barred all antihunting protests from taking place on federal lands. Meanwhile, Republican leaders launched a full-scale assault on the $33 billion crime bill, calling it a wasteful piece of legislation laden with pork barrel spending. Anxious to win final approval, and with an eye toward the fall elections, Clinton and his congressional allies pushed for an early vote in the House. This proved to be a serious tactical blunder, however, because they had not lined up the necessary support. In a dramatic reversal on a procedural vote to adopt a rule for the bill, the House rejected the crime bill on August 11 by a vote of 225–210.

Under normal circumstances, a defeat on a rules vote would spell the end of the legislation. Yet President Clinton would not accept the bill's defeat. Clinton launched an intense public campaign, enlisting the assistance of police organizations and several members of his cabinet. Congressional leaders vowed to bring the bill back, and in another departure from normal procedure, they negotiated a new version of the bill, this time cutting the bill's spending by about 10 percent.

On August 21, after three days and two nights of intense negotiation, the revised bill was again brought before the House in a highly unusual Sunday session. This time, with the help of moderate Republicans and four members of the black caucus who were persuaded to vote with the president, the bill passed by a vote of 235–195. The bill then went to the Senate, where after considerable partisan wrangling, the bill was passed. Clinton signed the bill, HR 3355, on September 13. After the Republicans won control of Congress in the 1994 elections, party leaders promised to repeal the ban. In 1996, a measure to repeal passed in the House, but no Senate vote was taken, ending the effort to repeal.

The effectiveness of the federal ban was questioned by many, as manufacturers and dealers were able to make minor or cosmetic alterations to formerly banned weapons in order to avoid the regulations. Four states have also enacted assault weapons bans, including California, Connecticut, New Jersey, and New York, as have several cities (Spitzer 1998, 114–126).

The final significant congressional action toward gun control in the 1990s occurred shortly after the mass shooting at Columbine High School in Littleton, Colorado, on April 20, 1999, when two disgruntled students shot and killed twelve students and one teacher before killing themselves. National shock and outrage put unprecedented pressure on Congress to respond. One month later, on May 20, the Senate passed a bill that would have required background checks for firearms purchases at gun shows and pawn shops (the so-called gun show loophole), revocation of gun ownership for those convicted of gun crimes as juveniles, tougher penalties for juvenile offenders, required sale of locking devices or boxes sold with all new handgun purchases, and a ban on the import of high-capacity ammunition clips (those that could hold more than ten bullets).

The Senate-passed bill met a chilly reception in the House of Representatives. Republican House leaders had long records of opposition to stronger gun laws, and House stalling tactics gave bill foes, led by the NRA, the time they needed to mobilize opposition. From mid-May to mid-June, the NRA spent $750,000 on mass mailings and $300,000 on phone banks. HCI spent about $350,000 on similar activities. On June 17 and 18, a series of votes was taken that resulted in victory for control foes. A final, weakened gun bill was defeated by a coalition of gun control supporters and foes. A conference committee was named to produce a compromise bill, but none ever emerged, ending this final effort at gun control in the 1990s (Spitzer 1999).

Although the Second Amendment was invoked during congressional and national debate over these legislative initiatives, these invocations were purely rhetorical and symbolic. Virtually no one argued seriously that any of these proposed legal changes would run afoul of the Second Amendment. Even so, spinning off from these national legislative gyrations, three efforts to transform and revive the Second Amendment sprang up. The first is the modern so-called militia movement, spurred by individuals who believe that they are entitled to form their own private militias to fight what they believe to be a tyrannical U.S. government. The second is a recent effort by some writers and gun rights organizations to promote new meanings and interpretations of the Second Amendment in order to prod the courts to use this amendment to protect at least some elements of gun ownership. The third is the continuing effort to use constitutional symbolism and rhetoric to buttress the political goals of gun rights groups.

The New Militia Movement

The 1990s witnessed an upsurge of home-grown, self-styled "militias." Scattered around the country, thousands of Americans engaged in preparation for a new revolution in what was dubbed "the new patriot movement." This movement was by no means the first time that self-styled, self-organized militias organized to wreak violence. In the post–Civil War South, the Ku Klux Klan administered violence to terrorize and oppress African Americans. The vigilante-style Klan often considered itself a local militia, even though it operated without official government control (although many local white government officials approved of, and even participated in, the Klan's actions). In the late 1930s, an organization called the Christian Front organized thousands of supporters who adhered to a far-right, anti-Semitic, fascist ideology. A Nazi-sympathetic group called the Silver Shirts organized more than 20,000 members that prepared for armed confrontation and insurrection by amassing vast quantities of weapons and engaging in military-style drill. In 1938, Silver Shirt leader Roy Zachary gained national attention when he announced that if no one else was prepared to assassinate President Franklin D. Roosevelt, he would do so. Believing in a worldwide Jewish conspiracy, this and other right-wing groups studied a publication called *The Protocols of the Elders of Zion*, a nineteenth-century forgery (probably put together by Czarist Russian secret police) that purported to be the transcript of a secret meeting of Jewish leaders describing how they would dominate Christian nations through secret control of banks and other institutions ("Patriot Dreams" 1997). In the 1960s, right-wing groups including the Ku Klux Klan and the Minutemen gained strength as the country entered a period of political and social turmoil. Leftist groups like the Weathermen also engaged in violence and terrorism during this time (Jenkins 1995).

The fears that provoked the formation of neomilitia groups in the 1990s were fanned by four key events: the passage of the Brady Law by Congress in 1993; the assault weapons ban, passed by Congress in 1994 (both discussed earlier in this chapter); the federal government assault on the home of white supremacist Randy Weaver in 1992; and the federal government's siege and assault on the heavily fortified Branch Davidian compound in Waco, Texas in 1993.

The first two events—the Brady law and the assault weapons ban—were the culmination of furious multiyear political battles in Washington, D.C., but represented very modest changes in existing gun law. In fact, even the National Rifle Association (NRA) had favored a waiting period for handgun purchases until the mid-1970s (Davidson 1993, 194). Yet both enactments were seen by right-wing groups and conspiracy theorists as the first steps toward the federal government confiscation of firearms, which in turn was viewed by these groups as the end of liberty in the United States. Closely tied to these enactments, in the view of conspiracy-minded Americans, were the Ruby Ridge and Waco incidents.

Former Vietnam War Green Beret Randy Weaver ran afoul of the law when he failed to appear before a judge to answer an illegal weapons charge. Authorities were suspicious of Weaver, a separatist who had moved to rural northern Idaho in 1983, because of his ties to the violent white supremacist neo-Nazi group Aryan Nations. Weaver refused to turn himself in to authorities, prompting federal agents to lay siege to his cabin, located in Ruby Ridge, Idaho, in 1992. During the standoff, a federal agent was killed by a live-in friend of Weaver, and Weaver's wife and son were killed by federal agents. Weaver eventually gave himself up. In his criminal trial, he was acquitted of most serious charges, and he was later awarded a $3.1 million judgment from the government for the wrongful deaths of his wife and son.

In 1993, four agents of the Bureau of Alcohol, Tobacco, and Firearms (ATF) were killed, and twenty wounded, in an initial assault on the heavily fortified and armed compound of the Branch Davidian religious cult in Waco, Texas, in February 1993. The Branch Davidians, an offshoot of the Seventh-Day Adventists that was led by self-proclaimed messiah David Koresh, believed that the end of the world was fast approaching and that the government was an instrument of this apocalyptic event. Agents had sought to arrest cult leader David Koresh for possession of illegal weapons and explosives and to search the compound. After the initial, failed assault, in which six Branch Davidians were also killed, federal officials laid siege to the compound for fifty-one days. Finally, on April 19, 1993, federal officials sent armored vehicles into the compound. The Davidians had laced the buildings with flammable material that was ignited when the attack began. In the fire that ensued, seventy-four Davidians died; nine escaped the fire (Karl 1995). Subsequent efforts by survivors and their families to win criminal and civil judgments against the government failed. An extensive investigation, headed by former Missouri Republican Senator John Danforth, exonerated law enforcement's role in the event.

These two events sparked outrage among many Americans, including those who maintained no sympathy for the conspiracy-minded views of right-wing separatists. In both the Ruby Ridge and Waco incidents, federal agents were sharply criticized by government investigators and the press for mishandling the operations, including the use of excessive force. For the new militia movement and its sympathizers, however, these events confirmed their worst fears that the U.S. government had fallen into the hands of tyrants. Conspiracists predicted martial law, war, and a totalitarian one-world government run by the hated United Nations. They also charged, among other things, that black helicopters (helicopters allegedly painted in flat black paint with no markings or identification numbers) were monitoring citizens' behavior, that foreign troops were being brought to U.S. soil as part of the government's plot to subvert democracy, that the U.S. government and the United Nations had developed technology to selectively create natural disasters like floods and hurricanes to use against enemies, and that the government was implanting bar codes on money so that government agents could drive by people's homes to count their cash. Many people insisted that these fanciful and paranoid claims had already come true (Stern 1996). Just as the extremist groups of the 1930s closely read *The Protocols of the Elders of Zion,* far right-wing groups of the 1990s studied *The Turner Diaries,* a work of fiction laced with violence, anti-Semitism, and racism that describes a full-scale revolution and race war, ending with worldwide nuclear war and final domination by the white race. The book was first published in 1978 by William Pierce under the pseudonym Andrew Macdonald (1978). Pierce led the National Alliance, a neo-Nazi hate group.

A variety of armed, right-wing paramilitary groups began to spring up around the country in the early 1990s. Although they had no attachment to federal or state governments, these organizations proclaimed themselves militias in the tradition of the Revolutionary War Minutemen. The views of these self-proclaimed militias were often aired in various publications, including magazines like *Soldier of Fortune,* the *American Rifleman,* and other gun publications. In many of these writings, the Second Amendment was cited as a basis for their activities. For example, a typical article in *Soldier of Fortune* charged that "this country is rapidly turning into a police state. A preventative measure against such tyranny lies in citizens [sic] militias. . . . these armed citizens view themselves as a final defense line against a federal government that . . . has become their enemy. The Second Amendment is at the core of their existence. It is viewed as the last constitutional defense against a government bent on oppression" (Williams 1995, 48).

In testimony presented before the U.S. Senate Judiciary Committee's Subcommittee on Terrorism, Technology, and Government Information on June 15, 1995, Michigan militia leader Norman Olson said that "the Second Amendment recognizes that the militia's existence and the security of the state rests [sic] ultimately in the people who volunteer their persons to constitute the militia and their arms to supply its firepower." Olson expressed the prevailing view among self-styled militias that, on the one hand, the Second Amendment provided an inherent right of citizens to form their own militias free from, and even in opposition to, the government. On the other hand, Olson and others also argued that this alleged right did not depend on the Second Amendment, but was a natural right that was beyond the power of the government to regulate. In testimony given at the same hearing, militia of Montana leaders John E. Trochmann and Bob Fletcher complained that their actions were necessary because the presidency had become "a position of dictatorial oppression," that the government "defines human beings as a biological resource under the United Nations ecosystem management program," that the U.S. military was "controlled by foreigners," and that the government had "destroyed" the Second Amendment.

Although estimates of the size and strength of these groups varied widely, at their height in the mid-1990s, they probably rallied around 20,000 hard-core adherents in about 850 groups found in nearly every state (McFadden 1995). Even though many of these groups engaged in paramilitary training, most states have laws prohibiting such activity. Seventeen states maintain antimilitia laws (that is, laws barring privately organized and operated militias), another seventeen outlaw paramilitary training, and seven states outlaw both. States with antimilitia laws (laws barring private militias) are Alabama, Arizona, Iowa, Kansas, Kentucky, Maine, Maryland, Massachusetts, Minnesota, Mississippi, Nevada, New Hampshire, North Dakota, Texas, Washington, West Virginia, and Wyoming. States with laws barring paramilitary training are Arkansas, California, Colorado, Connecticut, Louisiana, Michigan, Missouri, Montana, Nebraska, New Jersey, New Mexico, Oklahoma, Oregon, Pennsylvania, South Carolina, Tennessee, and Virginia. States barring both are Florida, Georgia, Idaho, Illinois, New York, North Carolina, and Rhode Island (Klanwatch Project 1996). Local and state leaders have been reluctant to strictly enforce these laws, however, because the training activities that these laws bar typically occurred in secret and in unpopulated areas. Further, law enforcement authorities feared provoking armed confrontations with these organizations, wary of sparking confrontations similar to those of Ruby Ridge or Waco.

A critical turning point of this self-styled militia activity came on April 19, 1995, with the terrorist bombing of the Alfred P. Murrah Federal Office Building in Oklahoma City, in which 168 people died. Those killed in the blast included a variety of government employees, visitors to the office building, and nearly twenty children who were being cared for at the building's child care center. Convicted bombers Timothy McVeigh and Terry Nichols had maintained ties with militia groups, and Persian Gulf War veteran McVeigh in particular was outraged by Ruby Ridge, Waco, and congressional gun control enactments. In 2001, McVeigh stated expressly that the bombing was his retaliation against the U.S. government for the Ruby Ridge and Waco incidents. Before the bombing, McVeigh read, and sold copies of, *The Turner Diaries*, which included an account of a government office building bombing occurring on April 19 (Kifner 1995; Michel and Herbeck 2001), a fictional event brought to life by McVeigh and Nichols. The dates of April 19 and 20 were given special significance by right-wing groups because the 19th was the date of the battle of Lexington and Concord in 1775 and the government raid on the Branch Davidian compound in Waco in 1993. Adolph Hitler's birthday was April 20. The selection of April 19 by McVeigh for the Oklahoma City bombing was chosen deliberately, as he admitted shortly before he was executed in 2001. Nichols was sentenced to life in prison for his role in the bombing. A third conspirator, Michael Fortier, gave evidence to the government in exchange for a reduced sentence of twelve years. Two high school seniors also embraced the significance of these two dates when they chose to shoot and kill twelve students and a teacher at Columbine High School in Littleton, Colorado, on April 20, 1999. The intense media attention given to the horrifying explosion in Oklahoma City, and to the paranoid beliefs of the mostly secretive militias, helped turn opinion more strongly against these organizations, their leaders, and their ideas.

The National Rifle Association suffered a considerable loss of prestige after the bombing. Since the 1980s, the NRA had demonized the ATF, the federal agency charged with administering gun regulations, calling them fascists and gun-grabbers, and comparing them to Nazis. Just a few weeks before the bombing, NRA Executive Vice-President Wayne LaPierre sent out a six-page fund-raising letter that again compared government agents to Nazis, saying that ATF agents wore "Nazi bucket helmets and black storm trooper uniforms," further charging that they were out to "harass, intimidate, even murder law-abiding citizens." Shortly after the Oklahoma City bombing, in which some ATF agents died, former President George Bush resigned his NRA life membership because of his outrage over the letter. The NRA suffered added embarrassment when it was revealed that NRA leader Tanya Metaksa had met with leaders of the Michigan militia in a hotel lobby in Michigan a few months before the Oklahoma City bombing, although no one suggested that the NRA knew about the bombing plans (Spitzer 1998).

By the late 1990s, the size and potency of these home-grown militia organizations had waned, with fewer than 200 such groups in existence by 2001, owing to public outrage after the Oklahoma City bombing, extensive media attention focused on these and related formerly secretive right-wing activities and beliefs, public revulsion over these groups' predilections toward violence, and a strong economy (Dees and Potok 2001). Two key factors will surely encourage the reemergence of such groups in the future: an economic downturn and the enactment of new gun control laws. The role played by the economy is one that has a long history in the United States and in other nations, as extremist groups usually gain strength when people in economically desperate circumstances are attracted to the simple, all-encompassing explanations and nostrums offered by extremist beliefs. When economic conditions improve, extremist groups wane (Hofstadter 1965).

The Second Amendment has served as a key rallying point for these so-called militia groups. Yet as chapter 2 described, the militias mentioned in the Constitution and in U.S. law can only exist when created and regulated by the federal or state governments. They are instruments of the government that are to be used not only to defend the nation from external attacks, but to suppress rebellion within U.S. borders, as the Constitution specifically states. Thus, by law, the self-proclaimed militia groups that have sought to challenge the U.S. government's authority have no legal claim to the term *militia*. Nor does the Second Amendment protect any purported right of individuals to make war on the U.S. government, as chapter 3 detailed. The U.S. governmental system provides various peaceful means by which citizens who have grievances against the government, or against other citizens, can resolve those grievances without resort to force. In the Ruby Ridge and Waco incidents, armed confrontations and deaths would in all likelihood not have occurred had those individuals who challenged government agents not confronted the agents with armed force at the outset. Even after these tragic confrontations, survivors from both incidents used peaceful means—specifically, legal action through the courts—to hold the government accountable for its actions.

Recent Court Actions

The 1990s also witnessed continued court actions that include the Second Amendment. As discussed in chapter 2, lower federal courts consistently upheld the collective-militia view of the Second Amendment in more than twenty cases in the second half of the twentieth century, following the rulings of several Supreme Court cases. For example, in *United States v. Nelson* (859 F.2d 1318, 1320 (8th Cir. 1988)) the federal appeals court for the Eighth Circuit said that "cases have analyzed the second amendment purely in terms of protecting state militias, rather than individual rights." In *Fresno Rifle and Pistol Club v. Van De Kamp* (965 F.2d 723 [9th Cir. 1992]) the federal appeals court for the Ninth Circuit affirmed that the Second Amendment has never been incorporated and therefore did not apply to the states, or specifically to state gun control laws. In *Love v. Pepersack* (47 F.3d 120, 124 [4th Cir. 1995]), the appeals court for the Fourth Circuit noted that, since the 1939 *Miller* case, "the lower federal courts have uniformly held that the Second Amendment preserves a collective, rather than individual, right." In *Hickman v. Block* (81 F.3d 98, 101 [9th Cir. 1996]), the federal appeals court for the Ninth Circuit said: "We follow our sister circuits in holding that the Second Amendment is a right held by the states, and does not protect the possession of a weapon by a private citizen." In 2000, in the case of *United States v. Napier* (233 F.3d 394, 403, 404 [6th Cir.]), the appeals court for the Sixth Circuit said that the case law "overwhelmingly" showed that "it is well-established that the Second Amendment does not create an individual right.... We find no reason to retreat from our determination in *Warin* [a 1976 appeals court case] that the Second Amendment does not guarantee an individual right to bear arms."

In 1997, the Supreme Court considered a constitutional challenge to the Brady law, a federal law enacted in 1993 that required a five-business-day waiting period for purchase of a handgun.

During the five day period, local law enforcement officials were required to conduct a background check of the prospective buyer to make sure the individual was not a felon, and did not have a history of mental problems. (If evidence of either of these circumstances was found, the gun sale would not go ahead. According to the terms of the law, the five-day waiting period was replaced by a computerized federal instant background check system in 1998.) Opponents of the law, including the NRA, challenged its constitutionality—not based on its violation of the Second Amendment, but rather based on its violation of the Tenth Amendment, which protects states' rights. In its decision in *Printz v. United States* (521 U.S. 898, 938–939; 1997), the Supreme Court struck down the background check provision of the law, saying that the federal government had overstepped its authority, and infringed on states' rights, by requiring local law enforcement authorities to conduct the background checks (most states already conducted background checks of handgun purchasers and continued to do so after the court ruling). Although not a part of the law promulgated by the Court in its decision, the Second Amendment was mentioned in a concurring opinion by Justice Clarence Thomas, who noted that:

> The Court has not had recent occasion to consider the nature of the substantive right safeguarded by the Second Amendment. If, however, the Second Amendment is read to confer a *personal* right to "keep and bear arms," a colorable argument exists that the Federal Government's regulatory scheme... runs afoul of that Amendment's protection. As the parties did not raise this argument, however, we need not consider it here.

In a footnote to this comment, Justice Thomas cited several published articles that have advanced the individualist view of the Second Amendment. He did not cite or mention the many historical, legal, and court writings discussed here that support the standard view of the amendment. Even though he was noting that the Brady Law was not being challenged as a violation of the Second Amendment, Thomas was indicating his interest in hearing a case that raised these arguments about the right to bear arms. Thomas was not joined by any other justice in this opinion, and no other opinion in this case raised the Second Amendment.

This case, along with several others handed down by the high Court in the 1990s, indicated that the Supreme Court was interested in redefining the federalism balance more strongly in favor of state powers or "state sovereignty," and against the federal government (Alfange 2000). In another, earlier case involving a federal gun law, the Supreme Court struck down a federal law making it a crime to bring a gun to a public school. In *United States v. Lopez* (54 U.S. 549; 1995), the court ruled that Congress had exceeded its power to regulate interstate commerce when it made possession of a gun on school property a federal crime as part of the Gun-Free School Zones Act of 1990. Although gun control opponents may log future successes in striking down federal gun laws based on the argument that the federal government has overreached its authority, it is important to note that the Second Amendment was not an issue in *Lopez* or the other federalism cases.

The Second Amendment returned as a legal issue in 1999 when a Texas court judge heard a case that challenged a gun control law as a violation of the Second Amendment. In the case, a Texas physician named Timothy Joe Emerson was charged with violating a 1994 federal law that barred the possession of firearms to anyone who is subject to a restraining order. Emerson had been arrested for brandishing a gun in the presence of his estranged wife and child, in violation of the restraining order filed against him. In court, Emerson's lawyer challenged the charges against him on several grounds, including arguing that Emerson's Second Amendment rights were being violated by the restraining order. In a ruling that surprised observers on all sides of the gun debate

(*United States v. Emerson,* 46 F.Supp.2d 598 [N.D. Texas 1999]) Judge Sam R. Cummings stated that the Second Amendment protected an individual right to bear arms, and that the portion of the restraining order against Emerson that prevented him from possessing a gun was an unconstitutional violation of his Second Amendment rights. In support of his contention, Judge Cummings cited several law journal articles taking the individual rights point of view (articles also cited by Justice Thomas in the 1997 *Printz* case). The ruling was immediately criticized for elevating Emerson's right to own a gun above the safety of his estranged wife and child, for its failure to cite past Second Amendment Supreme Court cases except for *United States v. Miller,* and its failure to mention the many writings that support the conventional, sometimes called collective, view of the Second Amendment (Rovella 2000).

The ruling was appealed to the Federal Court of Appeals for the Fifth Circuit, which heard oral argument in the case on June 13, 2000.

The fact that a federal judge used some law journal articles as a basis for contradicting existing court precedent illustrates the potential of such writings to influence court rulings. It also reflects a critical fact about legal arguments raised concerning the Second Amendment: virtually all of the writing that has attempted to formulate new interpretations of the Second Amendment has been published by lawyers writing in law journals within the last few decades. The significance of this fact lies in four unique traits of law journals.

First, unlike scholarly publishing in every other academic field, control over what is and is not published in law journals is in the hands of law school students, instead of faculty scholars and other specialists. These student editorial boards are composed of people who, with rare exceptions, do not possess, and cannot be expected to possess, the expertise necessary to judge articles submitted to them based on their merits. Although this student control is an anomaly that has been widely criticized within the law school community, student control of law journals is an old and entrenched practice that dates back more than a century.

Second, professional journals in every other field rely on peer review (sending manuscripts out to experts in their respective fields to judge their quality) to evaluate manuscripts submitted to them in order to decide whether they should be published. Law journals rarely use peer review to evaluate manuscripts sent to them, relying instead on the decisions of student-controlled editorial boards.

Third, there are an enormous number of law reviews—over 800 by one recent count—a huge publishing realm compared to other academic disciplines. This means that, with persistence, virtually any manuscript can eventually find a place to be published.

Fourth, law reviews often publish articles precisely because they offer arguments or ideas that are unusual or offbeat. In the case of recent Second Amendment writings, the very fact that they offer new and unusual arguments makes it more likely that students who run law reviews will be interested in publishing them, even though these new arguments might be inaccurate or poorly supported. There is, in fact, reason to believe that law journals have provided a uniquely fertile breeding ground for inaccurate constitutional theories on Constitution-related subjects other than the Second Amendment.

Another instance where law journals have provided the breeding ground for wayward constitutional theory is an extensive and, briefly, influential body of law journal writing that argued that Article I, section 7 of the Constitution provided the president with an item veto (referred to as an inherent item veto). This startling proposition, which otherwise would have been met with dismissive scorn by presidential scholars, spawned and flourished in the fertile ground of law journals, reaching its apex in 1989 when President George Bush announced that he planned to exercise an item veto based on this very theory. (Bush repudiated this theory in 1992.) That a sitting president would contemplate such a move attests to the sway of law reviews, as well as to the extent to which these publications might serve as a breeding ground for wayward constitutional theories (Spitzer 2000b).

Escalating Second Amendment Rhetoric

As discussed in chapter 3, the key political organization that continues to oppose stronger gun control laws, the NRA, has long invoked the Second Amendment as a kind of constitutional mantra that undergirds and buttresses its many activities. As President Clinton and other gun control supporters, emboldened by a supportive public, pressed for stronger gun laws in the 1990s, the NRA increased its Second Amendment rhetoric. In 1997, for example, then-NRA Vice President Charlton Heston spoke before the National Press Club to describe the Second Amendment as "the doorway to all freedoms," meaning that it was the "most vital" amendment, "more essential" than even the First Amendment protections of free speech, press, religion, assembly, and petition of redress of grievances (Spitzer 1997).

As a matter of law, this assertion is false. The courts have, indeed, elevated some Bill of Rights protections above others, under the legal doctrine of "preferred freedoms." Dating from the 1930s, the preferred freedoms doctrine says, simply, that some Bill of Rights protections are even more important than others, and that any attempt to infringe on these key Bill of Rights protections will be examined with even greater skepticism by the courts than laws infringing on other rights. So, for example, a law that infringes on the First Amendment right of free speech is much more likely to be declared unconstitutional than a law infringing on the Seventh Amendment right to a jury trial for a civil suit.

Writing in 1937, Justice Benjamin Cardozo referred to "freedom of thought and speech" as "the matrix, the indispensable condition, of nearly every other form of freedom" (*Palko v. Connecticut,* 302 U.S. 319, 326–327). Those rights elevated in this manner by the courts include the just-listed First Amendment protections, but not the Second Amendment (Abraham 1972). And as discussed in chapters 2 and 3, First Amendment freedoms, as well as other key rights in the Bill of Rights, have been incorporated by the courts—applied to the states through the Fourteenth Amendment—whereas the Second Amendment has not.

In addition, the Supreme Court deliberately set a lower standard for deciding whether gun control laws would pass federal muster than it has applied to other Bill of Rights protections in the 1980 case of *Lewis v. United States* (445 U.S. 90; see chapter 2). In a challenge to the 1968 Gun Control Act, the Court said that there simply needed to be some "rational basis" for restrictions on firearms ownership. In this case, the Court found that the law in question was justifiable and that it did not infringe on the Second Amendment.

Heston's argument also referred to the winning of the American Revolution through force of arms. In this respect, of course, freedom from an outside government was won by force of arms. But when the treaty ending the Revolution was signed in 1783, so too did the need to continue systematic violence as a way to win or protect freedom within U.S. borders. Obviously, the Second Amendment was unnecessary to the American Revolution, as it did not become part of the country's governing document until 1791. Understanding that the Revolution used violence to achieve the political objective of changing the government that ruled the United States, U.S. leaders moved even before the Revolution was over to establish a system of government that would not require violence in order to change leaders and protect individual rights. The genius of the U.S. system is that political ideas are normally expressed through words, not guns, and that aggrieved citizens can seek relief through the nation's courts, legislatures, elections, lobbying, or other nonviolent modes of political expression.

The NRA's ever-greater invocation of Second Amendment mythology was also seen when the NRA launched its new magazine, the *American Guardian,* in 1998, which emphasized the NRA's heightened political and legal agenda. In 2000, that magazine was renamed *America's First Freedom* (a reference to the Second Amendment), which was launched, according to the NRA, to "tell the truth about the threats to our Second Amendment rights." Typical of the NRA's ever-greater effort to identify its political activities with the Second Amendment was NRA President Heston's speech before the NRA's 1999 Annual Convention, held in Denver, Colorado, coincidentally just a few miles from Littleton, Colorado, the site of the tragic school shooting that had occurred just days before. Under fierce criticism in the aftermath of the shooting, the organization cut its convention short. In his brief closing remarks, Heston mentioned the Second Amendment by name eight times and laced his speech with other references to the right to bear arms and the Bill of Rights. The debate over gun control, according to Heston, "would be accurately described as those who believe in the Second Amendment, versus those who don't." The NRA's mission, Heston said, "is to remain a steady beacon of strength and support for the Second Amendment" (NRA website, accessed 2001).

During the 2000 presidential race, the NRA fought an aggressive and expensive political campaign on behalf of George W. Bush and other gun rights supporters, targeting such key states as Kentucky, Michigan, Minnesota, Missouri, Pennsylvania, and Virginia. These states were targeted because they were considered swing states and because they included substantial gun-owning populations. The theme of their $20 million campaign was "Vote Freedom First," a specific reference to the Constitution and the right to bear arms (Eilperin 2000).

The political lesson is simple: the Constitution is a hallowed and revered document; therefore, anything the NRA can do to persuade the country that its actions are merely the expression of the terms of that document provides a formidable political shield. The louder the criticism of the NRA and its efforts, the tighter the organization wraps itself in the Constitution and the Bill of Rights. The unfortunate by-product of this action is that it distorts and misstates the actual meaning of the Second Amendment. The evidence of this is seen in public opinion polls that show most Americans believe that the Second Amendment does protect the right of individual citizens to own guns.

Second Amendment rhetoric has been thoroughly integrated into the modern debate on gun control, as seen in the fact that opponents of gun control typically cite the amendment as their reason for opposing stronger controls. This argument provides more comfortable political cover for public figures who may oppose gun laws because of pressure from constituents or from the NRA. For example, during the summer of 2000 Republican vice-presidential nominee Dick Cheney found that his congressional voting record from the 1980s, when he represented Wyoming in the House of Representatives, was subject to intense scrutiny and criticism after he was picked by Texas Governor George W. Bush to run on his ticket. In particular, Cheney was criticized for voting in Congress against banning armor-piercing bullets (so-called cop-killer bullets capable of piercing body armor) and against regulating plastic handguns that might evade detection by airport metal detectors. Cheney's defense for these votes was: "I'm a strong believer in the Second Amendment and support it" (Clymer 2000). Cheney's beliefs aside, there is no legal precedent that supports the view that such regulations would infringe on the Second Amendment. Even among those advancing the individualist view of the Second Amendment, few would argue that it would prohibit such limited regulations.

Cheney's argument found similar expression in the Republican Party's 2000 platform, which said: "we oppose federal licensing of law-abiding gun owners and national gun registration as a violation of the Second Amendment...." Again, no court case or law supports the flat assertion that such regulations would violate the Second Amendment. (Chapter 2 described a federal court ruling from the 1980s that upheld an outright ban on the possession of handguns, a regulation far more extreme than either licensing or registration.) This claim also diverts attention away from the fact that the National Rifle Association heavily financed the Bush campaign and the Republican Party's National Convention (Dao 2000b).

Yet this furious campaign activity by the NRA, and to a lesser extent by gun control groups, had little effect on the outcome of the 2000 presidential race. Among the swing states targeted by the NRA, most went to Vice President Al Gore. And in the final months of the campaign, both presidential candidates ignored the gun issue. Gore avoided the issue to hone in on his main campaign themes, including such issues as social security, medical care, and prescription drugs. In addition, he realized that his support for gun control could hurt him in swing states. For his part, Bush avoided the gun issue to hone in on his main issues, including education reform and tax cuts. In addition, he did not want to be seen as being in the pocket of the extremist NRA (Dao 2000b). Despite avoidance of the gun issue at the national level, there is no doubt that it will return to the national stage in the coming years.

After the election, however, Bush's attorney general, former Missouri Senator John Ashcroft, moved to codify and legitimize the NRA's view of the Second Amendment. In one of his first legal pronouncements, Ashcroft outlined his views on the meaning of the Second Amendment's right to bear arms in a letter sent May 2001 to NRA Executive Director James Jay Baker shortly before the NRA's annual convention. The letter embraced the argument that the amendment endorses an individual right to own guns, aside and apart from citizen service in a militia—a position Ashcroft had embraced as a U.S. senator. As a formal issuance from the nation's chief law enforcement officer, however, it merits particular scrutiny because it argued that the individualist view "is not a novel position." Yet the letter cited sources that do not support Ashcroft's claim, and it failed to cite the most important sources explaining what the right to bear arms does mean.

In support of his individualist view of the Second Amendment, Ashcroft cited five Supreme Court cases. Of these, only two (*Miller v. Texas,* 1893, and *Robertson v. Baldwin,* 1897) actually address the meaning of the Second Amendment. As discussed in chapter 2, *Miller* upheld a Texas law that barred carrying dangerous weapons as not being in violation of the Second Amendment. In *Robertson,* the court ruled that the Second Amendment was not infringed by a law that barred carrying concealed weapons. In neither case did the court state or imply that the Second Amendment protected an individual right for citizens to own guns apart from their service in a government-organized and regulated militia. Two additional cases cited in Ashcroft's letter have nothing whatsoever to do with interpreting the Second Amendment. One of the cases, *Logan v. United States* (1892) had to do with the propriety of a federal conspiracy prosecution. The other, *Maxwell v. Dow* (1899), had to do with procedures governing jury trials (both cases did raise the Fourteenth Amendment, noting that it did not extend Bill of Rights protections to the states). *Maxwell* did, however, quote from *Presser v. Illinois,* which did rule on the meaning of the Second Amendment. But as discussed earlier, it said that the right to bear arms is inseparable from citizen service in a government militia. In other words, the *Presser* case interpreted the amendment in diametric opposition to Ashcroft's claim. (Ashcroft did not cite *Presser* in his letter.)

The fifth case Ashcroft cited was *United States v. Verdugo-Urquidez.* Again, this 1990 case has nothing to do with interpreting the Second Amendment, but instead deals with search and seizure (see chapter 2). In a passing comment, the majority opinion mentioned several places in the Constitution where the phrase "the people" appears, including the Second Amendment. Nowhere did the court say, as Ashcroft claimed in his letter, that the phrase *the people* "should be interpreted consistently throughout"; in fact, the court has never adopted a single, uniform interpretation of the phrase, as its rulings on the Second Amendment alone make clear.

Aside from these errors, Ashcroft not only failed to cite *Presser*, but the other two most important cases that *do* interpret the amendment's meaning: *United States v. Cruikshank* and *United States v. Miller*. *Miller* in particular contradicts Ashcroft's view of the Second Amendment.

Furthermore, Ashcroft argued that his individualist view is a longstanding and bipartisan one by saying that Franklin D. Roosevelt's attorney general, Homer Cummings, also embraced the individualist view. To support his view, Ashcroft cited Cummings's testimony in 1934 before the Ways and Means Committee of the House of Representatives on a bill that was later enacted as the National Firearms Act. Although Cummings acknowledged at one point during the hearings that he had concerns about the constitutionality of a proposal to require all existing gun owners to register their handguns (a proposal based on the government's powers to tax and regulate interstate commerce), at no time did Cummings say that such a proposal might run afoul of the Second Amendment, nor did Cummings ever say that he supported or believed the idea that the Second Amendment protected an individual right to own guns. In fact, Cummings was the most pro–gun control attorney general in the nation's history, who aggressively advocated a wide range of gun control measures. At the time, the Ways and Means Committee took extensive testimony from two NRA officers, including NRA President Karl T. Frederick. At no point in their testimony did either object to the proposed law as a violation of the Second Amendment. Both representatives did raise objections to the legislation, but did so primarily because they were concerned that the law might interfere with honest citizens attempting to defend themselves from lawless individuals.

Finally, Ashcroft cited a 1986 federal gun law, the Firearms Owners Protection Act, as having "explicitly adopted" the individualist view. It does nothing of the sort. In fact, all the law does is refer to "the right of citizens to keep and bear arms under the second amendment." This passing mention does nothing to contradict the militia-based view laid down by the Supreme Court and more than twenty lower federal court decisions.

The U.S. attorney general has every right to argue in court, or in the court of public opinion, that the courts should reverse past rulings and reinterpret the Second Amendment along individualist lines. But the argument that existing law already supports this proposition foists a false claim on a public that has already experienced too much distortion of the law to serve political ends. Ashcroft's letter attempted to invent a legal past that simply does not exist. He extended this effort further during the summer of 2001 when he directed the U.S. Office of Legal Counsel to draft an opinion buttressing the individualist view.

The desire to assert or expand gun rights under the Constitution has also been reflected in continuing congressional activity. In 1998, for example, the U.S. Senate Judiciary Committee's Subcommittee on the Constitution, Federalism, and Property Rights held hearings on the question of whether the Second Amendment served as a basis for individual rights—a proposition that was supported and encouraged by the subcommittee chair, Sen. John Ashcroft (R-MO), and by most of those invited to testify.

Invocations of the Second Amendment crop up in even the most questionable of circumstances. For example, when the Nassau County Legislature in New York State proposed a sharp increase in pistol permit fees, discussed among local leaders as one of several fee increases for the cash-strapped county to raise much-needed revenue, angry citizens argued against the increase as an infringement on their right to bear arms (Cooper 2000). Whether the proposed fee increase was good or bad policy is not the question. No law, court decision, or rule supports the idea that the fee increase infringes in any way on the Second Amendment or the actual rights of gun owners.

Two other Second Amendment–related claims have surfaced with increasing regularity in the media pertaining to new interpretations of the Second Amendment in support of the individualist view. One is the claim, offered with considerable rhetorical flourish, that the individualist view is not limited only to conservatives, but has recently been embraced by liberals as well. Thus, for example, the *New York Times* noted with much ballyhoo that "the influential liberal constitutional law expert" Laurence Tribe now believed that the Second Amendment might protect an individual right to own firearms (Glaberson 1999). Columnist William Safire (1999) also noted that some liberals seemed to be shifting positions on the issue, an observation made as well by newspaper columnist Walter Shapiro (1999) and writer Daniel Lazare (1999). A recent headline in the *Wall Street Journal* (Levey 1999) summed up this alleged tidal shift in liberal thought this way: "Liberals Have Second Thoughts on the Second Amendment."

The effort to legitimize the individualist view of the Second Amendment by claiming that it is embraced by liberals as well as conservatives is not a new phenomenon, in that it has percolated up from the arguments of several legal and academic writers who oppose stronger gun laws (Kates 1979). But the personal ideological leanings of those who write on the Second Amendment offer no insight into the debate itself. This recent debate over whether some liberals have now embraced the individualist view is a false argument because the focus on ideological pedigree becomes a substitute for a substantive debate of the actual merits of the individualist claims and of the meaning of the Second Amendment. Indeed, the merits of the claims concerning the meaning of the Second Amendment are not even raised in most of the press articles just cited. If the debate over this, or any, legal or public policy issue becomes one of the ideological pedigree of those on each side rather than the facts of the case, then the facts of the case become irrelevant. As a political tactic, there may be some gain to be had in trying to legitimate an argument by extolling the people who hold it, or by noting that the position is held by people of multiple ideological stripes (assuming, of course, that one can accept such claims at face value). Such claims are, at best, an irrelevant distraction to determining what the Second Amendment actually means; at worst, they represent a shoddy effort to give legitimacy to an argument that cannot stand well purely on its merits.

Another example of the escalating ideological war over the individualist view was seen in the reaction of some to a book on the history of gun practices in the early United States, authored by historian Michael Bellesiles (2000). Awarded history's prestigious Bancroft Prize in 2001, Bellesiles argues that gun ownership from colonial times up to the Civil War was far less common than most have assumed, for the obvious reasons that early guns were expensive, cumbersome, difficult to operate, relatively unreliable, made of materials that were difficult to maintain, and were simply not as important to early American life as much popular culture assumed. Even though Bellesiles's arguments bore no direct relationship to the debate over the meaning of the Second Amendment, it was nevertheless viewed by some as an attack on the individualist view. For example, an article in the *Wall Street Journal* (Strassel 2001) charged that "what this [book] means for modern politics . . . is that the Second Amendment may not have been designed to protect individual gun rights." In an effort to discredit the book, the article cited various criticisms, chief among them an allegation from UCLA law professor Eugene Volokh, who charged that none of the three sources cited in a footnote on page 223 of Bellesiles's book supported Bellesiles's statement that most Antifederalists opposed the idea of propertyless men carrying arms in the militia. Yet an examination of the three sources used by Bellesiles shows that they do, in fact, support his claim. Worse, Volokh quotes one of the three sources in the article in apparent support of the opposite idea: "that militia should include everyone, 'high and low, and rich and poor.'" The quote within this quote is from a speech by Antifederalist George Mason, delivered to the Virginia ratifying convention in 1788. Yet here is the full quote from Mason: "I cannot say who will be the militia of the future day. If that paper on the table gets no alteration, the militia of the future day may not consist of all classes, high and low, and rich and poor, granting exclusion to the higher classes of the people" (Jensen 1976, 10, 1312; Bellesiles's book does make a small error by citing this source as volume 10, page 312 instead of 1312). The word *not* reverses the meaning of the quote; by omitting the word *not*, Volokh distorted Mason's meaning in order to find fault with Bellesiles.

The second rhetorical claim raised in recent media accounts—one that also percolates up from academic writings (Barnett and Kates 1996)—is the unilateral declaration that the individualist view represents a new academic consensus. So, for example, Lazare (1999) asserts that the debate over the Second Amendment is simply over by flatly asserting that the amendment protects personal uses of guns. Joyce Lee Malcolm is quoted as saying, "It is very hard . . . to find a historian who now believes that it is only a collective right. . . . There is no one for me to argue against anymore . . ." (Lazare 1999, 59). *USA Today* reported that "most constitutional scholars agree with" the individualist view (Shapiro 1999).

Aside from the fact that these unilateralist claims are false (Spitzer 2000b), they are also roughly akin to a participant in a contest who suddenly stops competing, declares victory, and leaves, in the hope that the declaration may become the fact. The media's acceptance of this claim to victory for the individualist view belies the actual nature of the debate over the meaning of the Second Amendment—the very focus of this book.

Conclusion

The Second Amendment will continue to play an integral role in the nation's ongoing debate over gun control. Unlike other Bill of Rights freedoms, however, the amendment's role will probably not arise from a regular succession of court rulings on the meaning of the amendment, which in turn often has direct effects on the daily behavior of Americans, as occurs with such Bill of Rights protections as free speech, freedom of religion, or right to counsel. Even if the push to win a new court interpretation of the Second Amendment succeeds, it is highly unlikely that it will spawn the volume of court actions that one finds with other civil liberties. Even most supporters of the individualist view concede that their view would not bar most of the proposed or actual gun control laws that are the focus of public discussion and debate. Rather, the amendment continues to be far more significant for the political-symbolic value it holds to those who support broader gun rights and fewer gun regulations, a feature in evidence during debate over the Brady bill, the assault weapons ban, and the post-Columbine legislative effort.

Many of those involved in the revival of private militia activity in the early 1990s used the Second Amendment to legitimize their desire to arm their members in order to fight the government. Ironically, the militias referred to in the Constitution and in the Second Amendment were actually designed to suppress private, paramilitary activities if they posed a threat to the government or its citizens. No government, including our own, could operate with a provision in its laws that allowed or invited violence against itself. Even so, the long strain of antigovernment sentiment that traces back to early U.S. history, and the penchant of a few to attempt violence against the government and its leaders, surely means that such movements will crop up in the future. No doubt, they will continue to voice the fictional belief that the Second Amendment invites or supports violence against the government.

The effort by legal writers and interest groups to win a broader or different interpretation of the Second Amendment will also undeniably continue. Controversies over constitutional meaning occur in many areas, and it is no criticism to say that politics lies behind many of these efforts. Throughout U.S. history, many political forces have sought to win new or different interpretations of basic rights. As discussed in chapters 2 and 3, the historical, legal, and factual arguments in support of these new interpretations of the Second Amendment are painfully thin. Nevertheless, unlike the modern militia movement, this effort falls well within both the law and the politics of the U.S. system, even if the arguments raised are not very strong. Such views may find greater sympathy in the years to come in a federal court system dominated by conservative appointees from the Reagan, Bush, and second Bush administrations.

Dovetailing with this effort is the ever-greater political and symbolic invocation of the Second Amendment. As discussed earlier, Americans are quick to claim a constitutional basis for all kinds of actions, ideas, and causes. Such claims often aid political causes, but that does not make them correct as a matter of law. Unfortunately, this is one reason why Americans often have a poor understanding of what the Constitution actually says or means. As long as gun control remains an active and controversial issue in U.S. politics, partisans will invoke the rhetoric of the Second Amendment.

References and Further Reading

Abraham, Henry J. 1972. *Freedom and the Court.* New York: Oxford University Press.

Alfange, Dean Jr. 2000. "The Supreme Court and Federalism." In Robert J. Spitzer, ed., *Politics and Constitutionalism.* Albany, NY: SUNY Press.

Barnett, Randy E., and Don B. Kates. 1996. "Under Fire: The New Consensus on the Second Amendment." *Emory Law Journal* 45 (Fall): 1139–1159.

Bellesiles, Michael. 2000. *Arming America: The Origins of a National Gun Culture.* New York: Alfred A. Knopf.

Clymer, Adam. 2000. "In Philadelphia, 2000 Delegates Await the Arrival of the Star." *New York Times* (31 July).

Cooper, Michael. 2000. "Pistol Owners Raise Protest As Nassau Increases Fees." *New York Times* (15 June).

Dao, James. 2000a. "National Rifle Association Unleashes Attack on Gore." *New York Times* (21 May).

———. 2000b. "Gore Tables Gun Issue As He Courts Midwest." *New York Times* (20 September).

Davidson, Osha Gray. 1993. *Under Fire.* New York: Henry Holt.

Dees, Morris, and Mark Potok. 2001. "The Future of American Terrorism." *New York Times* (June 10).

Eilperin, Juliet. 2000. "A Pivotal Election Finds NRA's Wallet Open." *Washington Post* (1 November).

Glaberson, William. 1999. "Right to Bear Arms: A Second Look." *New York Times* (30 May).

Hofstadter, Richard. 1965. *The Paranoid Style in American Politics.* New York: Vintage.

Jenkins, Philip. 1995. "Home-Grown Terror." *American Heritage* (September): 38–46.

Jensen, Merrill, et al., eds. 1976–1995. *The Documentary History of the Ratification of the Constitution,* 18 vols. Madison, WI: State Historical Society.

Karl, Jonathan. 1995. *The Right to Bear Arms.* New York: HarperCollins.

Kates, Don B., ed. 1979. *Restricting Handguns: The Liberal Skeptics Speak Out.* Croton-on-Hudson, NY: North River Press.

Kifner, John. 1995. "Oklahoma Bombing Suspect." *New York Times* (31 December).

Klanwatch Project. 1996. *False Patriots: The Threat of Antigovernment Extremists.* Montgomery, AL: Southern Poverty Law Center.

Lazare, Daniel. 1999. "Your Constitution Is Killing You." *Harper's Magazine* (October): 57–65.

Levey, Collin. 1999. "Liberals Have Second Thoughts on the Second Amendment." *Wall Street Journal* (22 November).

Macdonald, Andrew. 1978. *The Turner Diaries.* Hillsboro, WV: National Vanguard Books.

McFadden, Robert D. 1995. "Links in Blast." *New York Times* (22 April).

Michel, Lou, and Dan Herbeck. 2001. *American Terrorist.* New York: Regan Books.

"Patriot Dreams." 1997. *Intelligence Report* (Fall): 14–15.

Rovella, David E. 2000. "Circuit Sights Gun Right." *National Law Journal* (31 May).

Safire, William. 1999. "An Appeal for Repeal." *New York Times* (10 June).

Shapiro, Walter. 1999. "It's High Time to Gun Down the 2nd Amendment." *USA Today* (17 September).

Spitzer, Robert J. 1997. "Door No. 1: Muskets? Or Door No. 2: Free Speech?" *Christian Science Monitor* (19 September).

———. 1998. *The Politics of Gun Control.* New York: Chatham House.

———. 1999. "The Gun Dispute." *American Educator* (Summer): 10–15.

———. 2000a. "Lost and Found: Researching the Second Amendment." *Chicago-Kent Law Review* 76: 349–401.

———. 2000b. "Saving the Constitution from Lawyers." In Robert J. Spitzer, ed., *Politics and Constitutionalism.* Albany, NY: SUNY Press.

Stern, Kenneth S. 1996. *A Force upon the Plain.* New York: Simon and Schuster.

Strassel, Kimberly. 2001. "Scholars Take Aim at Gun History." *Wall Street Journal* (9 April).

Subcommittee on Crime, Judiciary Committee, House of Representatives. 1989. "Semiautomatic Assault Weapons Act of 1989." 101st Cong., 1st sess., hearings 5 and 6 April. Washington, DC: Government Printing Office.

Subcommittee on the Constitution, Federalism, and Property Rights, Judiciary Committee, U.S. Senate. 1998. "Whose Right to Keep and Bear Arms? The Second Amendment as a Source of Individual Rights." 105th Cong., 2nd sess., hearing 23 September. Washington, DC: Government Printing Office.

Williams, Mike. 1995. "Citizen Militias." *Soldier of Fortune* 20 (April): 48–53.

5

Key People, Cases, and Events

Academics for the Second Amendment (ASA)

An organization formed in 1992 by a group of lawyers and academics who seek to promote an individualist interpretation of the Second Amendment.

Adams v. Williams *(1972)*

In a Supreme Court case dealing with the Fourth Amendment protection from unreasonable searches and seizures, two justices wrote in a dissent that the Second Amendment posed no obstacle to gun regulations. Although consistent with other Court rulings on the subject, these comments were *dicta* that did not bear directly on the case itself.

Alcohol, Tobacco, and Firearms, Bureau of (ATF)

The federal agency charged with implementing national gun control laws. The agency has been fiercely criticized by the National Rifle Association and its allies for alleged heavy-handed tactics.

American Bar Association (ABA)

The nation's preeminent organization of lawyers, the ABA has long endorsed the militia-based understanding of the meaning of the Second Amendment.

American Firearms Association (AFA)

A gun organization created as a more moderate alternative to the National Rifle Association, the AFA, based on Fairfax, Virginia, advocates gun rights balanced with reasonable gun control.

Antifederalists

The term applied to those who opposed ratification of the Constitution of 1787, generally because of fears that it gave too much power to the national government and too little to the states. Antifederalists pushed for inclusion of a Bill of Rights during the nation's ratification debate over the Constitution.

Articles of Confederation

First constitution of the United States that governed the nation from 1777–1789. Its weak national government made no provision for a national standing army, and it left primary military responsibilities to state militias. The deficiencies of this system lent support to giving the national government greater military authority under the Constitution of 1787.

Assault Weapons Ban of 1994 (PL 103–322; 108 Stat. 1796)

A provision of the Violent Crime Control and Law Enforcement Act of 1994 passed by Congress. The assault weapons ban barred the possession of nineteen named types of assault weapons, including several dozen copycat models. These are semiautomatic weapons that also possess at least two features of military style weaponry.

Aymette v. State *(1840)*

A Tennessee state court ruling that discussed the Second Amendment, saying that the purpose of keeping and bearing arms was for "common defence," and that the phrase "bear arms" referred to military use, not to individuals wanting to carry weapons for their own purposes.

The Bell Campaign

A national organization of parents, some of whose children were killed by guns, that advocates for stricter gun laws. Their demonstrations usually include ringing of bells for every child killed by a gun that year.

Bill of Rights

The first ten amendments to the Constitution, added as a group to the document in 1791 largely in response to the concerns of Antifederalists who feared that the new and more powerful national government would usurp rights and liberties.

Bliss v. Commonwealth *(1822)*

A Kentucky state court ruling that struck down a state restriction on weapons-carrying as a violation of the Kentucky Constitution's right-to-bear-arms-type clause, the wording of which was broader and different than that of the Second Amendment in the U.S. Constitution. The case is sometimes erroneously cited as offering an interpretation of the Second Amendment.

Brady Handgun Violence Prevention Act of 1993 (PL 103–159; 107 Stat. 1536)

Also known as the Brady Law, passed by Congress and named after former President Reagan's press secretary James Brady (who was wounded during the 1981 assassination attempt against Reagan), this law imposed a national five-business-day waiting period for purchase of a handgun, during which time the government would conduct a background check of the purchaser. In 1998, under the terms of the law, the five-day wait was replaced by a national, instant background check system. In 1997, the Supreme Court struck down the provision of the law requiring local law enforcement authorities to conduct the checks in the case of *Printz v. United States* as a violation of the Tenth Amendment, pertaining to states' rights.

Brady, Sarah

Wife of former Press Secretary James Brady and daughter of an FBI Agent, Brady spearheaded gun control efforts as head of Handgun Control, Inc. after her husband was shot and wounded during the 1981 assassination attempt against President Reagan.

Branch Davidians

A heavily armed religious doomsday cult based in Waco, Texas, led by David Koresh. After a failed effort to arrest Koresh, federal agents laid siege to the heavily armed compound, eventually storming it. Most of the occupants died from fires started by the Davidians. Survivors failed to win judgments against the government. The incident has been a rallying cause for antigovernment groups.

British Bill of Rights

Enacted in 1689 by the British Parliament, this document sought to protect basic rights in the aftermath of King James II's oppressive rule. Article 7 of the document said that "the subjects which are protestants, may have arms for their defence suitable to their conditions, and as allowed by law." This is considered the forerunner of the Second Amendment.

Calling Forth Act of 1792 (1 U.S. Stat. 264)

A law passed by Congress that placed state militias under presidential authority, but that also made it somewhat more difficult for militias to be used against domestic insurrections than against foreign invasions, reflecting continuing federal-state tensions over militia use and control.

Center to Prevent Handgun Violence

A Washington-based group that advances legal and political arguments on behalf of stronger handgun laws. In 2001, it was renamed the Brady Center to Prevent Gun Violence.

Christian Front

A far-right-wing group organized in the United States in the 1930s that adhered to an anti-Semitic, fascist ideology.

Cincinnatus Complex

The colonial-era belief that no professional army could fight as effectively as a citizen militia.

Citizens Committee for the Right to Keep and Bear Arms

An anti–gun control group formed in 1971 that emphasizes Second Amendment rights arguments. Its research arm is the Second Amendment Foundation.

Coalition to Stop Gun Violence

A political and educational coalition of religious, medical, labor, and other groups committed to reducing gun violence through advocacy of tougher gun control laws.

Columbine High School Massacre

In the worst school shooting in the country's history, two disgruntled high school boys entered Columbine High School in Littleton, Colorado, on April 20, 1999, with four guns and explosives. They killed twelve students and one teacher, wounded twenty-three others, and then killed themselves. The incident spurred renewed calls for stronger gun laws.

Common Law

Guiding legal principles derived from the cumulative precedents of past court rulings that, taken together, guide contemporary court rulings. The American common law tradition extends back to colonial times and to the British common law tradition.

Constitution of 1787

The modern Constitution, written in 1787 and put into effect in 1789. Rectifying the problems with the old Articles of Confederation, this document gave the national government explicit and sweeping power to create, finance, and regulate both a standing army and militias in Article I, section 8. It also specified that militias were to be used by the government to not only "repel invasions," but to enforce domestic laws and "suppress insurrections."

Constitutional Law

That type of law arising from the governing documents that create the branches of government, assign powers, and define rights and responsibilities. Courts contribute to constitutional law when they interpret the meaning of laws or actions in the light of the governing document. Executives and legislatures also contribute to constitutional law through their actions.

Declaration of Independence

Written in 1776, this document explained to the world why the United States sought independence from Great Britain. Included in the document were several complaints against the high-handed tactics of professional British soldiers, which enforced Americans' mistrust of standing armies.

Dicta

Opinions expressed by a judge in a case that do not bear on the legal resolution of the case, and thus are not binding in that or subsequent cases.

Dual Citizenship

The idea that all persons born or naturalized in the United States are simultaneously considered U.S. citizens and citizens of the state in which they reside. This reflects the fact that every state government, in addition to the national government, is a sovereign governing entity created by a state constitution that includes rights and protections affecting its citizens.

Dunne v. People *(1879)*

An Illinois state court ruling that included an extensive discussion of the Second Amendment, in which the court noted that the amendment provided no basis for any citizens' right to own guns for their own private purposes.

Federalism

The dividing of governmental powers between the national government and the states. The federalism-based fear that the national government would be given too much power over military matters, and that state governments might not retain adequate authority over their state militias under the new Constitution, was the primary basis for the insertion of the Second Amendment in the Bill of Rights.

Federalist Papers

A series of eighty-five essays, written by Alexander Hamilton, James Madison, and John Jay, that argued for and defended the newly written Constitution of 1787. Several of these papers, including numbers 24, 25, 28, 29, and 46, discussed the relative merits of armies and militias.

Federalists

Those who favored adoption of the Constitution of 1787, and generally stronger powers for the new national government.

Fourteenth Amendment

Added to the Constitution in 1868, this amendment opened the door to selective application of parts of the Bill of Rights to the

States through a process called incorporation. The Second Amendment, plus some other parts of the Bill of Rights, have not been incorporated.

Gun Culture

The historical, emotional attachment of some Americans to gun ownership and use, generally linked to hunting and sporting activities, but also to the romanticized frontier-militia tradition extending back to colonial times.

Gun Owners of America (GOA)

An anti–gun control group formed in 1975 considered more radical than the NRA, the smaller GOA aggressively promotes a right of revolution interpretation of the Second Amendment.

Gun Show Loophole

The ability of prospective gun purchasers to buy handguns at gun shows and flea markets without having to undergo a background check, whereas such background checks would otherwise be required if the purchases were made from licensed gun dealers.

Handgun Control, Inc. (HCI)

The nation's largest gun control group, HCI was formed in 1974 to work for stronger gun laws. It grew in the 1980s and 1990s under the leadership of Sarah Brady. Seeking to counterbalance the power of the National Rifle Association, HCI raises and spends campaign money, lobbies Congress, and promotes arguments for stronger gun laws. In resources, it is roughly one-tenth of the size of the NRA. In 2001, it was renamed the Brady Campaign to Prevent Gun Violence.

Henigan, Dennis

Gun control supporter and lawyer who has served as the long-time director of the Legal Action Project at the Center to Prevent Handgun Violence. Henigan writes and comments frequently on constitutional and legal issues in support of stronger gun laws.

Heston, Charlton

Academy-Award-winning actor and longtime political activist, Heston became president of the National Rifle Association in 1998 in the effort to improve the NRA's image and head off a takeover by a more extreme element within the NRA. He was reelected in 1999, 2000, and 2001, after the organization repealed its two-term limit for presidents. Heston was first elected NRA vice president in 1997.

Incorporation

The process by which the due process and equal protection clauses of the Fourteenth Amendment (added to the Constitution in 1868) have been used to apply parts of the Bill of Rights to the states (also sometimes called *absorption*). The Supreme Court applied most key Bill of Rights freedoms to the states in the period from 1897–1969. The court has declined to incorporate the Second Amendment.

Individualist Argument

The argument advanced by some legal writers and others that the Second Amendment provides individuals with a constitutional right to own firearms, aside or apart from militia or other government service. This view has been rejected by the courts.

Insurrectionist Theory

The theory that Americans have a right to engage in rebellion or insurrection against the U.S. government if they believe it to be oppressive. Some claim that the Second Amendment protects such a right.

Ku Klux Klan

A secret organization first started by former Confederate soldiers after the Civil War, organized to oppress African Americans and oppose other ethnic and religious groups, the Klan often carried weapons and styled itself as a home-grown militia.

LaPierre, Wayne

Long-time activist within and spokesperson for the National Rifle Association, LaPierre has served as its chief executive officer for many years. He engineered the election of Charlton Heston as NRA president to head off a more radical faction within the organization.

Lawyer's Second Amendment Society (LSAS)

A group formed in 1994 by a small group of gun rights lawyers, the LSAS seeks to advance individualist views of the Second Amendment and also funds legal actions against gun control laws.

Lewis v. United States (1980)

Citing *United States v. Miller,* the Supreme Court upheld the constitutionality of a 1968 federal law barring felons from owning guns and noted that the Second Amendment posed no obstacle to such regulations.

Malloy v. Hogan *(1964)*

A modern Supreme Court case in which the Court cited the nineteenth century *Cruikshank* and *Presser* cases as still good law in interpreting the meaning of the Second Amendment, putting to rest the idea that these older cases are somehow no longer relevant to understanding the amendment because they were handed down before the Supreme Court began applying parts of the Bill of Rights to the states using the Fourteenth Amendment, known as the process of incorporation.

Maryland v. United States *(1965)*

In a case arising from a suit brought by the families of victims killed in an air crash with a National Guard pilot, the Supreme Court ruled that the Guard member was a state, not federal, employee. Even so, Guard activities are not the sole province of state governors, as the federal government may call the Guard into national service, superseding state wishes. In the case, the Court noted that the Guard was the modern militia referred to in the Constitution.

McVeigh, Timothy

A former soldier and right-wing, antigovernment zealot convicted of the 1995 bombing of a federal office building in Oklahoma City in which 168 people died. He was executed in 2001.

Militia Act of 1903 (32 Stat. 775)

Also called the Dick Act (named after Rep. Charles Dick, the bill's sponsor), this law reorganized the nation's militia system, separating the unorganized or reserve militia (the old-style general militia) from the organized militia, which under this act became the

National Guard. Congress did and does retain the right to mobilize the unorganized militia.

Militias

Part-time, amateur fighting forces that were to be called up by the government to service in times of military crisis, militias consisted of two types: unorganized or general militias that encompassed all eligible men between the ages of eighteen and forty-five; and volunteer (also called organized or select) militias that trained on a more regular basis. Both dated from colonial times. The former were last used in the War of 1812, where their abysmal performance essentially ended the nation's use of such forces. (In later wars, the nation would institute a military draft instead of calling up militias.) The latter forces continued to operate throughout the nineteenth century; in 1903, Congress enacted the Militia Act, which formally renamed volunteer militias as the National Guard and brought them under federal control. Although some private individuals have formed groups they have called *militias,* such groups do not conform to the definition of militias, as only the government can create a militia.

Miller v. Texas *(1894)*

This Supreme Court case concluded that a state law barring the carrying of dangerous weapons did not violate the Second Amendment and that the amendment did not apply to the states.

Minutemen

The name of Massachusetts militias formed to oppose the British Army in the American Revolution in the 1770s, so named because of the rapidity with which they could respond to a call-up. The name was appropriated by right-wing extremists who organized and armed themselves in the 1950s and 1960s to violently oppose the U.S. government.

National Defense Act of 1916 (39 Stat. 166)

A law passed by Congress that required the National Guard to be organized in the same manner as the regular army. It also placed the Guards more directly under federal guidelines.

National Rifle Association (NRA)

Formed in 1871 to improve marksmanship skills, the nation's oldest gun organization and staunchest opponent of stronger gun laws has become one of the most influential and effective interest groups. Since the late 1970s, the organization has devoted more of its resources to political efforts to block new gun laws and repeal existing ones. It also aggressively promotes the theory that the Second Amendment provides all citizens with a constitutionally-based right to have firearms. In recent years, the organization has maintained a membership of between 3 and 4 million members.

New Militia Movement

The term applied to individuals who have formed their own so-called *militias*, separate and apart from government control, usually organized to resist what the members consider to be potential or actual government tyranny. Although such organizations claim the label *militia*, they are not so under the constitutional and legal definition of the term. Such groups typically arm themselves and often espouse ethnic and racial hatred.

Nichols, Terry

Convicted to a life sentence for his role in the 1995 Oklahoma City bombing. He appealed the sentence, but the appeal was dismissed.

Oklahoma City Bombing

A rented truck filled with explosives was detonated in front of the Alfred P. Murrah Federal Office Building in Oklahoma City on April 19, 1995, killing 168 people. Timothy McVeigh and Terry Nichols were convicted of the bombing, which was staged as a political act against the U.S. government. McVeigh was executed in 2001; Nichols was sentenced to life imprisonment.

Patsone v. Commonwealth *(1914)*

This Supreme Court case concluded that a state law barring unnaturalized, foreign-born persons from possessing firearms was constitutional.

People, The *(Meaning in the Bill of Rights)*

Some argue that the phrase *the people* as it appears in the Second Amendment has the same uniform meaning throughout the Bill of Rights. In congressional debate during approval of the Bill of Rights by Congress, and in subsequent court rulings, the phrase *the people* in the Second Amendment was applied only to militia-eligible males. In other parts of the document, such as the First Amendment, the meaning of the people has been defined more broadly.

Perpich v. Department of Defense *(1990)*

When a state governor challenged the right of the president to send National Guard troops abroad, the Supreme Court ruled that, while governors retain control over their state Guards for state purposes, governors may not contravene uses of the state Guards stipulated by the national government. The case also made clear that the National Guard is the modern descendent and last remnant of the militias.

Presser v. Illinois *(1886)*

This Supreme Court case confirmed that the Second Amendment applied to citizens only when they were called into militia service by the government. It also noted that private citizens had no right to form their own private militias (i.e., without government authority or permission) and confirmed that the Second Amendment did not apply to the states.

Printz v. United States *(1997)*

Supreme Court case brought as a challenge to the constitutionality of the background check provision of the 1993 Brady Law. The Court struck down the requirement in the law that local law enforcement agencies be required to conduct background checks of prospective handgun buyers as a violation of states' rights under the Tenth Amendment. The challenge, brought in part by the National Rifle Association, did not challenge the law as a violation of the Second Amendment. Despite the ruling, most law enforcement officials continued to conduct background checks.

Protocols of the Elders of Zion, The

A nineteenth-century manuscript forgery that alleged to be a transcript of a secret meeting of Jewish leaders describing how they would secretly dominate Christian nations. This writing is often taken as true by right-wing, self-styled militia groups.

Quilici v. Village of Morton Grove *(1982)*

In the most well-known lower federal court ruling on the meaning of the Second Amendment, two lower federal courts upheld a local law that barred possession of working handguns, except for police and others who needed handguns for their work, saying that the right to keep and bear arms pertained only to citizens participating in a militia. When the case was appealed to the Supreme Court, it declined to hear the case, letting the lower court ruling stand. This case is one of nearly twenty lower federal court rulings handed down from the 1940s to the 1990s coming to this conclusion.

Right of Revolution

The belief of some that the Second Amendment affords individuals a right to keep firearms in order to overthrow, or threaten to overthrow, the U.S. government if they believe it to be tyrannical. This view has been repeatedly rejected by the courts and statutory law.

Right to Bear Arms

The phrase from the Second Amendment often cited by gun control opponents to support their belief in a constitutional right for citizens to own firearms for their own purposes. The phrase refers to a citizen right when citizens are called in to military service by the government and need to bring their own firearms owing to the failure of the government to provide firearms. This was a typical circumstance in the country's early history, but it came to an end when the government began providing military issue.

Rights Talk

The tendency of Americans to frame political and policy debates in terms of *rights*, regardless of whether actual rights appertain to the issue in question or not.

Robertson v. Baldwin *(1897)*

This Supreme Court case ruled that a law barring the carrying of concealed weapons did not violate the Second Amendment.

Ruby Ridge

See Weaver, Randy

Second Amendment

"A well-regulated Militia, being necessary to the security of a free State, the right of the people to keep and bear Arms, shall not be infringed." This amendment was included in the Bill of Rights to reassure states' rights advocates and Antifederalists that the states would be able to maintain state-based militias under the new constitutional system that vested vastly expanded military powers in the hands of the national government under the Constitution of 1787.

Second Amendment Foundation (SAF)

The research arm of the Citizens Committee for the Right to Keep and Bear Arms, this organization promotes the view that the Second Amendment provides individuals with a constitutional right to own guns for their own purposes.

Second Amendment Rhetoric

The political tactic of connecting gun ownership practices with the Second Amendment as a way of enshrining and elevating any and all matters related to guns in order to obtain political benefit by claiming that gun possession and use is directly protected by the Constitution, regardless of whether the Constitution actually provides such protections or not.

Self-defense

The right of citizens to defend themselves from personal attack, or intrusion into their homes, is a right long established in the common law tradition and is now codified in state criminal laws.

Shays's Rebellion

An uprising of farmers in Massachusetts in January 1787, led by former Army captain Daniel Shays to protest foreclosure of debt-ridden lands, it underscored the national government's military weakness and the unreliability of state militias in responding to emergencies.

Silver Shirts

A right-wing U.S. neo-Nazi group formed in the 1930s, this group openly advocated armed insurrection in the United States, including the assassination of the president.

Standing Armies

Early Americans harbored a deep mistrust of regular, professional, standing armies, fearing that such a permanent military force would be tempted to take over the government and deprive citizens of their liberties, as had often happened in world history. This fear was eclipsed, however, by the realization that a professional army was a more effective and reliable fighting force than volunteer militias, so the Constitution of 1787 gave the national government the power to create and regulate both a standing army and the militias. Fears of a military takeover in the United States never materialized, as the country has maintained a long tradition of effective civilian control over its military.

Statutory Law

Law created by enactment of legislatures.

Straw Purchaser

The act of one person to buy numerous guns on behalf of others who would not otherwise be able to make such purchases. Guns purchased by straw buyers account for a significant number of guns used in crimes.

Tenth Amendment

Amendment in the Bill of Rights that reserves those powers to the states that do not already belong to the national government and that are not barred from state exercise. In recent years, the Supreme Court has been receptive to legal challenges to federal power based on Tenth Amendment claims of infringing on states' rights. Such a claim prevailed in *Printz v. United States,* which struck down a part of the 1993 Brady Law as a violation of the amendment.

Third Amendment

Amendment in the Bill of Rights barring the quartering of troops in people's homes during peacetime without their consent. Arising from Americans' experience with this practice under British rule, this fear never materialized, so the amendment is considered an anachronism. Like the Second Amendment, this amendment arose from eighteenth century concerns that disappeared because of changing circumstances and practices; moreover, neither amendment has been incorporated by the courts.

Turner Diaries, The

A 1978 novel written by William Pierce under the pseudonym Andrew Macdonald laced with violence, anti-Semitism, and racism that describes revolution and a race war. Convicted Oklahoma City bomber Timothy McVeigh styled his bombing attack after events in the novel.

Uniform Militia Act of 1792 (1 U.S. Stat. 271)

A law passed by Congress that defined militia service and that stipulated that militia-eligible men maintain firearms and other military accessories should their services be required by the government. Lacking any sanctions or methods of enforcement this and similar state laws were widely ignored.

United States v. Cruikshank *(1876)*

The first Supreme Court case to expressly address the meaning of the Second Amendment. In the case, the court noted that the Second Amendment posed no obstacle to at least some regulation of guns, and it said that the amendment did not apply to the states (i.e., was not incorporated).

United States v. Lopez *(1995)*

A Supreme Court ruling that struck down a federal law, the Gun-Free School Zones Act of 1990, that made possession of a gun on public school property a federal crime. The law was declared unconstitutional by the Court on the grounds that Congress had exceeded its power to regulate interstate commerce. The Second Amendment was not raised as an issue in this case.

United States v. Miller *(1939)*

The Supreme Court ruled in this case that a federal law barring transport of certain firearms across state lines did not violate the Second Amendment rights of two men convicted under the law. Again, the Court noted that the Second Amendment only came in to play when citizens were serving in a government-organized and regulated militia. This is the most important Supreme Court ruling on the meaning of the Second Amendment of the nineteenth and twentieth centuries.

United States v. Verdugo-Urquidez *(1990)*

This Supreme Court case dealt with the application of the Fourth Amendment protection against unlawful searches and seizures as applied to an illegal alien. This case is sometimes cited erroneously as one in which the Court ruled that all citizens had a right to bear arms because the decision mentions, in *dicta,* that the phrase *the people* appears several times in the document, including in the Second Amendment.

Vigilantism

The belief that citizens have a right to take the law into their own hands if they believe they, or the nation, is at risk. The vigilante belief has been used by many individuals and groups, from the Ku Klux Klan to modern so-called militia groups, to support their extralegal activities.

Violence Policy Center

A Washington-based research and advocacy group that supports stronger gun laws, headed by founder Josh Sugarmann.

Waco Incident

See Branch Davidians

War of 1812

The last major conflict fought with general (unorganized) militias. Their disastrous performance during the war effectively ended the use of these militias to meet military emergencies. The volunteer (organized) militias survived and eventually became the National Guard (see Militia Act of 1903).

Washington, George

Commander-in-chief of U.S. forces during the Revolutionary War and later the nation's first president, Washington was harshly critical of militias as a fighting force, but was impelled to keep his criticisms private because of the militias' political popularity.

Weaver, Randy

A white supremacist who lived in rural Ruby Ridge, Idaho. After failing to appear before a judge to answer to an illegal weapons charge in 1992, Weaver met federal government agents with gunfire when they sought him out. After they lay siege to his home, Weaver eventually gave himself up. His criminal trial resulted in acquittal of most serious charges, and he won a $3.1 million civil judgment against the government for the wrongful shooting of his wife and son. This incident has been a rallying cause for antigovernment groups.

6

Documents

THIS CHAPTER PRESENTS EIGHT primary documents. The first two, the Calling Forth Act of 1792 and the Uniform Militia Act of 1792, are early legislative enactments that shed light on the meaning of militias as discussed in the Second Amendment and the Constitution insofar as they detail the roles of the states and the national government in militia-related matters. The third, fourth, and fifth documents are the Supreme Court cases that discuss in greatest detail the meaning of the Second Amendment: *United States v. Cruikshank* (1876), *Presser v. Illinois* (1886), and *United States v. Miller* (1939). The sixth, *Quilici v. Morton Grove*, was a 1982 decision of the U.S. Court of Appeals for the Seventh Circuit that exemplifies the thinking of lower federal courts on the meaning of the Second Amendment in recent decades. The seventh document is a listing of the right-to-bear-arms-type provisions to be found in the forty-four state constitutions that have them. The eighth includes excerpts from Republican and Democratic Party Platforms that deal with gun control.

The Calling Forth Act of 1792, 1 U.S. Stat. 264

The Calling Forth Act represented the culmination of three years of political wrangling over how to implement congressional authority over militias. The compromise was to delegate this power to the president, leaving him a relatively free hand in the case of invasion, but circumscribing this power some in the case of domestic insurrection, when the president needed to seek approval from a federal judge. This balance reflected Antifederalist fears of an overly strong national government. The Second Amendment's assurance to the states that they would be able to form and maintain their own militias would not, this act said, absolve them of national connections, needs, or obligations. Any state that refused to call forth or commit its militias in appropriate circumstances could expect to find other state militias sent to its soil.

Chap. XXVIII—An Act to provide for calling forth the Militia to execute the laws of the Union, suppress insurrections and repel invasions.

SECTION 1. Be it enacted by the Senate and House of Representatives of the United States of America in Congress assembled, That whenever the United States shall be invaded, or be in imminent danger of invasion from any foreign nation or Indian tribe, it shall be lawful for the President of the United States, to call forth such number of the militia of the state or states most convenient to the place of danger or scene of action, as he may judge necessary to repel such invasion, and to issue his orders for that purpose, to such officer or officers of the militia as he shall think proper; and in case of an insurrection in any state, against the government thereof, it shall be lawful for the President of the United States, on application of the legislature of such state, or of the executive (when the legislature cannot be convened) to call forth such number of the militia of any other state or states, as may be applied for, or as he may judge sufficient to suppress such insurrection.

SEC. 2. And be it further enacted, That whenever the laws of the United States shall be opposed, or the execution thereof obstructed, in any state, by combinations too powerful to be suppressed by the ordinary course of judicial proceedings, or by the powers vested in the marshals by this act, the same being notified to the President of the United States, by an associate justice or the district judge, it shall be lawful for the President of the United States to call forth the militia of such state to suppress such combinations, and to cause the laws to be duly executed. And if the militia of a state, where such combinations may happen, shall refuse, or be insufficient to suppress the same, it shall be lawful for the President, if the legislature of the United States be not in session, to call forth and employ such numbers of the militia of any other state or states most convenient thereto, as may be necessary, and the use of militia, so to be called forth, may be continued, if necessary, until the expiration of thirty days after the commencement of the ensuing session.

SEC. 3. Provided always, and be it further enacted, That whenever it may be necessary, in the judgment of the President, to use the military force hereby directed to be called forth, the President shall forthwith, and previous thereto, by proclamation, command such insurgents to disperse, and retire peaceably to their respective abodes, within a limited time.

SEC. 4. And be it further enacted, That the militia employed in the service of the United States, shall receive the same pay and allowances, as the troops of the United States, who may be in service at the same time, or who were last in service, and shall be subject to the same rules and articles of war: And that no officer, non-commissioned officer or private of the militia shall be compelled to serve more than three months in any one year, nor more than in due rotation with every other able-bodied man of the same rank in the battalion to which be belongs.

SEC. 5. And be it further enacted, That every officer, non-commissioned officer or private of the militia, who shall fail to obey the orders of the President of the United States in any of the cases before recited, shall forfeit a sum not exceeding one year's pay, and not less than one month's pay, to be determined and adjudged by a court martial; and such officer shall, moreover, be liable to be cashiered by sentence of a court martial: and such non-commissioned officers and privates shall be liable to be imprisoned by a like sentence, on failure of payment of the fines adjudged against them, for the space of one calendar month for every five dollars of such fine.

SEC. 6. And be it further enacted, That courts martial for the trial of militia shall be composed of militia officers only.

SEC. 7. And be it further enacted, That all fines to be assessed, as aforesaid, shall be certified by the presiding officer of the court martial before whom the same shall be assessed, to the marshal of the district, in which the delinquent shall reside, or to one of his deputies; and also to the supervisor of the revenue of the same district, who shall record the said certificate in a book to be kept for that purpose. The said marshal or his deputy shall forthwith proceed to levy the said fines with costs, by distress and sale of the goods and chattels of the delinquent, which costs and the manner of proceeding, with respect to the sale of the goods distrained, shall be agreeable to the laws of the state, in which the same shall be, in other cases of distress; and where any non-commissioned officer or private shall be adjudged to suffer imprisonment, there being no goods or chattels to be found, whereof to levy the said fines, the marshal of the district or his deputy may commit such delinquent to gaol, during the term, for which he shall be so adjudged to imprisonment, or until the fine shall be paid, in the same manner as other persons condemned to fine and imprisonment at the suit of the United States, may be committed.

SEC. 8. And be it further enacted, That the marshals and their deputies shall pay all such fines by them levied to the supervisor of the revenue, in the district in which they are collected, within two months after they shall have received the same, deducting therefrom five per centum, as a compensation for their trouble; and in case of failure, the same shall be recoverable by action of debt or information in any court of the United States, of the district, in which such fines shall be levied, having cognizance thereof, to be sued for, prosecuted and recovered, in the name of the supervisor of the district, with interest and costs.

SEC. 9. And be further enacted, That the marshals of the several districts and their deputies, shall have the same powers in executing the laws of the United States, as sheriffs and their deputies in the several states have by law, in executing the laws of their respective states.

SEC. 10. And be it further enacted, That this act shall continue and be in force, for and during the term of two years, and from thence to the end of the next session of Congress thereafter, and no longer.

APPROVED, May 2, 1792.

The Uniform Militia Act of 1792,
1 U.S. Stat. 271

The Uniform Militia Act, passed by Congress one year after the adoption of the Bill of Rights, reveals in considerable detail what the country's leaders meant by the concept of militia at a time when it was still considered to be the backbone of the U.S. military. Congress intended the militias to be organized according to military principles; membership was limited not only to white males, but to those between eighteen and forty-five who were fit for service, underscoring the fact that white males over the age of forty-five, and the infirm, were excluded from militias, even though they were eligible to exercise other rights and freedoms; they were to provide their own arms and other military accessories (since neither the states nor the national government could be relied on to provide weapons and the like); and the militias were to be put to any use specified by the government. Thus, militias were not to be privately formed or operated, nor were they to be used against the government, as some modern commentators have suggested. For all of this, however, the act included no penalties against states or men who did not comply—another compromise owing to continued tensions between Federalists and Antifederalists—and the terms of this act, along with similar state enactments, were largely ignored. Aside from the general military and organizational failure of the old-style general militias, two nineteenth-century developments put an end to the militia system described here: the military draft and governmental issue of firearms, uniforms, and the other accoutrements of war. Congress finally revamped the old militia system in a series of enactments beginning with the Militia Act of 1903 (also called the Dick Act). Both the Calling Forth Act and the Uniform Militia Act also demonstrate how Congress participates in the process of interpreting the Constitution, as both of these acts represent congressional efforts to specify the nature and purposes of the militias discussed in the Constitution and the Second Amendment.

CHAP. XXXIII—An Act more effectually to provide for the National Defence by establishing an Uniform Militia throughout the United States.

SECTION I. Be it enacted by the Senate and House of Representatives of the United States of America in Congress assembled, That each and every free able-bodied white male citizen of the respective states, resident therein, who is or shall be of the age of eighteen years, and under the age of forty-five years (except as is herein after excepted) shall severally and respectively be enrolled in the militia by the captain or commanding officer of the company, within whose bounds such citizen shall reside, and that within twelve months after the passing of this act. And it shall at all times hereafter be the duty of every such captain or commanding officer of a company to enrol every such citizen, as aforesaid, and also those who shall, from time to time, arrive at the age of eighteen years, or being of the age of eighteen years and under the age of forty-five years (except as before excepted) shall come to reside within his bounds; and shall without delay notify such citizen of the said enrolment, by a proper non-commissioned officer of the company, by whom such notice may be proved. That every citizen so enrolled and notified, shall, within six months thereafter, provide himself with a good musket or firelock, a sufficient bayonet and belt, two spare flints, and a knapsack, a pouch with a box therein to contain not less than twenty-four cartridges, suited to the bore of his musket or firelock, each cartridge to contain a proper quantity of powder and ball: or with a good rifle, knapsack, shot-pouch and powder-horn, twenty balls suited to the bore of his rifle, and a quarter of a pound of powder; and shall appear, so armed, accoutred and provided, when called out to exercise, or into service, except, that when called out on company days to exercise only, he may appear without a knapsack. That the commissioned officers shall severally be armed with a sword or hanger and espontoon, and that from and after five years from the passing of this act, all muskets for arming the militia as herein required, shall be of bores sufficient for balls of the eighteenth part of a pound. And every citizen so enrolled, and providing himself with the arms, ammunition and accoutrements required as aforesaid, shall hold the same exempted from all suits, distresses, executions or sales, for debt or for the payment of taxes.

SEC. 2. And be it further enacted, That the Vice President of the United States; the officers judicial and executive of the government of the United States; the members of both Houses of Congress, and their respective officers; all custom-house officers with their clerks; all postofficers, and stage drivers, who are employed in the care and conveyance of the mail of the post-office of the United States; all ferrymen employed at any ferry on the post road; all inspectors of exports; all pilots; all mariners actually employed in the sea service of any citizen or merchant within the United States; and all persons who now are or may hereafter be exempted by the laws of the respective states, shall be, and are hereby exempted from militia duty, notwithstanding their being above the age of eighteen, and under the age of forty-five years.

SEC. 3. And be it further enacted, That within one year after the passing of this act, the militia of the respective states shall be arranged into divisions, brigades, regiments, battalions and companies, as the legislature of each state shall direct; and each division, brigade and regiment, shall be numbered at the formation thereof; and a record made of such numbers in the adjutant-general's office in the state; and when in the field, or in service in the state, each division, brigade and regiment shall respectively take rank according to their numbers, reckoning the first or lowest number highest in rank. That if the same be convenient, each brigade shall consist of four regiments; each regiment of two battalions; each battalion of five companies; each company of sixty-four privates. That the said militia shall be officered by the respective states, as follows: To each division, one major-general and two aids-de-camp, with the rank of major; to each brigade, one brigadier-general, with one brigade inspector, to serve also as brigade-major, with the rank of a major; to each regiment, one lieutenant-colonel commandant; and to each battalion one major; to each company one captain, one lieutenant, one ensign, four sergeants, four corporals, one drummer and one fifer or bugler. That there shall be a regimental staff, to consist of one adjutant and one quartermaster, to rank as lieutenants; one paymaster; one surgeon, and one surgeon's mate; one sergeant-major; one drum-major, and one fife-major.

SEC. 4. And be it further enacted, That out of the militia enrolled, as is herein directed, there shall be formed for each battalion at least one company of grenadiers, light infantry or riflemen; and that to each division there shall be at least one company of artillery, and one troop of horse: there shall be to each company of artillery, one captain, two lieutenants, four sergeants, four corporals, six gunners, six bombadiers, one drummer, and one fifer. The officers to be armed with a sword or hanger, a fusee, bayonet and belt, with a cartridge-box to contain twelve cartridges; and each private or matross shall furnish himself with all the equipments of a private in the infantry, until proper ordnance and field artillery is provided. There shall be to each troop of horse, one captain, two lieutenants, one cornet, four sergeants, four corporals, one saddler, one farrier, and one trumpeter. The commissioned officers to furnish themselves with good horses of at least fourteen hands and an half high, and to be armed with a sword and pair of pistols, the holsters of which to be covered with bearskin caps. Each dragoon to furnish himself with a serviceable horse, at least fourteen hands and a half high, a good saddle, bridle, mailpillion and valise, holsters, and a breast-plate and crupper, a pair of boots and spurs, a pair of pistols, a sabre, and a cartoucb-box, to contain twelve cartridges for pistols. That each company of artillery and troop of horse shall be formed of volunteers from the brigade, at the discretion of the commander-in-chief of the state, not exceeding one company of each to a regiment, nor more in number than one eleventh part of the infantry, and shall be uniformly clothed in regimentals, to be furnished at their own expense; the colour and fashion to be determined by the brigadier commanding the brigade to which they belong.

SEC. 5. And be it further enacted, That each battalion and regiment shall be provided with the state and regimental colours by the field officers, and each company with a drum and fife, or bugle-horn, by the commissioned officers of the company, in such manner as the legislature of the respective states shall direct.

SEC. 6. And be it further enacted, That there shall be an adjutant-general appointed in each state, whose duty it shall be to distribute all orders from the commander-in-chief of the state to the several corps; to attend all public reviews when the commander-in-chief of the state shall review the militia, or any part thereof; to obey all orders from him relative to carrying into execution and perfecting the system of military discipline established by this act; to furnish blank forms of different returns that may be required, and to explain the principles on which they should be made; to receive from the several officers of the different corps throughout the state, returns of the militia under their command, reporting the actual situation of their arms, accoutrements, and ammunition, their delinquencies, and every other thing which relates to the general advancement of good order and discipline: all which the several officers of the divisions, brigades, regiments, and battalions, are hereby required to make in the usual manner, so that the said adjutant-general may be duly furnished therewith: from all which returns he shall make proper abstracts, and lay the same annually before the commander-in-chief of the state.

SEC. 7. And be it further enacted, That the rules of discipline, approved and established by Congress in their resolution of the twenty-ninth of March, one thousand seven hundred and seventy-nine, shall be the rules of discipline to be observed by the militia throughout the United States, except such deviations from the said rules as may be rendered necessary by the requisitions of this act, or by some other unavoidable circumstances. It shall be the duty of the commanding officer at every muster, whether by battalion, regiment, or single company, to cause the militia to be exercised and trained agreeably to the said rules of discipline.

SEC. 8. And be it further enacted, That all commissioned officers shall take rank according to the date of their commissions; and when two of the same grade bear an equal date, then their rank to be determined by lot, to be drawn by them before the commanding officer of the brigade, regiment, battalion, company, or detachment.

SEC. 9. And be it further enacted, That if any person, whether officer or soldier, belonging to the militia of any state, and called out into the service of the United States, be wounded or disabled while in actual service, he shall be taken care of and provided for at the public expense.

SEC. 10. And be it further enacted, That it shall be the duty of the brigade-inspector to attend the regimental and battalion meetings of the militia composing their several brigades, during the time of their being under arms, to inspect their arms, ammunition, and accoutrements; superintend their exercise and manoeuvres, and introduce the system of military discipline before described throughout the brigade, agreeable to law, and such orders as they shall from time to time receive from the commander-in-chief of the state; to make returns to the adjutant-general of the state, at least once in every year, of the militia of the brigade to which he belongs, reporting therein the actual situation of the arms, accoutrements, and ammunition of the several corps, and every other thing which, in his judgment, may relate to their government and the general advancement of good order and military discipline; and the adjutant-general shall make a return of all the militia of the state to the commander-in-chief of the said state, and a duplicate of the same to the President of the United States.

And whereas sundry corps of artillery, cavalry, and infantry now exist in several of the said states, which by the laws, customs, or usages thereof have not been incorporated with, or subject to the general regulations of the militia:

SEC. 11. Be it further enacted, That such corps retain their accustomed privileges, subject, nevertheless, to all other duties required by this act, in like manner with the other militia.

APPROVED, May 8, 1792.

United States v. Cruikshank, 92 U.S. 542 (1876)

Tensions ran high between African Americans and whites in the South after the Civil War, and violent confrontations often occurred between blacks and whites who could not accept the free status of these former slaves. In one instance, a band of whites who were reputedly members of the Ku Klux Klan attacked and burned a courthouse in Louisiana that was defended by armed blacks trying to assert their right to vote. In the process, two blacks were killed. A group of the attacking whites was charged with violating a federal civil rights law, and with violating various other federal rights of the blacks, including the Second Amendment's right to bear arms. A lower court upheld the convictions, but the Supreme Court reversed the lower court in Cruikshank, *noting that the Second Amendment as well as the rest of the Bill of Rights did not apply to the states. While much of the Bill of Rights has since been applied to the states through the process of incorporation (using the Fourteenth Amendment to apply parts of the Bill of Rights to the states), the Second Amendment has not. This case also established the principle that laws may be properly enacted to restrict or regulate the carrying of weapons, including firearms. This case also reveals much of how the court defined Federalism and dual citizenship in the era before the incorporation process began.*

Argued March 30, 31, April 1, 1875. Decided March 27, 1876.

MR. CHIEF JUSTICE WAITE delivered the opinion of the court.

This case comes here with a certificate by the judges of the Circuit Court for the District of Louisiana that they were divided in opinion upon a question which occurred at the hearing. It presents for our consideration an indictment containing sixteen counts, divided into two series of eight counts each, based upon sect. 6 of the Enforcement Act of May 31, 1870. That section is as follows:—

That if two or more persons shall band or conspire together, or go in disguise upon the public highway, or upon the premises of another, with intent to violate any provision of this act, or to injure, oppress, threaten, or intimidate any citizen, with intent to prevent or hinder his free exercise and enjoyment of any right or privilege granted or secured to him by the constitution or laws of the United States, or because of his having exercised the same, such persons shall be held guilty of felony, and, on conviction thereof, shall be fined or imprisoned, or both, at the discretion of the court,-the fine not to exceed $5,000, and the imprisonment not to exceed ten years; and shall, moreover, be thereafter ineligible to, and disabled from holding, any office or place of honor, profit, or trust created by the constitution or laws of the United States. 16 Stat. 141.

The question certified arose upon a motion in arrest of judgment after a verdict of guilty generally upon the whole sixteen counts, and is stated to be, whether "the said sixteen counts of said indictment are severally good and sufficient in law, and contain charges of criminal matter indictable under the laws of the United States."

The general charge in the first eight counts is that of "banding," and in the second eight, that of "conspiring" together to injure, oppress, threaten, and intimidate Levi Nelson and Alexander Tillman, citizens of the United States, of African descent and persons of color, with the intent thereby to hinder and prevent them in their free exercise and enjoyment of rights and privileges "granted and secured" to them "in common with all other good citizens of the United States by the constitution and laws of the United States."

The offences provided for by the statute in question do not consist in the mere "banding" or "conspiring" of two or more persons together, but in their banding or conspiring with the intent, or for any of the purposes, specified. To bring this case under the operation of the statute, therefore, it must appear that the right, the enjoyment of which the conspirators intended to hinder or prevent, was one granted or secured by the constitution or laws of the United States. If it does not so appear, the criminal matter charged has not been made indictable by any act of Congress.

We have in our political system a government of the United States and a government of each of the several States. Each one of these governments is distinct from the others, and each has citizens of its own who owe it allegiance, and whose rights, within its jurisdiction, it must protect. The same person may be at the same time a citizen of the United States and a citizen of a State, but his rights of citizenship under one of these governments will be different from those he has under the other. . . .

Citizens are the members of the political community to which they belong. They are the people who compose the community, and who, in their associated capacity, have established or submitted themselves to the dominion of a government for the promotion of their general welfare and the protection of their individual as well as their collective rights. In the formation of a government, the people may confer upon it such powers as they choose. The government, when so formed, may, and when called upon should, exercise all the powers it has for the protection of the rights of its citizens and the people within its jurisdiction; but it can exercise no other. The duty of a government to afford protection is limited always by the power it possesses for that purpose.

Experience made the fact known to the people of the United States that they required a national government for national purposes. The separate governments of the separate States, bound together by the articles of confederation alone, were not sufficient for the promotion of the general welfare of the people in respect to foreign nations, or for their complete protection as citizens of the confederated States. For this reason, the people of the United States, "in order to form a more perfect union, establish justice, insure domestic tranquillity, provide for the common defence, promote the general welfare, and secure the blessings of liberty" to themselves and their posterity (Const. Preamble), ordained and established the government of the United States, and defined its powers by a constitution, which they adopted as its fundamental law, and made its rule of action.

The government thus established and defined is to some extent a government of the States in their political capacity. It is also, for certain purposes, a government of the people. Its powers are limited in number, but not in degree. Within the scope of its powers, as enumerated and defined, it is supreme and above the States; but beyond, it has no existence. It was erected for special purposes, and endowed with all the powers necessary for its own preservation and the accomplishment of the ends its people had in view. It can neither grant nor secure to its citizens any right or privilege not expressly or by implication placed under its jurisdiction.

The people of the United States resident within any State are subject to two governments: one State, and the other National; but there need be no conflict between the two. The powers which one possesses, the other does not. They are established for different purposes, and have separate jurisdictions. Together they make one whole, and furnish the people of the United States with a complete government, ample for the protection of all their rights at home and abroad. True, it may sometimes happen that a person is amenable to both jurisdictions for one and the same act. Thus, if a marshal of the United States is unlawfully resisted while executing the process of the courts within a State, and the resistance is accompanied by an assault on the officer, the sovereignty of the United States is violated by the resistance, and that of the State by the breach of peace, in the assault. So, too, if one passes counterfeited coin of the United States within a State, it may be an offence against the United States and the State: the United States, because it discredits the coin; and the State, because of the fraud upon him to whom it is passed. This does not, however, necessarily imply that the two governments possess powers in common, or bring them into conflict with each other. It is the natural consequence of a citizenship which owes allegiance to two sovereignties, and claims protection from both. The citizen cannot complain, because he has voluntarily submitted himself to such a form of government. He owes allegiance to the two departments, so to speak, and within their respective spheres must pay the penalties which each exacts for disobedience to its laws. In return, he can demand protection from each within its own jurisdiction.

The government of the United States is one of delegated powers alone. Its authority is defined and limited by the Constitution. All powers not granted to it by that instrument are reserved to the

States or the people. No rights can be acquired under the constitution or laws of the United States, except such as the government of the United States has the authority to grant or secure. All that cannot be so granted or secured are left under the protection of the States.

We now proceed to an examination of the indictment, to ascertain whether the several rights, which it is alleged the defendants intended to interfere with, are such as had been in law and in fact granted or secured by the constitution or laws of the United States.

The first and ninth counts state the intent of the defendants to have been to hinder and prevent the citizens named in the free exercise and enjoyment of their "lawful right and privilege to peaceably assemble together with each other and with other citizens of the United States for a peaceful and lawful purpose." The right of the people peaceably to assemble for lawful purposes existed long before the adoption of the Constitution of the United States. In fact, it is, and always has been, one of the attributes of citizenship under a free government. It "derives its source," to use the language of Chief Justice Marshall, in *Gibbons v. Ogden*, 9 Wheat. 211, "from those laws whose authority is acknowledged by civilized man throughout the world." It is found wherever civilization exists. It was not, therefore, a right granted to the people by the Constitution. The government of the United States when established found it in existence, with the obligation on the part of the States to afford it protection. As no direct power over it was granted to Congress, it remains, according to the ruling in *Gibbons v. Ogden,* id. 203, subject to State jurisdiction. Only such existing rights were committed by the people to the protection of Congress as came within the general scope of the authority granted to the national government.

The first amendment to the Constitution prohibits Congress from abridging "the right of the people to assemble and to petition the government for a redress of grievances." This, like the other amendments proposed and adopted at the same time, was not intended to limit the powers of the State governments in respect to their own citizens, but to operate upon the National government alone.... It is now too late to question the correctness of this construction. As was said by the late Chief Justice, in *Twitchell v. The Commonwealth,* 7 Wall. 325, "the scope and application of these amendments are no longer subjects of discussion here." They left the authority of the States just where they found it, and added nothing to the already existing powers of the United States.

The particular amendment now under consideration assumes the existence of the right of the people to assemble for lawful purposes, and protects it against encroachment by Congress. The right was not created by the amendment; neither was its continuance guaranteed, except as against congressional interference. For their protection in its enjoyment, therefore, the people must look to the States. The power for that purpose was originally placed there, and it has never been surrendered to the United States.

The right of the people peaceably to assemble for the purpose of petitioning Congress for a redress of grievances, or for any thing else connected with the powers or the duties of the national government, is an attribute of national citizenship, and, as such, under the protection of, and guaranteed by, the United States. The very idea of a government, republican in form, implies a right on the part of its citizens to meet peaceably for consultation in respect to public affairs and to petition for a redress of grievances. If it had been alleged in these counts that the object of the defendants was to prevent a meeting for such a purpose, the case would have been within the statute, and within the scope of the sovereignty of the United States. Such, however, is not the case. The offence, as stated in the indictment, will be made out, if it be shown that the object of the conspiracy was to prevent a meeting for any lawful purpose whatever.

The second and tenth counts are equally defective. The right there specified is that of "bearing arms for a lawful purpose." This is not a right granted by the Constitution. Neither is it in any manner dependent upon that instrument for its existence. The second amendment declares that it shall not be infringed; but this, as has been seen, means no more than that it shall not be infringed by Congress. This is one of the amendments that has no other effect than to restrict the powers of the national government, leaving the people to look for their protection against any violation by their fellow-citizens of the rights it recognizes, to what is called, in *The City of New York v. Miln,* 11 Pet. 139, the "powers which relate to merely municipal legislation, or what was, perhaps, more properly called internal police," "not surrendered or restrained" by the Constitution of the United States.

The third and eleventh counts are even more objectionable. They charge the intent to have been to deprive the citizens named, they being in Louisiana, "of their respective several lives and liberty of person without due process of law." This is nothing else than alleging a conspiracy to falsely imprison or murder citizens of the United States, being within the territorial jurisdiction of the State of Louisiana. The rights of life and personal liberty are natural rights of man. "To secure these rights," says the Declaration of Independence, "governments are instituted among men, deriving their just powers from the consent of the governed." The very highest duty of the States, when they entered into the Union under the Constitution, was to protect all persons within their boundaries in the enjoyment of these "unalienable rights with which they were endowed by their Creator." Sovereignty, for this purpose, rests alone with the States. It is no more the duty or within the power of the United States to punish for a conspiracy to falsely imprison or murder within a State, than it would be to punish for false imprisonment or murder itself.

The fourteenth amendment prohibits a State from depriving any person of life, liberty, or property, without due process of law; but this adds nothing to the rights of one citizen as against another. It simply furnishes an additional guaranty against any encroachment by the States upon the fundamental rights which belong to every citizen as a member of society. As was said by Mr. Justice Johnson, in *Bank of Columbia v. Okely,* 4 Wheat. 244, it secures "the individual from the arbitrary exercise of the powers of government, unrestrained by the established principles of private rights and distributive justice." These counts in the indictment do not call for the exercise of any of the powers conferred by this provision in the amendment.

The fourth and twelfth counts charge the intent to have been to prevent and hinder the citizens named, who were of African descent and persons of color, in "the free exercise and enjoyment of their several right and privilege to the full and equal benefit of all laws and proceedings, then and there, before that time, enacted or ordained by the said State of Louisiana and by the United States; and then and there, at that time, being in force in the said State and District of Louisiana aforesaid, for the security of their respective persons and property, then and there, at that time enjoyed at and within said State and District of Louisiana by white persons, being citizens of said State of Louisiana and the United States, for the protection of the persons and property of said white citizens." There is no allegation that this was done because of the race or color of the persons conspired against. When stripped of its verbiage, the case as presented amounts to nothing more than that the defendants conspired to prevent certain citizens of the United States, being within the State of Louisiana, from enjoying the equal protection of the laws of the State and of the United States.

The fourteenth amendment prohibits a State from denying to any person within its jurisdiction the equal protection of the laws; but this provision does not, any more than the one which precedes it, and which we have just considered, add any thing to the rights which one citizen has under the Constitution against another. The equality of the rights of citizens is a principle of republicanism. Every republican government is in duty bound to protect all its citizens in the enjoyment of this principle, if within its power. That duty was originally assumed by the States; and it still remains there. The only obligation resting upon the United States is to see that the States do not deny the right. This the amendment guarantees, but no more. The power of the national government is limited to the enforcement of this guaranty.

No question arises under the Civil Rights Act of April 9, 1866 (14 Stat. 27), which is intended for the protection of citizens of the United States in the enjoyment of certain rights, without discrimination on account of race, color, or previous condition of servitude, because, as has already been stated, it is nowhere alleged in these counts that the wrong contemplated against the rights of these citizens was on account of their race or color.

Another objection is made to these counts, that they are too vague and uncertain. This will be considered hereafter, in connection with the same objection to other counts.

The sixth and fourteenth counts state the intent of the defendants to have been to hinder and prevent the citizens named, being of African descent, and colored, "in the free exercise and enjoyment of their several and respective right and privilege to vote at any election to be thereafter by law had and held by the people in and of the said State of Louisiana, or by the people of and in the parish of Grant aforesaid." In *Minor v. Happersett*, 21 Wall. 178, we decided that the Constitution of the United States has not conferred the right of suffrage upon any one, and that the United States have no voters of their own creation in the States. In *United States v. Reese et al.*, supra, p. 214, we hold that the fifteenth amendment has invested the citizens of the United States with a new constitutional right, which is, exemption from discrimination in the exercise of the elective franchise on account of race, color, or previous condition of servitude. From this it appears that the right of suffrage is not a necessary attribute of national citizenship; but that exemption from discrimination in the exercise of that right on account of race, &c., is. The right to vote in the States comes from the States; but the right of exemption from the prohibited discrimination comes from the United States. The first has not been granted or secured by the Constitution of the United States; but the last has been.

Inasmuch, therefore, as it does not appear in these counts that the intent of the defendants was to prevent these parties from exercising their right to vote on account of their race, &c., it does not appear that it was their intent to interfere with any right granted or secured by the constitution or laws of the United States. We may suspect that race was the cause of the hostility; but it is not so averred. This is material to a description of the substance of the offence, and cannot be supplied by implication. Every thing essential must be charged positively, and not inferentially. The defect here is not in form, but in substance.

The seventh and fifteenth counts are no better than the sixth and fourteenth. The intent here charged is to put the parties named in great fear of bodily harm, and to injure and oppress them, because, being and having been in all things qualified, they had voted "at an election before that time had and held according to law by the people of the said State of Louisiana, in said State, to wit, on the fourth day of November, A.D. 1872, and at divers other elections by the people of the State, also before that time had and held according to law." There is nothing to show that the elections voted at were any other than State elections, or that the conspiracy was formed on account of the race of the parties against whom the conspirators were to act. The charge as made is really of nothing more than a conspiracy to commit a breach of the peace within a State. Certainly it will not be claimed that the United States have the power or are required to do mere police duly in the States. If a State cannot protect itself against domestic violence, the United States may, upon the call of the executive, when the legislature cannot be convened, lend their assistance for that purpose. This is a guaranty of the Constitution (art. 4, sect. 4); but it applies to no case like this.

We are, therefore, of the opinion that the first, second, third, fourth, sixth, seventh, ninth, tenth, eleventh, twelfth, fourteenth, and fifteenth counts do not contain charges of a criminal nature made indictable under the laws of the United States, and that consequently they are not good and sufficient in law. They do not show that it was the intent of the defendants, by their conspiracy, to hinder or prevent the enjoyment of any right granted or secured by the Constitution.

We come now to consider the fifth and thirteenth and the eighth and sixteenth counts, which may be brought together for that purpose. The intent charged in the fifth and thirteenth is "to hinder and prevent the parties in their respective free exercise and enjoyment of the rights, privileges, immunities, and protection granted and secured to them respectively as citizens of the United States, and as citizens of said State of Louisiana," "for the reason that they, . . . being then and there citizens of said State and of the United States, were persons of African descent and race, and persons of color, and not white citizens thereof;" and in the eighth and sixteenth, to hinder and prevent them "in their several and respective free exercise and enjoyment of every, each, all, and singular the several rights and privileges granted and secured to them by the constitution and laws of the United States." The same general statement of the rights to be interfered with is found in the fifth and thirteenth counts.

According to the view we take of these counts, the question is not whether it is enough, in general, to describe a statutory offence in the language of the statute, but whether the offence has here been described at all. The statute provides for the punishment of those who conspire "to injure, oppress, threaten, or intimidate any citizen, with intent to prevent or hinder his free exercise and enjoyment of any right or privilege granted or secured to him by the constitution or laws of the United States." These counts in the indictment charge, in substance, that the intent in this case was to hinder and prevent these citizens in the free exercise and enjoyment of "every, each, all, and singular" the rights granted them by the Constitution, &c. There is no specification of any particular right. The language is broad enough to cover all.

In criminal cases, prosecuted under the laws of the United States, the accused has the constitutional right "to be informed of the nature and cause of the accusation." Amend. VI. In United States v. Mills, 7 Pet. 142, this was construed to mean, that the indictment must set forth the offence "with clearness and all necessary certainty, to apprise the accused of the crime with which he stands charged;" and in United States v. Cook, 17 Wall. 174, that "every ingredient of which the offence is composed must be accurately and clearly alleged." It is an elementary principle of criminal pleading, that where the definition of an offence, whether it be at common law or by statute, "includes generic terms, it is not sufficient that the indictment shall charge the offence in the same generic terms as in the definition; but it must state the species,—it must descend to particulars." 1 Arch. Cr. Pr. and Pl., 291. The object of the indictment is, first, to furnish the accused with such a description of the charge against him as will enable him to make his defence, and avail himself of his conviction or acquittal for protection against a further prosecution for the same cause; and, second, to inform the court of the facts alleged, so that it may decide whether they are sufficient in law to support a conviction, if one should be had. For this, facts are to be stated, not conclusions of law alone. A crime is made up of acts and intent; and these must be set forth in the indictment, with reasonable particularity of time, place, and circumstances.

It is a crime to steal goods and chattels; but an indictment would be bad that did not specify with some degree of certainty the articles stolen. This, because the accused must be advised of the essential particulars of the charge against him, and the court must be able to decide whether the property taken was such as was the subject of larceny. So, too, it is in some States a crime for two or more persons to conspire to cheat and defraud another out of his property; but it has been held that an indictment for such an offence must contain allegations setting forth the means proposed to be used to accomplish the purpose. This, because, to make such a purpose criminal, the conspiracy must be to cheat and defraud in a mode made criminal by statute; and as all cheating and defrauding has not been made criminal, it is necessary for the indictment to state the means proposed, in order that the court may see that they are in fact illegal. . . . In Maine, it is an offence for two or more to conspire with the intent unlawfully and wickedly to commit any crime punishable by imprisonment in the State prison (*State v. Roberts*); but we think it will hardly be claimed that an indictment would be good under this statute, which charges the object of the conspiracy to have been "unlawfully and wickedly to commit each, every, all, and singular the crimes punishable by imprisonment in the State prison." All crimes are not so punishable. Whether a particular crime be such a one or not, is a question of law. The accused has, therefore, the right to have a specification of the charge against him in this respect, in order that he may decide whether he should present his defence by motion to quash, demurrer, or plea; and the court, that it may determine whether the facts will sustain the indictment. So here, the crime is made to consist in the unlawful combination with an intent to prevent the enjoyment of any right granted or secured by the Constitution, &c. All rights are not so granted or secured. Whether one is so or not is a question of law, to be decided by the court, not the prosecutor. Therefore, the indictment should state the particulars, to inform the court as well as the accused. It must be made to appear—that is to say, appears from the indictment, without going further—that the acts charged will, if proved, support a conviction for the offence alleged.

But it is needless to pursue the argument further. The conclusion is irresistible, that these counts are too vague and general. They lack the certainty and precision required by the established rules of criminal pleading. It follows that they are not good and sufficient in law. They are so defective that no judgment of conviction should be pronounced upon them.

The order of the Circuit Court arresting the judgment upon the verdict is, therefore, affirmed; and the cause remanded, with instructions to discharge the defendants.

MR. JUSTICE CLIFFORD dissenting.

I concur that the judgment in this case should be arrested, but for reasons quite different from those given by the court. Power is vested in Congress to enforce by appropriate legislation the prohibition contained in the fourteenth amendment of the Constitution; and the fifth section of the Enforcement Act provides to the effect, that persons who prevent, hinder, control, or intimidate, or who attempt to prevent, hinder, control, or intimidate, any person to whom the right of suffrage is secured or guaranteed by that amendment, from exercising, or in exercising such right, by means of bribery or threats; of depriving such person of employment or occupation; or of ejecting such person from rented house, lands, or other property; or by threats of refusing to renew leases or contracts for labor; or by threats of violence to himself or family—such person so offending shall be deemed guilty of a misdemeanor, and, on conviction thereof, shall be fined or imprisoned, or both, as therein provided. 16 Stat. 141.

Provision is also made, by sect. 6 of the same act, that, if two or more persons shall band or conspire together, or go in disguise, upon the public highway, or upon the premises of another, with intent to violate any provision of that act, or to injure, oppress, threaten, or intimidate any citizen with intent to prevent or hinder his free exercise and enjoyment of any right or privilege granted or secured to him by the constitution and laws of the United States, or because of his having exercised the same, such persons shall be deemed guilty of felony, and, on conviction thereof, shall be fined or imprisoned, or both, and be further punished as therein provided.

More than one hundred persons were jointly indicted at the April Term, 1873, of the Circuit Court of the United States for the

District of Louisiana, charged with offences in violation of the provisions of the Enforcement Act. By the record, it appears that the indictment contained thirty-two counts, in two series of sixteen counts each: that the first series were drawn under the fifth and sixth sections of the act; and that the second series were drawn under the seventh section of the same act; and that the latter series charged that the prisoners are guilty of murder committed by them in the act of violating some of the provisions of the two preceding sections of that act.

Eight of the persons named in the indictment appeared on the 10th of June, 1874, and went to trial under the plea of not guilty, previously entered at the time of their arraignment. Three of those who went to trial—to wit, the three defendants named in the transcript—were found guilty by the jury on the first series of the counts of the indictment, and not guilty on the second series of the counts in the same indictment.

Subsequently the convicted defendants filed a motion for a new trial, which motion being overruled they filed a motion in arrest of judgment. Hearing was had upon that motion; and the opinions of the judges of the Circuit Court being opposed, the matter in difference was duly certified to this court, the question being whether the motion in arrest of judgment ought to be granted or denied.

Two only of the causes of arrest assigned in the motion will be considered in answering the questions certified: (1.) Because the matters and things set forth and charged in the several counts in question do not constitute offences against the laws of the United States, and do not come within the purview, true intent, and meaning of the Enforcement Act. (2.) Because the several counts of the indictment in question are too vague, insufficient, and uncertain to afford the accused proper notice to plead and prepare their defence, and do not set forth any offence defined by the Enforcement Act.

Four other causes of arrest were assigned; but, in the view taken of the case, it will be sufficient to examine the two causes above set forth.

Since the questions were certified into this court, the parties have been fully heard in respect to all the questions presented for decision in the transcript. Questions not pressed at the argument will not be considered; and, inasmuch as the counsel in behalf of the United States confined their arguments entirely to the thirteenth, fourteenth, and sixteenth counts of the first series in the indictment, the answers may well be limited to these counts, the others being virtually abandoned. Mere introductory allegations will be omitted as unimportant, for the reason that the questions to be answered relate to the allegations of the respective counts describing the offence.

As described in the thirteenth count, the charge is, that the defendants did, at the time and place mentioned, combine, conspire, and confederated together, between and among themselves, for and with the unlawful and felonious intent and purpose one Levi Nelson and one Alexander Tillman, each of whom being then and there a citizen of the United States, of African descent, and a person of color, unlawfully and feloniously to injure, oppress, threaten, and intimidate, with the unlawful and felonious intent thereby the said persons of color, respectively, then and there to hinder and prevent in their respective and several free exercise and enjoyment of the rights, privileges, and immunities, and protection, granted and secured to them respectively as citizens of the United States and citizens of the State, by reason of their race and color; and because that they, the said persons of color, being then and there citizens of the State and of the United States, were then and there persons of African descent and race, and persons of color, and not white citizens thereof; the same being a right or privilege granted or secured to the said persons of color respectively, in common with all other good citizens of the United States, by the Federal Constitution and the laws of Congress.

Matters of law conceded, in the opinion of the court, may be assumed to be correct without argument; and, if so, then discussion is not necessary to show that every ingredient of which an offence is composed must be accurately and clearly alleged in the indictment, or the indictment will be bad, and may be quashed on motion, or the judgment may be arrested before sentence, or be reversed on a writ of error. *United States v. Cook,* 17 Wall. 174.

Offences created by statute, as well as offences at common law, must be accurately and clearly described in an indictment; and, if the offence cannot be so described without expanding the allegations beyond the mere words of the statute, then it is clear that the allegations of the indictment must be expanded to that extent, as it is universally true that no indictment is sufficient which does not accurately and clearly allege all the ingredients of which the offence is composed, so as to bring the accused within the true intent and meaning of the statute defining the offence. Authorities of great weight, besides those referred to by me, in the dissenting opinion just read, may be found in support of that proposition.

Every offence consists of certain acts done or omitted under certain circumstances; and, in the indictment for the offence, it is not sufficient to charge the accused generally with having committed the offence, but all the circumstances constituting the offence must be specially set forth. . . .

Persons born or naturalized in the United States, and subject to the jurisdiction thereof, are citizens thereof; and the fourteenth amendment also provides, that no State shall make or enforce any law which shall abridge the privileges or immunities of citizens of the United States. Congress may, doubtless, prohibit any violation of that provision, and may provide that any person convicted of violating the same shall be guilty of an offence, and be subject to such reasonable punishment as Congress may prescribe.

Conspiracies of the kind described in the introductory clause of the sixth section of the Enforcement Act are explicitly forbidden by the subsequent clauses of the same section; and it may be that if the indictment was for a conspiracy at common law, and was pending in a tribunal having jurisdiction of common-law offences, the indictment in its present form might be sufficient, even though it contains no definite allegation whatever of any particular overt act committed by the defendants in pursuance of the alleged conspiracy.

Decided cases may doubtless be found in which it is held that an indictment for a conspiracy, at common law, may be sustained where there is an unlawful agreement between two or more persons to do an unlawful act, or to do a lawful act by unlawful means; and authorities may be referred to which support the proposition, that the indictment, if the conspiracy is well pleaded, is sufficient, even though it be not alleged that any overt act had been done in pursuance of the unlawful combination.

Suffice it to say, however, that the authorities to that effect are opposed by another class of authorities equally respectable, and even more numerous, which decide that the indictment is bad unless it is alleged that some overt act was committed in pursuance of the intent and purpose of the alleged conspiracy; and in all the latter class of cases it is held, that the overt act, as well as the unlawful combination, must be clearly and accurately alleged.

Two reasons of a conclusive nature, however, may be assigned which show, beyond all doubt, that it is not necessary to enter into the inquiry which class of those decisions is correct.

1. Because the common law is not a source of jurisdiction in the circuit courts, nor in any other Federal court.

Circuit Courts have no common-law jurisdiction of offences of any grade or description; and it is equally clear that the appellate jurisdiction of the Supreme Court does not extend to any case or any question, in a case not within the jurisdiction of the subordinate Federal courts. . . .

2. Because it is conceded that the offence described in the indictment is an offence created and defined by an act of Congress.

Indictments for offences created and defined by statute must in all cases follow the words of the statute: and, where there is no departure from that rule, the indictment is in general sufficient, except in cases where the statute is elliptical, or where, by necessary implication, other constituents are component parts of the offence; as where the words of the statute defining the offence have a compound signification, or are enlarged by what immediately precedes or follows the words describing the offence, and in the same connection. Cases of the kind do arise, as where, in the dissenting opinion in *United States v. Reese et al.*, supra, p. 222, it was held, that the words offer to pay a capitation tax were so expanded by a succeeding clause of the same sentence that the word "offer" necessarily included readiness to perform what was offered, the provision being that the offer should be equivalent to actual performance if the offer failed to be carried into execution by the wrongful act or omission of the party to whom the offer was made.

Two offences are in fact created and defined by the sixth section of the Enforcement Act, both of which consist of a conspiracy with an intent to perpetrate a forbidden act. They are alike in respect to the conspiracy; but differ very widely in respect to the act embraced in the prohibition.

1. Persons, two or more, are forbidden to band or conspire together, or go in disguise upon the public highway, or on the premises of another, with intent to violate any provision of the Enforcement Act, which is an act of twenty-three sections.

Much discussion of that clause is certainly unnecessary, as no one of the counts under consideration is founded on it, or contains any allegations describing such an offence. Such a conspiracy with intent to injure, oppress, threaten, or intimidate any person, is also forbidden by the succeeding clause of that section, if it be done with intent to prevent or hinder his free exercise and enjoyment of any right or privilege granted or secured to him by the constitution or laws of the United States, or because of having exercised the same. Sufficient proof appears in the thirteenth count to warrant the conclusion, that the grand jury intended to charge the defendants with the second offence created and defined in the sixth section of the Enforcement Act.

Indefinite and vague as the description of the offence there defined, is, it is obvious that it is greatly more so as described in the allegations of the thirteenth count. By the act of Congress, the prohibition is extended to any right or privilege granted or secured by the constitution or laws of Congress; leaving it to the pleader to specify the particular right or privilege which had been invaded, in order to give the accusation that certainty which the rules of criminal pleading everywhere require in an indictment; but the pleader in this case, overlooking any necessity for any such specification, and making no attempt to comply with the rules of criminal pleading in that regard, describes the supposed offence in terms much more vague and indefinite than those employed in the act of Congress.

Instead of specifying the particular right or privilege which had been invaded, the pleader proceeds to allege that the defendants, with all the others named in the indictment, did combine, conspire, and confederate together, with the unlawful intent and purpose the said persons of African descent and persons of color then and there to injure, oppress, threaten, and intimidate, and thereby then and there to hinder and prevent them in the free exercise and enjoyment of the rights, privileges, and immunities and protection granted and secured to them as citizens of the United States and citizens of the State, without any other specification of the rights, privileges, immunities, and protection which had been violated or invaded, or which were threatened, except what follows; to wit, the same being a right or privilege granted or secured in common with all other good citizens by the constitution and laws of the United States.

Vague and indefinite allegations of the kind are not sufficient to inform the accused in a criminal prosecution of the nature and cause of the accusation against him, within the meaning of the sixth amendment of the Constitution.

Valuable rights and privileges, almost without number, are granted and secured to citizens by the constitution and laws of

Congress; none of which may be, with impunity, invaded in violation of the prohibition contained in that section. Congress intended by that provision to protect citizens in the enjoyment of all such rights and privileges; but in affording such protection in the mode there provided Congress never intended to open the door to the invasion of the rule requiring certainty in criminal pleading, which for ages has been regarded as one of the great safeguards of the citizen against oppressive and groundless prosecutions.

Judge Story says the indictment must charge the time and place and nature and circumstances of the offence with clearness and certainty, so that the party may have full notice of the charge, and be able to make his defence with all reasonable knowledge and ability. 2 Story, Const., sect. 1785.

Nothing need be added to show that the fourteenth count is founded upon the same clause in the sixth section of the Enforcement Act as the thirteenth count, which will supersede the necessity of any extended remarks to explain the nature and character of the offence there created and defined. Enough has already been remarked to show that that particular clause of the section was passed to protect citizens in the free exercise and enjoyment of every right or privilege granted or secured to them by the constitution and laws of Congress, and to provide for the punishment of those who band or conspire together, in the manner described, to injure, oppress, or intimidate any citizen, to prevent or hinder him from the free exercise and enjoyment of all such rights or privileges, or because of his having exercised any such right or privilege so granted or secured.

What is charged in the fourteenth count is, that the defendants did combine, conspire, and confederate the said citizens of African descent and persons of color to injure, oppress, threaten, and intimidate, with intent the said citizens thereby to prevent and hinder in the free exercise and enjoyment of the right and privilege to vote at any election to be thereafter had and held according to law by the people of the State, or by the people of the parish; they, the defendants, well knowing that the said citizens were lawfully qualified to vote at any such election thereafter to be had and held.

Confessedly, some of the defects existing in the preceding count are avoided in the count in question; as, for example, the description of the particular right or privilege of the said citizens which it was the intent of the defendants to invade is clearly alleged; but the difficulty in the count is, that it does not allege for what purpose the election or elections were to be ordered, nor when or where the elections were to be had and held. All that is alleged upon the subject is, that it was the intent of the defendants to prevent and hinder the said citizens of African descent and persons of color in the free exercise and enjoyment of the right and privilege to vote at any election thereafter to be had and held, according to law, by the people of the State, or by the people of the parish, without any other allegation whatever as to the purpose of the election, or any allegation as to the time and place when and where the election was to be had and held.

Elections thereafter to be held must mean something different from pending elections; but whether the pleader means to charge that the intent and purpose of the alleged conspiracy extended only to the next succeeding elections to be held in the State or parish, or to all future elections to be held in the State or parish during the lifetime of the parties, may admit of a serious question, which cannot be easily solved by any thing contained in the allegations of the count.

Reasonable certainty, all will agree, is required in criminal pleading; and if so it must be conceded, we think, that the allegation in question fails to comply with that requirement. Accused persons, as matter of common justice, ought to have the charge against them set forth in such terms that they may readily understand the nature and character of the accusation, in order that they, when arraigned, may know what answer to make to it, and that they may not be embarrassed in conducting their defence; and the charge ought also to be laid in such terms that, if the party accused is put to trial, the verdict and judgment may be pleaded in bar of a second accusation for the same offence.

Tested by these considerations, it is quite clear that the fourteenth count is not sufficient to warrant the conviction and sentence of the accused.

Defects and imperfections of the same kind as those pointed out in the thirteenth count also exist in the sixteenth count, and of a more decided character in the latter count than in the former; conclusive proof of which will appear by a brief examination of a few of the most material allegations of the charge against the defendants. Suffice it to say, without entering into details, that the introductory allegations of the count are in all respects the same as in the thirteenth and fourteenth counts. None of the introductory allegations allege that any overt act was perpetrated in pursuance of the alleged conspiracy; but the jurors proceed to present that the unlawful and felonious intent and purpose of the defendants were to prevent and hinder the said citizens of African descent and persons of color, by the means therein described, in the free exercise and enjoyment of each, every, all, and singular the several rights and privileges granted and secured to them by the constitution and laws of the United States in common with all other good citizens, without any attempt to describe or designate any particular right or privilege which it was the purpose and intent of the defendants to invade, abridge, or deny.

Descriptive allegations in criminal pleading are required to be reasonably definite and certain, as a necessary safeguard to the accused against surprise, misconception, and error in conducting his defence, and in order that the judgment in the case may be a bar to a second accusation for the same charge. Considerations of the kind are entitled to respect; but it is obvious, that, if such a description of the ingredient of an offence created and defined by an act of Congress is held to be sufficient, the indictment must become a snare to the accused; as it is scarcely possible that an allegation can be framed which would be less certain, or more at variance with the universal rule that every ingredient of the offence must be clearly and accurately described so as to bring the defendant within the true intent and meaning of the provision defining the offence. Such a vague and indefinite description of a material ingredient of the offence is not a compliance with the rules of pleading in framing an indictment. On the contrary, such an indictment is insufficient, and must be held bad on demurrer or in arrest of judgment.

Certain other causes for arresting the judgment are assigned in the record, which deny the constitutionality of the Enforcement Act; but, having come to the conclusion that the indictment is insufficient, it is not necessary to consider that question.

Presser v. State of Illinois, 116 U.S. 252 (1886)

In 1876, the Supreme Court for the first time addressed the meaning of the Second Amendment in the case of United States v. Cruikshank. *Although it only devoted a few paragraphs to the subject, it did establish two principles: that laws may be properly enacted to restrict or regulate the carrying of weapons, including firearms; and that the Second Amendment does not apply to the states (that is, is not incorporated under the Fourteenth Amendment). Ten years later, in the* Presser *case, the Supreme Court reaffirmed* Cruikshank's *conclusion that the Second Amendment did not apply to the states, a position that the Court has maintained from that day to this, even while it has applied most other Bill of Rights freedoms to the states in the meantime. Beyond that, the Court discussed at length the meaning of the term* militia *as it appears in the Second Amendment, and in other parts of the Constitution, rejecting the ideas that citizens may lawfully create their own, private militias, or that there is any citizen right to own or carry weapons under the Second Amendment. Only the government has the power to create militias. Both* Cruikshank *and* Presser *are still considered good law.*

Mr. Justice Woods delivered the opinion of the Court:

Herman Presser, the plaintiff in error, was indicted on September 24, 1879, in the criminal court of Cook county, Illinois, for a violation of the following sections of article 11 of the Military Code of that state (Act May 28, 1879; Laws 1876, 192):

"Sec. 5. It shall not be lawful for any body of men whatever, other than the regular organized volunteer militia of this state, and the troops of the United States, to associate themselves together as a military company or organization, or to drill or parade with arms in any city or town of this state, without the license of the governor thereof, which license may at any time be revoked: and provided, further, that students in educational institutions, where military science is a part of the course of instruction, may, with the consent of the governor, drill and parade with arms in public, under the superintendence of their instructors, and may take part in any regimental or brigade encampment, under command of their military instructor; and while so encamped shall be governed by the provisions of this act. They shall be entitled only to transportation [116 U.S. 252, 254] and subsistence, and shall report and be subject to the commandant of such encampment: Provided, that nothing herein contained shall be construed so as to prevent benevolent or social organizations from wearing swords.

Sec. 6. Whoever offends against the provisions of the preceding section, or belongs to, or parades with, any such unauthorized body of men with arms, shall be punished by a fine not exceeding the sum of ten dollars, ($10,) or by imprisonment in the common jail for a term not exceeding six months, or both." The indictment charged in substance that Presser, on September 24, 1879, in the county of Cook, in the state of Illinois, "did unlawfully belong to, and did parade and drill in the city of Chicago with, an unauthorized body of men with arms, who had associated themselves together as a military company and organization, without having a license from the governor, and not being a part of, or belonging to, 'the regular organized volunteer militia' of the state of Illinois, or the troops of the United States."

A motion to quash the indictment was overruled. Presser then pleaded not guilty, and, both parties having waived a jury, the case was tried by the court, which found Presser guilty and sentenced him to pay a fine of $10.

The bill of exceptions taken upon the trial set out all the evidence, from which it appeared that Presser was 31 years old, a citizen of the United States and of the state of Illinois, and a voter; that he belonged to a society called the *Lehr und Wehr Verein,* a corporation organized April 16, 1875, in due form, under chapter 32, Revised Statutes of Illinois, called the General Incorporation Laws of Illinois, "for the purpose," as expressed by its certificate of association, "of improving the mental and bodily condition of its members so as to qualify them for the duties of citizens of a republic. Its members shall, therefore, obtain, in the meetings of the association, a knowledge of our laws and political economy, and shall also be instructed in military and gymnastic exercises;" that Presser, in December, 1879, marched at the head of said company, about 400 in number, in the streets of the city [116 U.S. 252, 255] of Chicago, he riding on horseback and in command; that the company was armed with rifles, and Presser with a cavalry sword; that the company had no license from the Governor of Illinois to drill or parade as a part of the militia of the state, and was not a part of the regular organized militia of the state, nor a part of troops of the United States, and had no organization under the militia law of the United States. The evidence showed no other facts. Exceptions were reserved to the ruling of the court upon the motion to quash the indictment, to the finding of guilty, and to the judgment thereon. The case was taken to the Supreme Court of Illinois, where the judgment was affirmed. Thereupon Presser brought the present writ of error for a review of the judgment of affirmance.

The position of the plaintiff in error in this court was that the entire statute under which he was convicted was invalid and void because its enactment was the exercise of a power by the legislature of Illinois forbidden to the states by the Constitution of the

United States. The clauses of the Constitution of the United States referred to in the assignments of error were as follows:

Article 1, 8. "The Congress shall have power . . . to raise and support armies; . . . to provide for calling forth the militia to execute the laws of the Union, suppress insurrections, and repel invasions; to provide for organizing, arming, and disciplining the militia, and for governing such part of them as may be employed in the service of the United States, reserving to the states, respectively, the appointment of the officers, and the authority of training the militia, according to the discipline prescribed by congress; . . . to make all laws which shall be necessary and proper, for carrying into execution the foregoing powers," etc.

Article 1, 10. "No state shall, without the consent of congress, keep troops . . . in time of peace."

Art. 2 of Amendments. "A well regulated militia being necessary to the security of a free State, the right of the people to keep and bear arms shall not be infringed."

The plaintiff in error also contended that the enactment of the fifth and sixth sections of article 11 of the Military Code [116 U.S. 252, 261] was forbidden by subdivision 3 of section 9 of article 1, which declares "no bill of attainder or ex post facto law shall be passed," and by article 14 of Amendments, which provides that "no state shall make or enforce any law which shall abridge the privileges or immunities of citizens of the United States, nor shall any state deprive any person of life, liberty, or property without due process of law."

The first contention of counsel for plaintiff in error is that the Congress of the United States having, by virtue of the provisions of article 1 of section 8, above quoted, passed the act of May 8, 1792, entitled "An Act More Effectually to Provide for the National Defense by Establishing an Uniform Militia Throughout the United States," (1 St. 271,) the act of February 28, 1795, "To Provide for Calling Forth the Militia to Execute the Laws of the Union, Suppress Insurrections, and Repel Invasions," (1 St. 424,) and the Act of July 22, 1861, "To Authorize the Employment of Volunteers to Aid in Enforcing the Laws and Protecting Public Property," (12 St. 268,) and other subsequent Acts, now forming "Title 16, The Militia," of the Revised Statutes of the United States, the legislature of Illinois had no power to pass the act approved May 28, 1879, "To Provide for the Organization of the State Militia, entitled the Military Code of Illinois," under the provisions of which (sections 5 and 6 of article 11) the plaintiff in error was indicted.

The argument in support of this contention is, that the power of organizing, arming, and disciplining the militia being confided by the Constitution to Congress, when it acts upon the subject, and passes a law to carry into effect the constitutional provision, such action excludes the power of legislation by the state on the same subject.

It is further argued that the whole scope and object of the Military Code of Illinois is in conflict with that of the law of Congress. It is said that the object of the act of Congress is to provide for organizing, arming, and disciplining all the able-bodied male citizens of the states, respectively, between certain ages, that they may be ready at all times to respond to the call of the nation to enforce its laws, suppress insurrection, and [116 U.S. 252, 262] repel invasion, and thereby avoid the necessity for maintaining a large standing army, with which liberty can never be safe, and that, on the other hand, the effect if not object of the Illinois statute is to prevent such organizing, arming, and disciplining of the militia.

The plaintiff in error insists that the Act of Congress requires absolutely all able-bodied citizens of the state, between certain ages, to be enrolled in the militia; that the Act of Illinois makes the enrollment dependent on the necessity for the use of troops to execute the laws and suppress insurrections, and then leaves it discretionary with the governor by proclamation to require such enrollment; that the Act of Congress requires the entire enrolled militia of the state, with a few exemptions made by it and which may be made by state laws, to be formed into companies, battalions, regiments, brigades, and divisions; that every man shall be armed and supplied with ammunition; provides a system of discipline and field exercises for companies, regiments, etc., and subjects the entire militia of the state to the call of the president to enforce the laws, suppress insurrection, or repel invasion, and provides for the punishment of the militia officers and men who refuse obedience to his orders. On the other hand, it is said that the state law makes it unlawful for any of its able-bodied citizens, except 8,000, called the Illinois National Guard, to associate themselves together as a military company, or to drill or parade with arms without the license of the Governor, and declares that no military company shall leave the state with arms and equipments without his consent; that even the 8,000 men styled the Illinois National Guard are not enrolled or organized as required by the Act of Congress, nor are they subject to the call of the President, but they constitute a military force sworn to serve in the military service of the state, to obey the orders of the Governor, and not to leave the state without his consent; and that, if the state act is valid, the national act providing for organizing, arming, and disciplining the militia is of no force in the state of Illinois, for the Illinois act, so far from being in harmony with the act of Congress, is an insurmountable obstacle to its execution. [116 U.S. 252, 263].

We have not found it necessary to consider or decide the question thus raised as to the validity of the entire Military Code of Illinois, for, in our opinion, the sections under which the plaintiff in error was convicted may be valid, even if the other sections of the act were invalid. For it is a settled rule "that statutes that are constitutional in part only will be upheld so far as they are not in conflict with the Constitution, provided the allowed and prohibited parts are separable." *Packet Co. v. Keokuk,* 95 U.S. 80; *Penniman's Case,* 103 U.S. 714, 717; *Unity v. Burrage,* Id. 459. See, also, *Trade-Mark Cases,* 100 U.S. 82.

We are of opinion that this rule is applicable in this case. The first two sections of article 1 of the Military Code provide that all able bodied male citizens of the state between the ages of 18 and 45 years, except those exempted, shall be subject to military duty, and be designated the "Illinois State Militia," and declare how they shall be enrolled and under what circumstances. The residue of the Code, except the two sections on which the indictment against the plaintiff in error is based, provides for a volunteer active militia, to consist of not more than 8,000 officers and men, declares how it shall be enlisted and brigaded, and the term of service of its officers and men; provides for brigade generals and their staffs, for the organization of the requisite battalions and companies and the election of company officers; provides for inspections, parades, and encampments, arms and armories, rifle practice, and courts-martial; provides for the pay of the officers and men, for medical service, regimental bands, books of instructions and maps; contains provisions for levying and collecting a military fund by taxation, and directs how it shall be expended; and appropriates $25,000 out of the treasury, in advance of the collection of the military fund, to be used for the purposes specified in the Military Code.

It is plain from this statement of the substance of the Military Code that the two sections upon which the indictment against the plaintiff in error is based may be separated from the residue of the Code, and stand upon their own independent provisions. These sections might have been left out of the [116 U.S. 252, 264] Military Code and put in an act by themselves, and the act thus constituted and the residue of the Military Code would have been coherent and sensible acts. If it be conceded that the entire Military Code, except these sections, is unconstitutional and invalid, for the reasons stated by the plaintiff in error, these sections are separable, and, put in an act by themselves, could not be considered as forbidden by the clauses of the Constitution having reference to the militia, or to the clause forbidding the states, without the consent of Congress, to keep troops in time of peace. There is no such connection between the sections which prohibit any body of men, other than the organized militia of the state and the troops of the United States, from associating as a military company and drilling with arms in any city or town of the state, and the sections which provide for the enrollment and organization of the state militia, as makes it impossible to declare one, without declaring both, invalid.

This view disposes of the objection to the judgment of the Supreme Court of Illinois, which judgment was in effect that the legislation on which the indictment is based is not invalid by reason of the provisions of the Constitution of the United States which vest Congress with power to raise and support armies, and to provide for calling out, organizing, arming, and disciplining the militia, and governing such part of them as may be employed in the service of the United States, and that provision which declares that "no state shall, without the consent of Congress, . . . keep troops . . . in time of peace."

We are next to inquire whether the fifth and sixth sections of article 11 of the Military Code are in violation of the other provisions of the Constitution of the United States relied on by the plaintiff in error. The first of these is the Second Amendment, which declares: "A well regulated militia being necessary to the security of a free State, the right of the people to keep and bear arms shall not be infringed."

We think it clear that the sections under consideration, which only forbid bodies of men to associate together as military organizations, or to drill or parade with arms in cities [116 U.S. 252, 265] and towns unless authorized by law, do not infringe the right of the people to keep and bear arms. But a conclusive answer to the contention that this amendment prohibits the legislation in question lies in the fact that the amendment is a limitation only upon the power of Congress and the national government, and not upon that of the states. It was so held by this court in the case of

U. S. v. Cruikshank, 92 U.S. 542, 553, in which the Chief Justice, in delivering the judgment of the court, said that the right of the people to keep and bear arms "is not a right granted by the Constitution. Neither is it in any manner dependent upon that instrument for its existence. The Second Amendment declares that it shall not be infringed, but this, as has been seen, means no more than that it shall not be infringed by Congress. This is one of the amendments that has no other effect than to restrict the powers of the national government, leaving the people to look for their protection against any violation by their fellow-citizens of the rights it recognizes to what is called in *City of New York v. Miln,* 11 Pet. [116 U.S. 252, 102], the 'powers which relate to merely municipal legislation, or what was perhaps more properly called internal police,' 'not surrendered or restrained' by the Constitution of the United States." . . .

It is undoubtedly true that all citizens capable of bearing arms constitute the reserved military force or reserve militia of the United States as well as of the states, and, in view of this prerogative of the general government, as well as of its general powers, the states cannot, even laying the constitutional provision in question out of view, prohibit the people from keeping and bearing arms, so as to deprive the United States of their rightful resource for maintaining the public security, and disable the people from performing their duty to the general government. But, as already stated, we think it clear that the sections under consideration do not have this effect.

The plaintiff in error next insists that the sections of the Military Code of Illinois, under which he was indicted, are an invasion of that clause of the first section of the Fourteenth Amendment to the Constitution of the United States which declares: "No state shall make or enforce any law which shall abridge the privileges or immunities of citizens of the United States."

It is only the privileges and immunities of citizens of the United States that the clause relied on was intended to protect. A state may pass laws to regulate the privileges and immunities of its own citizens, provided that in so doing it does not abridge their privileges and immunities as citizens of the United States. The inquiry is therefore pertinent: What privilege or immunity of a citizen of the United States is abridged by sections 5 and 6 of article 11 of the Military Code of Illinois?

The plaintiff in error was not a member of the organized volunteer militia of the State of Illinois, nor did he belong to the troops of the United States or to any organization under the militia law of the United States. On the contrary, the fact that he did not belong to the organized militia or the troops of the United States was an ingredient in the offense for which he was convicted and sentenced. The question is, therefore: Had he a right as a citizen of the United States, in disobedience of the state law, to associate with others as a military company, and to drill and parade with arms in the towns and cities of the state? . . .

We have not been referred to any statute of the United States which confers upon the plaintiff in error the privilege which he asserts. The only clause in the Constitution which, upon any pretense, could be said to have any relation whatever to his right to associate with others as a military company, is found in the First Amendment, which declares that "Congress shall make no laws . . . abridging . . . the right of the people peaceably to assemble and to petition the government for a redress of grievances." This is a right which it was held in *U. S. v. Cruikshank,* above cited, was an attribute of national citizenship, and, as such, under the protection of, and guaranteed by, the United States. But it was held in the same case that the right peaceably to assemble was not protected by the clause referred to, unless the purpose of the assembly was to petition the government for a redress of grievances.

The right voluntarily to associate together as a military company or organization, or to drill or parade with arms, without, and independent of, an act of Congress or law of the state authorizing the same, is not an attribute of national citizenship. Military organization and military drill and parade under arms are subjects especially under the control of the government of every country. They cannot be claimed as a right independent of law. Under our political system they are subject to the regulation and control of the state and federal governments, acting in due regard to their respective prerogatives and powers. The Constitution and laws of the United States will be searched in vain for any support to the view that these rights are privileges and immunities of citizens of the United States independent of some specific legislation on the subject.

It cannot be successfully questioned that the state governments, unless restrained by their own constitutions, have the power to regulate or prohibit associations and meetings of the people, except in the case of peaceable assemblies to perform the duties or exercise the privileges of citizens of the United States, and have also the power to control and regulate the organization, drilling, and parading of military bodies and associations, except when such bodies or associations, are [116 U.S. 252, 268] authorized by the militia laws of the United States. The exercise of this power by the states is necessary to the public peace, safety, and good order. To deny the power would be to deny the right of the state to disperse assemblages organized for sedition and treason, and the right to suppress armed mobs bent on riot and rapine. . . .

The argument of the plaintiff in error that the legislation mentioned deprives him of either life, liberty, or property without due process of law, or that it is a bill of attainder or ex post facto law, is so clearly untenable as to require no discussion.

It is next contended by the plaintiff in error that sections 5 and 6 of article 11 of the Military Code, under which he was indicted, are in conflict with the acts of Congress for the organization of the militia. But this position is based on what seems to us to be an unwarranted construction of the sections referred to. It is clear that their object was to forbid voluntary military associations, unauthorized by law, from organizing or [116 U.S. 252, 269] drilling and parading with arms in the cities or towns of the state, and not to interfere with the organization, arming and drilling of the militia under the authority of the acts of Congress. If the object and effect of the sections were in irreconcilable conflict with the acts of Congress, they would of course be invalid. But it is a rule of construction that a statute must be interpreted so as, if possible, to make it consistent with the Constitution and the paramount law.... If we yielded to this contention of the plaintiff in error, we should render the sections invalid by giving them a strained construction, which would make them antagonistic to the law of Congress. We cannot attribute to the legislature, unless compelled to do so by its plain words, a purpose to pass an act in conflict with an act of Congress on a subject over which Congress is given authority by the constitution of the United States. We are, therefore, of opinion that, fairly construed, the sections of the Military Code referred to do not conflict with the laws of Congress on the subject of the militia.

The plaintiff in error further insists that the organization of the *Lehr und Wehr Verein* as a corporate body, under the general corporation law of the state of Illinois, was in effect a license from the Governor, within the meaning of section 5 of article 11 of the Military Code, and that such corporate body fell within the exception of the same section "of students in educational institutions where military science is a part of the course of instruction." In respect to these points we have to say that they present no federal question. It is not, therefore, our province to consider or decide them....

All the federal questions presented by the record were rightly decided by the Supreme Court of Illinois. Judgment affirmed.

United States v. Miller, 307 U.S. 174 (1939)

When two men were convicted of violating a 1934 federal law that barred transport of a sawed-off shotgun (a weapon modified by gangsters to increase a shotgun's lethality) across state lines, they appealed their conviction through the federal courts, arguing that the law violated their Second Amendment right to keep and bear such a firearm. Reversing a lower federal court ruling, the Supreme Court ruled unanimously against the men, saying that the Second Amendment only came in to play when citizens were serving in a government organized and regulated militia, and that there was no individual right to keep and bear arms aside from this purpose. Most of the decision is devoted to a painstaking description of the history of militias, emphasizing that any law-based right to have firearms was always linked to militia service. (The court also cited the Cruikshank *and* Presser *cases to buttress their interpretation of the Second Amendment.) Note that Miller and Layton did not send lawyers to represent them before the court.*

Argued March 30, 1939.

Decided May 15, 1939.

Appeal from the District Court of the United States for the Western District of Arkansas. [307 U.S. 174, 175] Mr. Gordon Dean, of Washington, D.C., for the United States.

No appearance for appellees.

Mr. Justice McREYNOLDS delivered the opinion of the Court.

An indictment in the District Court Western District Arkansas, charged that Jack Miller and Frank Layton "did unlawfully, knowingly, wilfully, and feloniously transport in interstate commerce from the town of Claremore in the State of Oklahoma to the town of Siloam Springs in the State of Arkansas a certain firearm, to-wit, a double barrel 12-gauge Stevens shotgun having a barrel less than 18 inches in length, bearing identification number 76230, said defendants, at the time of so transporting said firearm in interstate commerce as aforesaid, not having registered said firearm as required by Section 1132d of Title 26, United States Code, 26 U.S.C.A. 1132d (Act of June 26, 1934, c. 757, Sec. 5, 48 Stat. 1237), and not having in their possession a stamp-affixed written order for said firearm as provided by Section 1132c, Title 26, United States Code, 26 U.S.C.A. 1132c (June 26, 1934, c. 757, Sec. 4, 48 Stat. 1237) and the regulations issued under authority of the said Act of Congress known as the 'National Firearms Act' approved June 26, 1934, contrary to the form of the statute in such case made and provided, and against the peace and dignity of the United States." [307 U.S. 174, 176].

A duly interposed demurrer alleged: The National Firearms Act is not a revenue measure but an attempt to usurp police power reserved to the States, and is therefore unconstitutional. Also, it offends the inhibition of the Second Amendment to the Constitution—"A well regulated Militia, being necessary to the security of a free State, the right of the people to keep and bear Arms, shall not be infringed." [307 U.S. 174, 177].

The District Court held that section 11 of the Act violates the Second Amendment. It accordingly sustained the demurrer and quashed the indictment.

The cause is here by direct appeal . . . the objection that the Act usurps police power reserved to the States is plainly untenable.

In the absence of any evidence tending to show that possession or use of a "shotgun having a barrel of less than eighteen inches in length" at this time has some reasonable relationship to the preservation or efficiency of a well regulated militia, we cannot say that the Second Amendment guarantees the right to keep and bear such an instrument. Certainly it is not within judicial notice that this weapon is any part of the ordinary military equipment or that its use could contribute to the common defense . . .

The Constitution as originally adopted granted to the Congress power—"To provide for calling forth the Militia to execute the Laws of the Union, suppress Insurrections and repel Invasions; To provide for organizing, arming, and disciplining, the Militia, and for governing such Part of them as may be employed in the Service of the United States, reserving to the States respectively, the Appointment of the Officers, and the Authority of training the

Militia according to the discipline prescribed by Congress." ... With obvious purpose to assure the continuation and render possible the effectiveness of such forces the declaration and guarantee of the Second Amendment were made. It must be interpreted and applied with that end in view.

The Militia which the States were expected to maintain and train is set in contrast with Troops which they [307 U.S. 174, 179] were forbidden to keep without the consent of Congress. The sentiment of the time strongly disfavored standing armies; the common view was that adequate defense of country and laws could be secured through the Militia—civilians primarily, soldiers on occasion.

The signification attributed to the term Militia appears from the debates in the Convention, the history and legislation of Colonies and States, and the writings of approved commentators. These show plainly enough that the Militia comprised all males physically capable of acting in concert for the common defense. "A body of citizens enrolled for military discipline." And further, that ordinarily when called for service these men were expected to appear bearing arms supplied by themselves and of the kind in common use at the time.

Blackstone's Commentaries, Vol. 2, Ch. 13, p. 409 points out "that king Alfred first settled a national militia in this kingdom" and traces the subsequent development and use of such forces.

Adam Smith's *Wealth of Nations,* Book V. Ch. 1, contains an extended account of the Militia. It is there said: "Men of republican principles have been jealous of a standing army as dangerous to liberty." "In a militia, the character of the labourer, artificer, or tradesman, predominates over that of the soldier: in a standing army, that of the soldier predominates over every other character; and in this distinction seems to consist the essential difference between those two different species of military force."

"The American Colonies In The 17th Century," *Osgood,* Vol. 1, ch. XIII, affirms in reference to the early system of defense in New England—

"In all the colonies, as in England, the militia system was based on the principle of the assize of arms. This implied the general obligation of all adult male inhabitants to possess arms, and, with certain exceptions, to [307 U.S. 174, 180] cooperate in the work of defence." "The possession of arms also implied the possession of ammunition, and the authorities paid quite as much attention to the latter as to the former." "A year later [1632] it was ordered that any single man who had not furnished himself with arms might be put out to service, and this became a permanent part of the legislation of the colony [Massachusetts]."

Also "Clauses intended to insure the possession of arms and ammunition by all who were subject to military service appear in all the important enactments concerning military affairs. Fines were the penalty for delinquency, whether of towns or individuals. According to the usage of the times, the infantry of Massachusetts consisted of pikemen and musketeers. The law, as enacted in 1649 and thereafter, provided that each of the former should be armed with a pike, corselet, head-piece, sword, and knapsack. The musketeer should carry a 'good fixed musket,' not under bastard musket bore, not less than three feet, nine inches, nor more than four feet three inches in length, a priming wire, scourer, and mould, a sword, rest, bandoleers, one pound of powder, twenty bullets, and two fathoms of match. The law also required that two-thirds of each company should be musketeers."

The General Court of Massachusetts, January Session 1784 (Laws and Resolves 1784, c. 55, pp. 140, 142), provided for the organization and government of the Militia. It directed that the Train Band should "contain all able bodied men, from sixteen to forty years of age, and the Alarm List, all other men under sixty years of age,...." Also, "That every non-commissioned officer and private soldier of the said militia not under the controul of parents, masters or guardians, and being of sufficient ability therefor in the judgment of the Selectmen of the town in which he shall dwell, shall equip himself, and be constantly provided with a good fire arm, &c."

By an Act passed April 4, 1786 (Laws 1786, c. 25), the New York Legislature directed: "That every able-bodied Male Person, being [307 U.S. 174, 181] a Citizen of this State, or of any of the United States, and residing in this State, (except such Persons as are herein after excepted) and who are of the Age of Sixteen, and under the Age of Forty-five Years, shall, by the Captain or commanding Officer of the Beat in which such Citizens shall reside, within four Months after the passing of this Act, be enrolled in the Company of such Beat.... That every Citizen so enrolled and notified, shall, within three Months thereafter, provide himself, at his own Expense, with a good Musket or Firelock, a sufficient Bayonet and Belt, a Pouch with a Box therein to contain not less than Twenty-four Cartridges suited to the Bore of his Musket or Firelock, each Cartridge containing a proper Quantity of Powder and Ball, two spare Flints, a Blanket and Knapsack;..."

The General Assembly of Virginia, October, 1785 (12 Hening's Statutes c. 1, p. 9 et seq.), declared: "The defense and safety of the commonwealth depend upon having its citizens properly armed and taught the knowledge of military duty."

It further provided for organization and control of the Militia and directed that "All free male persons between the ages of eighteen and fifty years," with certain exceptions, "shall be inrolled or formed into companies." "There shall be a private muster of every company once in two months."

Also that "Every officer and soldier shall appear at his respective muster-field on the day appointed, by eleven o'clock in the forenoon, armed, equipped, and accoutred, as follows:... every non-commissioned officer and private with a good, clean musket carrying an ounce ball, and three feet eight inches long in the barrel, with a good bayonet and iron ramrod well fitted thereto, a cartridge box properly made, to contain and secure twenty cartridges fitted to his musket, a good knapsack and canteen, and moreover, each non-commissioned officer and private shall have at every muster one pound of good [307 U.S. 174, 182] powder, and four pounds of lead, including twenty blind cartridges; and each sergeant shall have a pair of moulds fit to cast balls for their respective companies, to be purchased by the commanding officer out of the monies arising on delinquencies. Provided, That the militia of the counties westward of the Blue Ridge, and the counties below adjoining thereto, shall not be obliged to be armed with muskets, but may have good rifles with proper accoutrements, in lieu thereof. And every of the said officers, non-commissioned officers, and privates, shall constantly keep the aforesaid arms, accoutrements, and ammunition, ready to be produced whenever called for by his commanding officer. If any private shall make it appear to the satisfaction of the court hereafter to be appointed for trying delinquencies under this act that he is so poor that he cannot purchase the arms herein required, such court shall cause them to be purchased out of the money arising from delinquents."

Most if not all of the States have adopted provisions touching the right to keep and bear arms. Differences in the language employed in these have naturally led to somewhat variant conclusions concerning the scope of the right guaranteed. But none of them seem to afford any material support for the challenged ruling of the court below.... [307 U.S. 174, 183].

We are unable to accept the conclusion of the court below and the challenged judgment must be reversed. The cause will be remanded for further proceedings.

Reversed and remanded.

Quilici v. Village of Morton Grove, 695 F.2d 261 (1982)

In 1981, the village of Morton Grove, Illinois, passed a local ordinance banning the possession of working handguns, with exceptions for police officers, security guards, and licensed gun collectors. Residents were not actually denied their handguns, however, as they could keep them in licensed gun clubs. Long guns were not affected by the law.

Gun control opponents immediately filed suit, claiming that the law violated the Second, Fifth, Ninth, and Fourteenth Amendments to the U.S. Constitution, as well as Article I, Section 22 of the Illinois State Constitution. A federal court for the Northern District of Illinois ruled in favor of the village law. On appeal, the Seventh Circuit of the U.S. Court of Appeals also upheld the law. In its decision, it swept aside the arguments made by those who say that the Second Amendment provides an individual right to bear arms. Citing Presser *and* Miller, *the court noted that the Second Amendment applies only to maintenance of a well-regulated militia; that there was no basis for arguing that the Bill of Rights enshrined a right of personal self-defense; and that the Second Amendment had not been incorporated by the courts, meaning that it did not apply to the states. The ruling was appealed to the Supreme Court, but it declined to hear the case (cert. denied 464 U.S. 863; 1983), letting the lower court ruling stand, and therefore keeping in place the handgun ban.*

Victor D. QUILICI, Robert Stengl, et al., George L. Reichert, and Robert E. Metier, Plaintiffs-Appellants,

VILLAGE OF MORTON GROVE, et al., Defendants-Appellees.

Nos. 82-1045, 82-1076 and 82-1132.

U.S. Court of Appeals, Seventh Circuit.

Argued May 28, 1982.

Decided Dec. 6, 1982.

As Amended Dec. 10, 1982.

Rehearing and Rehearing En Banc Denied March 2, 1983.

Victor D. Quilici, Bennsonville, Ill., Don B. Kates, Jr., O'Brien & Hallisey, San Francisco, Cal., Richard V. Houpt, Pedersen & Houpt, Donald J. Moran, Chicago, Ill., for plaintiffs-appellants.

Eugene R. Wedoff, Jenner & Block, Chicago, Ill., for defendants-appellees.

Before BAUER, WOOD, and COFFEY, Circuit Judges.
BAUER, Circuit Judge.

This appeal concerns the constitutionality of the Village of Morton Grove's Ordinance No. 81-11, which prohibits the possession of handguns within the Village's borders. The district court held that the Ordinance was constitutional. We affirm.

I

Victor D. Quilici initially challenged Ordinance No. 81-11 in state court. Morton Grove removed the action to federal court where it was consolidated with two similar actions, one brought by George L. Reichert and Robert E. Metier (collectively Reichert) and one brought by Robert Stengl, Martin Gutenkauf, Alice Gutenkauf, Walter J. Dutchak and Geoffrey Lagonia (collectively Stengl). Plaintiffs alleged that Ordinance No. 81-11 violated article 1, section 22 of the Illinois Constitution and the second, ninth and fourteenth amendments of the United States Constitution. They sought an order declaring the Ordinance unconstitutional and permanently enjoining its enforcement. The parties filed cross motions for summary judgment. The district court granted Morton Grove's motion for summary judgment and denied plaintiffs' motions for summary judgment.

In its opinion, *Quilici v. Village of Morton Grove,* 532 F.Supp. 1169 (N.D.Ill. 1981), the district court set forth several reasons for upholding the handgun ban's validity under the state and federal constitutions. First, it held that the Ordinance which banned only certain kinds of arms was a valid exercise of Morton Grove's police power and did not conflict with section 22's conditional right to keep and bear arms. Second, relying on *Presser v. Illinois,* 116 U.S. 252 (1886), the court concluded that the second amendment's guarantee of the right to bear arms has not been incorporated into the fourteenth amendment and, therefore, is inapplicable to Morton Grove. Finally, it stated that the ninth amendment does not include the right to possess handguns for self-defense. Appellants contend that the district court incorrectly construed the relevant constitutional provisions, assigning numerous errors based on case law, historical analysis, common law traditions and public policy concerns.

While we recognize that this case raises controversial issues which engender strong emotions, our task is to apply the law as it has been interpreted by the Supreme Court, regardless of whether that Court's interpretation comports with various personal views of what the law should be. We are also aware that we must resolve the controversy without rendering unnecessary constitutional decisions.... With these principles in mind we address appellants' contentions.

II

We consider the state constitutional issue first. The Illinois Constitution provides:

Subject only to the police power, the right of the individual citizen to keep and bear arms shall not be infringed. (Ill. Const. art. I, section 22)

The parties agree that the meaning of this section is controlled by the terms "arms" and "police power" but disagree as to the scope of these terms.

Relying on the statutory construction principles that constitutional guarantees should be broadly construed and that constitutional provisions should prevail over conflicting statutory provisions, appellants allege that section 22's guarantee of the right to keep and bear arms prohibits a complete ban of any one kind of arm. They argue that the constitutional history of section 22 establishes that the term "arms" includes those weapons commonly employed for "recreation or the protection of person and property," 6 Record of Proceedings, Sixth Illinois Constitutional Convention 87 (Proceedings), and contend that handguns have consistently been used for these purposes.

Appellants concede that the phrase "subject to the police power" does not prohibit reasonable regulation of arms. Thus, they admit that laws which require the licensing of guns or which restrict the carrying of concealed weapons or the possession of firearms by minors, convicted felons, and incompetents are valid. However, they maintain that no authority supports interpreting section 22 to permit a ban on the possession of handguns merely because alternative weapons are not also banned. They argue that construing section 22 in this manner would lead to the anomalous situation in which one municipality completely bans handguns while a neighboring municipality completely bans all arms but handguns.

In contrast, Morton Grove alleges that "arms" is a general term which does not include any specific kind of weapon. Relying on section 22's language, which they characterize as clear and explicit, Morton Grove reads section 22 to guarantee the right to keep only some, but not all, arms which are used for "recreation or the protection of person and property." It argues that the Ordinance passes constitutional muster because standard rifles and shotguns are also used for "recreation or the protection of person and property" and Ordinance No. 81-11 does not ban these weapons.

While Morton Grove does not challenge appellants' assertion that "arms" includes handguns, we believe that a discussion of the kind of arms section 22 protects is an appropriate place to begin our analysis. Because we disagree with Morton Grove's assertion that section 22's language is clear and explicit, we turn to the constitutional debates for guidance on the proper construction of arms. . . .

The debates indicate that the category of arms protected by section 22 is not limited to military weapons; the framers also intended to include those arms that "law-abiding persons commonly employ[ed]" for "recreation or the protection of person and property." 6 Proceedings 87. Handguns are undisputedly the type of arms commonly used for "recreation or the protection of person and property."

Our conclusion that the framers intended to include handguns in the class of protected arms is supported by the fact that in discussing the term the Proceedings refer to *People v. Brown*, 253 Mich. 537, 541–42, 235 N.W. 245, 246–47 (1931) and *State v. Duke*, 42 Tex. 455, 458 (1875). Brown defines weapons as those "relied upon ... for defense or pleasure," including "ordinary guns" and "revolvers." 253 Mich. at 542, 235 N.W. at 247. Duke states that "[t]he arms which every person is secured the right to keep and bear (in defense of himself or the State, subject to legislative regulation), must be such arms as are commonly kept, ... and are appropriate for ... self defense, as well as such as are proper for the defense of the State." 42 Tex. at 458. The delegates' statements and reliance on Brown and Duke convinces us that the term *arms* in section 22 includes handguns.

Having determined that section 22 includes handguns within the class of arms protected, we must now determine the extent to which a municipality may exercise its police power to restrict, or even prohibit, the right to keep and bear these arms. The district court concluded that section 22 recognizes only a narrow individual right which is subject to substantial legislative control. It noted that "[t]o the extent that one looks to the convention debate for assistance in reconciling the conflict between the right to arms and the exercise of the police power, the debate clearly supports its narrow construction of the individual right." *Quilici v. Village of Morton Grove*, 532 F.Supp. at 1174. It further noted that while the Proceedings cite some cases holding that the state's police power should be read restrictively, those cases were decided under "distinctly different constitutional provisions" and, thus, have little application to this case. Id. at 1176.

We agree with the district court that the right to keep and bear arms in Illinois is so limited by the police power that a ban on handguns does not violate that right. In reaching this conclusion we find two factors significant. First, section 22's plain language grants only the right to keep and bear arms, not handguns. Second, although the framers intended handguns to be one of the arms conditionally protected under section 22, they also envisioned that local governments might exercise their police power to restrict, or prohibit, the right to keep and bear handguns. For example, Delegate Foster, speaking for the majority, explained:

It could be argued that, in theory, the legislature now [prior to the adoption of the 1970 Illinois Constitution] has the right to ban all firearms in the state as far as individual citizens owning them is concerned. That is the power which we wanted to restrict—an absolute ban on all firearms. (3 Proceedings 1688)

Delegate Foster then noted that section 22 "would prevent a complete ban on all guns, but there could be a ban on certain categories." Id. at 1693.... It is difficult to imagine clearer evidence that section 22 was intended to permit a municipality to ban handguns if it so desired.

Appellants argue that construing section 22 to protect only some unspecified categories of arms, thereby allowing municipalities to exercise their police power to enact dissimilar gun control laws, leads to "untenable" and "absurd" results. Quilici br. at 14. This argument ignores the fact that the Illinois Constitution authorizes local governments to function as home rule units to "exercise any power and perform any function pertaining to its government and affairs." Illinois Const. art. VIII, section 6(a). Home rule government ... is based on the theory that local governments are in the best position to assess the needs and desires of the community and, thus, can most wisely enact legislation addressing local concerns.... Illinois home rule units have expansive powers to govern as they deem proper... including the authority to impose greater restrictions on particular rights than those imposed by the state.... The only limits on their autonomy are those imposed by the Illinois Constitution ... or by the Illinois General Assembly exercising its authority to preempt home rule in specific instances. Because we have concluded that the Illinois Constitution permits a ban on certain categories of arms, home rule units such as Morton Grove may properly enact different, even inconsistent, arms restrictions. This is precisely the kind of local control envisioned by the new Illinois Constitution.

Appellants concede that municipalities may, under the Illinois Constitution, exercise their police power to enact regulations which prohibit "possession of items legislatively found to be dangerous... ," *Quilici* br. at 9. They draw a distinction, however, between the exercise of the police power in general and the exercise of police power with respect to a constitutionally protected right. Indeed, they vehemently insist that a municipality may not exercise its police power to completely prohibit a constitutional guarantee.

We agree that the state may not exercise its police power to violate a positive constitutional mandate... but we reiterate that section 22 simply prohibits a[n] absolute ban on all firearms. Since Ordinance No. 81-11 does not prohibit all firearms, it does not prohibit a constitutionally protected right. There is no right under the Illinois Constitution to possess a handgun, nor does the state have an overriding state interest in gun control which requires it to retain exclusive control in order to prevent home rule units from adopting conflicting enactments.... Accordingly, Morton Grove may exercise its police power to prohibit handguns even though this prohibition interferes with an individual's liberty or property.

The Illinois Constitution establishes a presumption in favor of municipal home rule.... Once a local government identifies a problem and enacts legislation to mitigate or eliminate it, that enactment is presumed valid and may be overturned only if it is unreasonable, clearly arbitrary, and has no foundation in the police power.... Thus, it is not the province of this court to pass judgment on the merits of Ordinance No. 81-11; our task is simply to determine whether Ordinance No. 81-11's restrictions are rationally related to its stated goals.... As the district court noted, there is at least some empirical evidence that gun control legislation may reduce the number of deaths and accidents caused by handguns.... This evidence is sufficient to sustain the conclusion that Ordinance No. 81-11 is neither wholly arbitrary nor completely unsupported by any set of facts.... Accordingly, we decline to consider plaintiffs' arguments that Ordinance No. 81-11 will not make Morton Grove a safer, more peaceful place.

We agree with the district court that Ordinance No. 81-11: (1) is properly directed at protecting the safety and health of Morton Grove citizens; (2) is a valid exercise of Morton Grove's police power; and (3) does not violate any of appellants' rights guaranteed by the Illinois Constitution.

III

We next consider whether Ordinance No. 81-11 violates the second amendment to the United States Constitution. While appellants all contend that Ordinance No. 81-11 is invalid under the second amendment, they offer slightly different arguments to substantiate this contention. All argue, however, that the second amendment applies to state and local governments and that the second amendment guarantee of the right to keep and bear arms exists, not only to assist in the common defense, but also to protect the individual. While reluctantly conceding that *Presser v. Illinois,* 116 U.S. 252 (1886), held that the second amendment applied only to action by the federal government they nevertheless assert that *Presser* also held that the right to keep and bear arms is an attribute of national citizenship which is not subject to state restriction. Reichert br. at 36. Finally, apparently responding to the district court's comments that "[p]laintiffs... have not suggested that the Morton Grove Ordinance in any way interferes with the ability of the United States to maintain public security..." *Quilici v. Village of Morton Grove,* 532 F.Supp. at 1169, Quilici and Reichert argue in this court that the Morton Grove Ordinance interferes with the federal government's ability to maintain public security by preventing individuals from defending themselves and the community from "external or internal armed threats." Quilici br. at 12; Reichert br. at 37–38. These are the same arguments made in the district court. Accordingly, we comment only briefly on the points already fully analyzed in that court's decision.

As we have noted, the parties agree that *Presser* is controlling, but disagree as to what *Presser* held. It is difficult to understand how appellants can assert that *Presser* supports the theory that the second amendment right to keep and bear arms is a fundamental right which the state cannot regulate when the *Presser* decision plainly states that "[t]he Second Amendment declares that it shall not be infringed, but this ... means no more than that it shall not be infringed by Congress. This is one of the amendments that has no other effect than to restrict the powers of the National government..." *Presser v. Illinois,* 116 U.S. 252, 265 (1886). As the district court explained in detail, appellants' claim that *Presser* supports the proposition that the second amendment guarantee of the right to keep and bear arms is not subject to state restriction is based on dicta quoted out of context. *Quilici v. Village of Morton Grove,* 532 F.Supp. at 1181–82. This argument borders on the frivolous and does not warrant any further consideration.

Apparently recognizing the inherent weakness of their reliance on *Presser,* appellants urge three additional arguments to buttress their claim that the second amendment applies to the states. They contend that: (1) *Presser* is no longer good law because later Supreme Court cases incorporating other amendments into the fourteenth amendment have effectively overruled *Presser,* Reichert br. at 52; (2) *Presser* is illogical, Quilici br. at 12; and (3) the entire Bill of Rights has been implicitly incorporated into the fourteenth amendment to apply to the states, Reichert br. at 48–52.

None of these arguments has merit. First, appellants offer no authority, other than their own opinions, to support their arguments that *Presser* is no longer good law or would have been decided differently today. Indeed, the fact that the Supreme Court continues to cite *Presser, Malloy v. Hogan,* 378 U.S. 1, 4 n. 2 (1964), leads to the opposite conclusion. Second, regardless of whether appellants agree with the *Presser* analysis, it is the law of the land and we are bound by it. Their assertion that *Presser* is illogical is a policy matter for the Supreme Court to address. Finally, their theory of implicit incorporation is wholly unsupported. The Supreme Court has specifically rejected the proposition that the entire Bill of Rights applies to the states through the fourteenth amendment....

Since we hold that the second amendment does not apply to the states, we need not consider the scope of its guarantee of the right to bear arms. For the sake of completeness, however, and because appellants devote a large portion of their briefs to this issue, we briefly comment on what we believe to be the scope of the second amendment.

The second amendment provides that "A regulated Militia being necessary to the security of a free State, the right of the people to keep and bear Arms, shall not be infringed." U.S. Const. amend. II. Construing this language according to its plain meaning, it seems clear that the right to bear arms is inextricably connected to the preservation of a militia. This is precisely the manner in which the Supreme Court interpreted the second amendment in *United States v. Miller,* 307 U.S. 174 (1939), the only Supreme Court case specifically addressing that amendment's scope. There the Court held that the right to keep and bear arms extends only to those arms which are necessary to maintain a well regulated militia.

In an attempt to avoid the *Miller* holding that the right to keep and bear arms exists only as it relates to protecting the public security, appellants argue that "[t]he fact that the right to keep and bear arms is joined with language expressing one of its purposes in no way permits a construction which limits or confines the exercise of that right." Reichert br. at 35. They offer no explanation for how they have arrived at this conclusion. Alternatively, they argue that handguns are military weapons. Stengl's br. at 11–13. Our reading of *Miller* convinces us that it does not support either of these theories. As the Village correctly notes, appellants are essentially arguing that *Miller* was wrongly decided and should be overruled. Such arguments have no place before this court. Under the controlling authority of *Miller* we conclude that the right to keep and bear handguns is not guaranteed by the second amendment.

Because the second amendment is not applicable to Morton Grove and possession of handguns by individuals is not part of the right to keep and bear arms, Ordinance No. 81-11 does not violate the second amendment.

IV

Finally, we consider whether Ordinance No. 81-11 violates the ninth amendment. Appellants argue that, although the right to use commonly-owned arms for self-defense is not explicitly listed in the Bill of Rights, it is a fundamental right protected by the ninth amendment. Citing no authority which directly supports their contention, they rely on the debates in the First Congress and the writings of legal philosophers to establish that the right of an individual to own and possess firearms for self-defense is an absolute and inalienable right which cannot be impinged.

Since appellants do not cite, and our research has not revealed, any Supreme Court case holding that any specific right is protected by the ninth amendment, appellants' argument has no legal significance. Appellants may believe the ninth amendment should be read to recognize an unwritten, fundamental, individual right to own or possess firearms; the fact remains that the Supreme Court has never embraced this theory.

Reasonable people may differ about the wisdom of Ordinance No. 81-11. History may prove that the Ordinance cannot effectively promote peace and security for Morton Grove's citizens. Such issues, however, are not before the court. We simply hold the

Ordinance No. 81-11 is a proper exercise of Morton Grove's police power and does not violate art. 1, section 22 of the Illinois Constitution or the second, ninth, or fourteenth amendments of the United States Constitution. Accordingly, the decision of the district court is
AFFIRMED.

State Right-to-Bear-Arms Provisions

Alabama Constitution Article I, Section 26

That every citizen has a right to bear arms in defense of himself and the state.

Alaska Constitution Article I, Section 19

A well-regulated militia being necessary to the security of a free state, the right of the people to keep and bear arms shall not be infringed. The individual right to keep and bear arms shall not be denied or infringed by the State or a political subdivision of the State.

Arizona Constitution Article 2, Section 26

The right of the individual citizen to bear arms in defense of himself or the State shall not be impaired, but nothing in this section shall be construed as authorizing individuals or corporations to organize, maintain, or employ an armed body of men.

Arkansas Constitution Article II, Section 5

The citizens of this State shall have the right to keep and bear arms for their common defense.

Colorado Constitution Article II, Section 13

The right of no person to keep and bear arms in defense of his home, person and property, or in aid of the civil power when thereto legally summoned, shall be called in question; but nothing herein contained shall be construed to justify the practice of carrying concealed weapons.

Connecticut Constitution Article I, Section 15

Every citizen has a right to bear arms in defense of himself and the state.

Delaware Constitution Article I, Section 20

A person has the right to keep and bear arms for the defense of self, family, home and State, and for hunting and recreational use.

Florida Constitution Article I, Section 8(a)

The right of the people to keep and bear arms in defense of themselves and of the lawful authority of the state shall not be infringed, except that the manner of bearing arms may be regulated by law.

Georgia Constitution Article I, Section 1, Paragraph VIII.

The right of the people to keep and bear arms shall not be infringed, but the General Assembly shall have power to prescribe the manner in which arms may be borne.

Hawaii Constitution Article I, Section 17

A well regulated militia being necessary to the security of a free state, the right of the people to keep and bear arms shall not be infringed.

Idaho Constitution Article I, Section 11

The people have the right to keep and bear arms, which right shall not be abridged; but this provision shall not prevent the passage of laws to govern the carrying of weapons concealed on the person nor prevent passage of legislation providing minimum sentences for crimes committed while in possession of a firearm, nor prevent the passage of legislation providing penalties for the possession of firearms by a convicted felon, nor prevent the passage of any legislation punishing the use of a firearm. No law shall impose licensure, registration or special taxation on the ownership or possession of firearms or ammunition. Nor shall any law permit the confiscation of firearms, except those actually used in the commission of a felony.

Illinois Constitution Article I, Section 22

Subject only to the police power, the right of the individual citizen to keep and bear arms shall not be infringed.

Indiana Constitution Article I, Section 32

The people shall have a right to bear arms, for the defense of themselves and the State.

Kansas Constitution Bill of Rights 4

The people have the right to bear arms for their defense and security; but standing armies, in time of peace, are dangerous to liberty, and shall not be tolerated, and the military shall be in strict subordination to the civil power.

Kentucky Constitution Section 1

All men are, by nature, free and equal, and have certain inherent and inalienable rights, among which may be reckoned: . . . The right to bear arms in defense of themselves and of the State, subject to the power of the General Assembly to enact laws to prevent persons from carrying concealed weapons.

Louisiana Constitution Article I, Section 11

The right of each citizen to keep and bear arms shall not be abridged, but this provision shall not prevent the passage of laws to prohibit the carrying of weapons concealed on the person.

Maine Constitution Article 1, Section 16

Every citizen has a right to keep and bear arms and this right shall never be questioned.

Massachusetts Constitution Part The First, Article XVII

The people have a right to keep and to bear arms for the common defence. And as, in time of peace, armies are dangerous to liberty, they ought not to be maintained without the consent of the legislature; and the military power shall always be held in an exact subordination to the civil authority, and be governed by it.

Michigan Constitution Article I, Section 6

Every person has a right to keep and bear arms for the defense of himself and the state.

Mississippi Constitution Article III, Section 12

The right of every citizen to keep and bear arms in defense of his home, person, or property, or in aid of the civil power when thereto legally summoned, shall not be called in question, but the legislature may regulate or forbid carrying concealed weapons.

Missouri Constitution Article I, Section 23

That the right of every citizen to keep and bear arms in defense of his home, person and property, or when lawfully summoned in aid of the civil power, shall not be questioned; but this shall not justify the wearing of concealed weapons.

Montana Constitution Article II, Section 12

The right of any person to keep or bear arms in defense of his own home, person, and property, or in aid of the civil power when thereto legally summoned, shall not be called in question, but nothing herein contained shall be held to permit the carrying of concealed weapons.

Nebraska Constitution Article I, Section 1

All persons are by nature free and independent, and have certain inherent and inalienable rights; among these are life, liberty, the pursuit of happiness, and the right to keep and bear arms for security or defense of self, family, home, and others, and for lawful common defense, hunting, recreational use, and all other lawful purposes, and such rights shall not be denied or infringed by the state or any subdivision thereof.

Nevada Constitution Article 1, Section 11, [1.]

Every citizen has the right to keep and bear arms for security and defense, for lawful hunting and recreational use and for other lawful purposes.

New Hampshire Constitution Part First, Article 2-a

All persons have the right to keep and bear arms in defense of themselves, their families, their property and the state.

Part First, Article 13

No person, who is conscientiously scrupulous about the lawfulness of bearing arms, shall be compelled thereto.

New Mexico Constitution Article II, Section 6

No law shall abridge the right of the citizen to keep and bear arms for security and defense, for lawful hunting and recreational use and for other lawful purposes, but nothing herein shall be held to permit the carrying of concealed weapons. No municipality or county shall regulate, in any way, an incident of the right to keep and bear arms.

North Carolina Constitution Article I, Section 30

A well regulated militia being necessary to the security of a free State, the right of the people to keep and bear arms shall not be infringed; and, as standing armies in time of peace are dangerous to liberty, they shall not be maintained, and the military shall be kept under strict subordination to, and governed by, the civil power. Nothing herein shall justify the practice of carrying concealed weapons, or prevent the General Assembly from enacting penal statutes against that practice.

North Dakota Constitution Article I, Section 1

All individuals are by nature equally free and independent and have certain inalienable rights, among which are those of enjoying and defending life and liberty; acquiring, possessing and protecting property and reputation; pursuing and obtaining safety and happiness; and to keep and bear arms for the defense of their person, family, property, and the state, and for lawful hunting, recreational and other lawful purposes, which shall not be infringed.

Ohio Constitution Article I, Section 4

The people have the right to bear arms for their defense and security; but standing armies, in time of peace, are dangerous to liberty, and shall not be kept up; and the military shall be in strict subordination to the civil power.

Oklahoma Constitution Article II, Section 26

The right of a citizen to keep and bear arms in defense of his home, person, or property, or in aid of the civil power, when thereunto legally summoned, shall never be prohibited; but nothing herein contained shall prevent the Legislature from regulating the carrying of weapons.

Oregon Constitution Article I, Section 27

The people shall have the right to bear arms for the defence of themselves, and the State, but the Military shall be kept in strict subordination to the civil power.

Pennsylvania Constitution Article I, Section 21

The right of the citizens to bear arms in defense of themselves and the State shall not be questioned.

Rhode Island Constitution Article I, Section 22

The right of the people to keep and bear arms shall not be infringed.

South Carolina Constitution Article I, Section 20

A well regulated militia being necessary to the security of a free State, the right of the people to keep and bear arms shall not be infringed. As, in times of peace, armies are dangerous to liberty, they shall not be maintained without the consent of the General Assembly. The military power of the State shall always be held in subordination to the civil authority and be governed by it. No soldier shall in time of peace be quartered in any house without the consent of the owner nor in time of war but in the manner prescribed by law.

South Dakota Constitution Article VI, Section 24

The right of the citizens to bear arms in defense of themselves and the state shall not be denied.

Tennessee Constitution Article I, Section 26

That the citizens of this State have a right to keep and to bear arms for their common defense; but the Legislature shall have power, by law, to regulate the wearing of arms with a view to prevent crime.

Texas Constitution Article I, Section 23

Every citizen shall have the right to keep and bear arms in the lawful defense of himself or the State; but the Legislature shall have power, by law, to regulate the wearing of arms, with a view to prevent crime.

Utah Constitution Article I, Section 6

The individual right of the people to keep and bear arms for security and defense of self, family, others, property, or the state, as well as for other lawful purposes shall not be infringed; but nothing herein shall prevent the Legislature from defining the lawful use of arms.

Vermont Constitution Chapter 1, Article 16

That the people have a right to bear arms for the defence of themselves and the State—and as standing armies in time of peace are dangerous to liberty, they ought not to be kept up; and that the military should be kept under strict subordination to and governed by the civil power.

Virginia Constitution Article I, Section 13

That a well regulated militia, composed of the body of the people, trained to arms, is the proper, natural, and safe defense of a free state, therefore, the right of the people to keep and bear arms shall not be infringed; that standing armies, in time of peace, should be avoided as dangerous to liberty; and that in all cases the military should be under strict subordination to, and governed by, the civil power.

Washington Constitution Article I, Section 24

The right of the individual citizen to bear arms in defense of himself, or the state, shall not be impaired, but nothing in this section shall be construed as authorizing individuals or corporations to organize, maintain or employ an armed body of men.

West Virginia Constitution Article III, Section 22

A person has the right to keep and bear arms for the defense of self, family, home and state, and for lawful hunting and recreational use.

Wisconsin Constitution Article I, Section 25

The people have the right to keep and bear arms for security, defense, hunting, recreation or any other lawful purpose.

Wyoming Constitution Article I, Section 24

The right of citizens to bear arms in defense of themselves and of the state shall not be denied.

MAJOR PARTY PLATFORMS ON GUN CONTROL

The first references to gun control in any major party platforms appeared in 1968, when rising crime, political assassinations, and consideration of major gun control legislation in Congress spurred the parties to address the issue. In general, the Republicans have emphasized gun rights and crime control, whereas the Democrats have emphasized stronger gun laws, crime control, and, more recently, protecting gun rights for hunters and sportspeople.

Republican Party Platform Statements on Gun Control

1968: "Enactment of legislation to control indiscriminate availability of firearms, safeguarding the right of responsible citizens to collect, own and use firearms for legitimate purposes, retaining primary responsibility at the state level, with such federal laws as necessary to better enable the states to meet their responsibilities."

1972: "Intensify efforts to prevent criminal access to all weapons, including special emphasis on cheap, readily-obtainable handguns, retaining primary responsibility at the State level, with such Federal law as necessary to enable the States to meet their responsibilities.

"Safeguard the right of responsible citizens to collect, own and use firearms for legitimate purposes, including hunting, target shooting and self defense. We will strongly support efforts of all law enforcement agencies to apprehend and prosecute to the limit of the law all those who use firearms in the commission of crimes."

1976: "The federal criminal code should include automatic and mandatory minimum sentences for persons committing offenses under federal jurisdiction that involve the use of a dangerous weapon.... We support the right of citizens to keep and bear arms. We oppose federal registration of firearms. Mandatory sentences for crimes committed with a lethal weapon are the only effective solution to this problem."

1980: "We believe the right of citizens to keep and bear arms must be preserved. Accordingly, we oppose federal registration of firearms. Mandatory sentences for commission of armed felonies are the most effective means to deter abuse of this right. We therefore support Congressional initiatives to remove those provisions of the Gun Control Act of 1968 that do not significantly impact on crime but serve rather to restrain the law-abiding citizen in his legitimate use of firearms."

1984: "Republicans will continue to defend the constitutional right to keep and bear arms. When this right is abused and armed felonies are committed, we believe in stiff, mandatory sentencing. Law-abiding citizens exercising their constitutional rights must not be blamed for crime. Republicans will continue to seek repeal of legislation that restrains innocent citizens more than violent criminals."

1988: "Republicans defend the constitutional right to keep and bear arms. When this right is abused by an individual who uses a gun in the commission of a crime, we call for stiff, mandatory penalties."

1992: "Republicans defend the constitutional right to keep and bear arms. We call for stiff mandatory sentences for those who use firearms in a crime. We note that those who seek to disarm citizens in their homes are the same liberals who tried to disarm our Nation during the Cold War and are today seeking to cut our national defense below safe levels. We applaud congressional Republicans for overturning the District of Columbia's law blaming firearm manufacturers for street crime."

1996: "We defend the constitutional right to keep and bear arms. We will promote training in the safe usage of firearms, especially in programs for women and the elderly. We strongly support Bob Dole's National Instant Check Initiative, which will help keep all guns out of the hands of convicted felons. The point-of-purchase instant check has worked well in many states and now it is time to extend this system all across America. We applaud Bob Dole's commitment to have the national instant check system operational by the end of 1997. In one of the strangest actions of his tenure, Bill Clinton abolished Operation Triggerlock, the Republican initiative to jail any felon caught with a gun. We will restore that effort and will set by law minimum mandatory penalties for the use of guns in committing a crime: 5 years for possession, 10 years for brandishing, and 20 for discharge."

2000: "We defend the constitutional right to keep and bear arms, and we affirm the individual responsibility to safely use and store firearms. Because self-defense is a basic human right, we will promote training in their safe usage, especially in federal programs for women and the elderly. A Republican administration will vigorously enforce current gun laws, neglected by the Democrats, especially by prosecuting dangerous offenders identified as felons in instant background checks. Although we support background checks to ensure that guns do not fall into the hands of criminals, we oppose federal licensing of law-abiding gun owners and national gun registration as a violation of the Second Amendment and an invasion of privacy of honest citizens. Through programs like Project Exile, we will hold criminals individually accountable for their actions by strong enforcement of federal and state firearm laws, especially when guns are used in violent or drug-related crimes. With a special emphasis on school safety, we propose the crackdown on youth violence explained elsewhere in this platform."

Democratic Party Platform Statements on Gun Control

1968: "Promote the passage and enforcement of effective federal, state and local gun control legislation."

1972: "There must be laws to control the improper use of hand guns. Four years ago a candidate for the presidency was slain by a handgun. Two months ago, another candidate for that office was gravely wounded. Three out of four police officers killed in the line of duty are slain with hand guns. Effective legislation must include a ban on sale of hand guns known as Saturday night specials which are unsuitable for sporting purposes."

1976: "Handguns simplify and intensify violent crime. Ways must be found to curtail the availability of these weapons. The Democratic Party must provide the leadership for a coordinated federal and state effort to strengthen the presently inadequate controls over the manufacture, assembly, distribution and possession of handguns and to ban Saturday night specials.

"Furthermore, since people and not guns commit crimes, we support mandatory sentencing for individuals convicted of committing a felony with a gun.

"The Democratic Party, however, affirms the right of sportsmen to possess guns for purely hunting and target-shooting purposes."

1980: "The Democratic Party affirms the right of sportsmen to possess guns for purely hunting and target-shooting purposes.

However, handguns simplify and intensify violent crime. Ways must be found to curtail the availability of these weapons. The Democratic Party supports enactment of federal legislation to strengthen the presently inadequate regulations over the manufacture, assembly, distribution, and possession of handguns and to ban 'Saturday night specials.'"

1984: "We support tough restraints on the manufacture, transportation, and sale of snub-nosed handguns, which have no legitimate sporting use and are used in a high proportion of violent crimes."

1988: "We believe that the federal government should provide increased assistance to local criminal justice agencies, enforce a ban on 'cop killer' bullets that have no purpose other than the killing and maiming of law enforcement officers, reinforce our commitment to help crime victims, and assume a leadership role in securing the safety of our neighborhoods and homes. We further believe that the repeated toleration in Washington of unethical and unlawful greed among too many of those who have been governing our nation, procuring our weapons and polluting our environment has made far more difficult the daily work of the local policemen, teachers and parents who must convey to our children respect for justice and authority."

1992: "It is time to shut down the weapons bazaars. We support a reasonable waiting period to permit background checks for purchases of handguns, as well as assault weapons controls to ban the possession, sale, importation and manufacture of the most deadly assault weapons. We do not support efforts to restrict weapons used for legitimate hunting and sporting purposes. We will work for swift and certain punishment of all people who violate the country's gun laws and for stronger sentences for criminals who use guns. We will also seek to shut down the black market for guns and impose severe penalties on people who sell guns to children."

1996: "Today's Democratic Party believes the first responsibility of government is law and order. Four years ago, crime in America seemed intractable. The violent crime rate and the murder rate had climbed for seven straight years. Drugs seemed to flow freely across our borders and into our neighborhoods. Convicted felons could walk into any gun shop and buy a handgun. Military-style assault weapons were sold freely. Our people didn't feel safe in their homes, walking their streets, or even sending their children to school. Under the thumb of special interests like the gun lobby, Republicans talked tough about crime but did nothing to fight it.

"Bill Clinton promised to turn things around, and that is exactly what he did. After a long hard fight, President Clinton beat back fierce Republican opposition, led by Senator Dole and Speaker Gingrich, to answer the call of America's police officers and pass the toughest Crime Bill in history. The Democratic Party under President Clinton is putting more police on the streets and tougher penalties on the books; we are taking guns off the streets and working to steer young people away from crime and gangs and drugs in the first place. And it is making a difference. In city after city and town after town, crime rates are finally coming down....

Bob Dole, Newt Gingrich, and George Bush were able to hold the Brady Bill hostage for the gun lobby until Bill Clinton became President. With his leadership, we made the Brady Bill the law of the land. And because we did, more than 600,000 felons, fugitives, and stalkers have been stopped from buying guns. President Clinton led the fight to ban 19 deadly assault weapons, designed for one purpose only—to kill human beings. We oppose efforts to restrict weapons used for legitimate sporting purposes, and we are proud that not one hunter or sportsman was forced to change guns because of the assault weapons ban. But we know that the military-style guns we banned have no place on America's streets, and we are proud of the courageous Democrats who defied the gun lobby and sacrificed their seats in Congress to make America safer.

"Today's Democratic Party stands with America's police officers. We are proud to tell them that as long as Bill Clinton and Al Gore are in the White House, any attempt to repeal the Brady Bill or assault weapons ban will be met with a veto. We must do everything we can to stand behind our police officers, and the first thing we should do is pass a ban on cop-killer bullets. Any bullet that can rip through a bulletproof vest should be against the law; that is the least we can do to protect the brave police officers who risk their lives to protect us."

2000: "Bill Clinton and Al Gore.... stood up to the gun lobby, to pass the Brady Bill and ban deadly assault weapons and stopped nearly half a million felons, fugitives, and stalkers from buying guns.... serious crime is down seven years in a row, to its lowest level in a quarter-century. Violent crime is down by 24 percent. The number of juveniles committing homicides with guns is down by nearly 60 percent.... We can't surrender to the right-wing Republicans who threatened funding for new police, who tried to gut crime prevention, and who would invite the NRA into the Oval Office. Nor will we go back to the old approach which was tough on the causes of crime, but not tough enough on crime itself.... A shocking level of gun violence on our streets and in our schools has shown America that the need to keep guns away from those who shouldn't have them—in ways that respect the rights of hunters, sportsmen, and legitimate gun owners. The Columbine tragedy struck America's heart, but in its wake Republicans have done nothing to keep guns away from those who should not have them.

"Democrats believe that we should fight gun crime on all fronts —with stronger laws and stronger enforcement. That's why

Democrats fought and passed the Brady Law and the Assault Weapons Ban. We increased federal, state, and local gun crime prosecution by 22 percent since 1992. Now gun crime is down by 35 percent.

"Now we must do even more. We need mandatory child safety locks, to protect our children. We should require a photo license I.D., a full background check, and a gun safety test to buy a new handgun in America. We support more federal gun prosecutors, ATF agents and inspectors, and giving states and communities another 10,000 prosecutors to fight gun crime."

Chronology

1689	The British Bill of Rights, also known as the Declaration of Rights, is drafted, including in Article 7 a qualified right to bear arms. Some believe that this provision was the forerunner of the Second Amendment in the U.S. Constitution.
April 19, 1775	Battle of Lexington and Concord, beginning the Revolutionary War.
1776	The Continental Congress approves the Declaration of Independence, the document that declares and explains the nation's severing of ties with Great Britain.
1781	The Revolutionary War is concluded, and the United States wins its freedom from Great Britain.
1787	Shays's Rebellion is suppressed by militia forces.
1787	The modern Constitution is written and sent to the states for ratification.
1789	The modern Constitution takes effect.
1789	The First Congress approves twelve amendments to the Constitution, called the Bill of Rights. They are sent to the states for ratification, including the Second Amendment.
1791	Ten amendments are ratified by the states and added to the Constitution as the Bill of Rights.

1792	Congress passes the Uniform Militia Act and the Calling Forth Act, which attempt to implement the militia system for national defense and assert the primacy of federal government power over the militias.
1794	The Whiskey Rebellion is suppressed by militia forces.
1812–1814	The War of 1812 with Britain is fought. Owing to poor performance by U.S. troops, this is the last major military conflict when the United States relies on the old-style general militias.
1868	The Fourteenth Amendment is added to the Constitution. The due process and equal protection clauses of this amendment opened the door to the process by which parts of the Bill of Rights were applied to the states in what is called *incorporation*.
1871	The National Rifle Association (NRA) is formed by two Civil War veterans from New York to improve marksmanship skills.
1876	The first Supreme Court case in which the high court offers interpretation of the Second Amendment, *United States v. Cruikshank*, says that it does not apply to the states.
1886	The Supreme Court rules in *Presser v. Illinois* that the Second Amendment does not afford citizens the right to form their own militias, as this power belongs solely to the government, and reaffirms *Cruikshank*.
April 20, 1889	Adolph Hitler's date of birth, considered significant by some right-wing extremists.
1894	In *Miller v. Texas*, the Supreme Court upholds a law prohibiting the carrying of dangerous weapons, saying that it does not violate the Second Amendment.

1897	The Supreme Court begins the process of applying parts of the Bill of Rights to the states in the case of *Chicago, Burlington, and Quincy Railroad v. Chicago*.
1897	The Supreme Court rules in *Robertson v. Baldwin* that a law barring the carrying of concealed weapons did not violate the Second Amendment.
1903	Congress passes the Militia Act, also known as the Dick Act, which for the first time recognizes in law that the reserved or volunteer militias constitute the National Guard, as distinct from the unorganized or general militias. The act begins the process of consolidating federal control over what were once the militias.
1911	The New York legislature enacts the Sullivan Law, the first modern strict gun control law, which strictly regulates the sale, possession, and carrying of handguns.
1916	Congress passes the National Defense Act, implementing sweeping new federal control over the National Guard.
1919	Congress enacts the War Revenue Act, a revenue-raising measure that included a 10 percent federal excise tax on guns.
1919	The enactment of Prohibition prompts the creation of the Prohibition Unit, which in turn becomes the Bureau of Prohibition, the forerunner of the modern Bureau of Alcohol, Tobacco, and Firearms.
1927	Congress passes a bill, titled "An Act Declaring Pistols, Revolvers, and Other Firearms Capable of Being Concealed on the Person Nonmailable and Providing Penalties," to prohibit the sale of handguns by private individuals through the mail.
1934	Congress passes the National Firearms Act, which restricts the manufacture, sale, and transfer

	of automatic weapons, sawed-off shotguns, and other exotic weapons like cane guns.
1938	Congress passes the Federal Firearms Act, establishing a system of licensing for firearms dealers and regulating sales of guns to criminals.
1939	The Supreme Court rules in *Miller v. United States* that gun regulations in the National Firearms Act do not violate the Second Amendment, and that the amendment pertains only to citizen service in a government-organized and regulated militia.
November 22, 1963	President John F. Kennedy is assassinated in Dallas, Texas, with a rifle purchased through interstate mails. The assassination spurs national support for stronger gun control laws.
1968	Congress enacts the Gun Control Act, banning the interstate shipment of firearms to individuals and strengthening other licensing and regulatory measures. Support for the bill was spurred by the assassinations of Martin Luther King Jr. and Robert F. Kennedy in the months before the bill's passage.
1972	The modern Bureau of Alcohol, Tobacco, and Firearms is organized by being transferred from the Internal Revenue Service to the Department of Treasury, where it is given bureau status.
1972	Congress enacts legislation to create the Consumer Product Safety Commission. Just before enactment, a provision is inserted by gun control foes to exempt firearms and ammunition from agency scrutiny, making guns virtually the only commodity available to consumers exempted from the law.
1974	Handgun Control, Inc., the largest pro–gun control group, is formed by businessman Nelson "Pete" Shields. The organization was originally founded as the National Council to Control Handguns.

	The National Council to Ban Handguns, later renamed the Coalition to Stop Gun Violence in 1990, is formed by a coalition of religious groups.
1975	The National Rifle Association creates its Institute for Legislative Action, foreshadowing its greater emphasis on politics. The ILA would soon become the largest and most powerful element of the NRA.
1976	The National Rifle Association forms its own political action committee, called the Political Victory Fund. Its PAC would become one of the largest in the nation.
1977	Hardliners in the National Rifle Association win control of the organization at the NRA's annual convention, held in Cincinnati, beginning the organization's more political, and more right-wing, turn.
March 30, 1981	President Ronald Reagan is wounded, and his press secretary, James Brady, is gravely injured in an assassination attempt in Washington, D.C. After his recovery, Reagan continues to oppose stronger gun laws, a position he reverses after leaving office.
1986	Congress passes the Firearms Owners Protection Act, also known as the McClure-Volkmer bill, that repeals some gun regulations enacted in 1968, notably allowing interstate sale of long guns and eliminating some record-keeping requirements for licensed gun dealers.
1989	Loner Patrick Purdy kills five children and wounds twenty-nine others in a schoolyard massacre in Stockton, California, using an AK-47 assault weapon. The mass shooting shocks the nation and spurs calls for a ban on assault weapons.
1991	George Hennard kills twenty-two people and himself, and wounds twenty-three others, in a

	shooting at a cafeteria in Killeen, Texas. The event lends added support to gun control efforts.
1992	Federal law enforcement officials lay siege to the cabin of Randy Weaver in Ruby Ridge, Idaho, after he eludes capture. Two of his family members are killed, as is a federal agent. The incident becomes a rally event for those fearing government power.
	Academics for the Second Amendment (ASA) is formed by a group of lawyers and academics to promote the individualist view of the Second Amendment.
	Democrat Bill Clinton, a gun control supporter, is elected president, paving the way for the enactment of stronger gun laws.
April 19, 1993	Federal law enforcement officials storm the Branch Davidian compound in Waco, Texas after a fifty-one day siege. Seventy-four Davidians died in the fire that ensued.
	Congress enacts the Brady Handgun Violence Prevention Act, which imposes a five-business-day waiting period and background checks for handgun purchases. The waiting period is replaced by an instant check system in 1998.
1994	Congress enacts the assault weapons ban, barring possession of nineteen named assault weapons and several dozen copycat models.
	A small group of progun lawyers form the Lawyers' Second Amendment Society to advance the individualist view of the Second Amendment and fund challenges to gun laws.
April 19, 1995	Timothy McVeigh, motivated by antigovernment hatred, detonates a truck bomb in front of a federal office building in Oklahoma City, killing 168. McVeigh is convicted.

1998	Actor Charlton Heston becomes president of the National Rifle Association, a move orchestrated by NRA Vice President Wayne LaPierre, in an effort to defeat an even more extremist element within the NRA lead by Neal Knox. Heston is also brought in to rehabilitate the NRA's image.
April 20, 1999	Two high school boys kill twelve students and wound a teacher, who later dies, at Columbine High School in Littleton, Colorado, before turning their guns on themselves. The killings shock the nation; in response, the U.S. Senate passes a gun control bill, but it dies in a conference committee after the House of Representatives fails to pass a comparable measure.
2000	A group of women concerned about gun violence organize the Million Mom March, held on Mother's Day in Washington, D.C., with concurrent large marches held in numerous cities across the country to support stronger gun laws. The first modern mass demonstration on behalf of gun control, the march attracts over 700,000 participants, making it one of the largest mass demonstrations ever held in the nation's capital. Republican George W. Bush is elected president. Bush opposes most new gun control measures, having supported National Rifle Association positions as governor of Texas, and thus dimming the prospect of new national gun laws under his presidency.
2001	Convicted Oklahoma City bomber Timothy McVeigh is executed in federal prison in Terre Haute, Indiana.

TABLE OF CASES

Adams v. Williams, 407 U.S. 143 (1972), 37, 131
Adamson v. California, 332 U.S. 46 (1947), 70
Aymette v. State, 21 Tenn. 154 (1840), 7, 55, 133
Bliss v. Commonwealth, 2 Littell 90 (Ky. 1822), 54, 133
Burton v. Sills, 394 U.S. 812 (1969), 39
Cases v. United States, 131 F.2d 916 (1st Cir. 1942), cert. denied sub nom
Cody v. United States, 460 F.2d 34, (8th Cir. 1972), cert. denied, 409 U.S. 1010 (1972)
Dunne v. People, 94 Ill. 120 (1879), 55, 138
Eckert v. City of Philadelphia, 477 F.2d 610 (3d Cir. 1973)
Farmer v. Higgins, 907 F.2d 1041 (11th Cir. 1990), cert. denied, 111 S.Ct. 753 (1991)
Fresno Rifle & Pistol Club v. Van de Camp, 965 F.2d 723 (9th Cir. 1992), 69, 110
Hickman v. Block, 81 F.3d 168 (9th Cir. 1996), 110
Hill v. Georgia, 53 Ga. 472 (1874), 7
Lewis v. United States, 445 U.S. 90 (1980), 38, 116, 120, 141
Love v. Pepersack, 47 F.3d 120 (4th Cir. 1995), 110
Malloy v. Hogan, 378 U.S. 1 (1964), 39, 142
Maryland v. United States, 381 U.S. 41 (1965), 32, 41, 142
Miller v. Texas, 153 U.S. 535 (1894), 35, 120, 236
Nunn v. State, 1 Kelly 243 (1846), 40, 55
Palko v. Connecticut, 302 U.S. 319 (1937), 116

Patsone v. Commonwealth, 232 U.S. 138 (1914), 35, 145

Peoples Rights Organization, Inc. v. City of Columbus, 152 F.3d 522 (6th Cir. 1998)

Perpich v. Department of Defense, 496 U.S. 334 (1990), 32, 41, 145

Presser v. Illinois, 116 U.S. 252 (1886), 33–35, 37, 38, 56, 72, 120, 146, 189–200, 207, 208, 215, 236

Printz v. United States, 521 U.S. 898 (1997), 76, 95, 110–112, 146, 150

Quilici v. Village of Morton Grove, 695 F.2d 261 (7th Cir. 1982), cert. denied, 464 U.S. 863 (1983), 39–40, 146–147, 206–218

Robertson v. Baldwin, 165 U.S. 275 (1897), 35, 120, 147, 237

Staples v. United States, 511 U.S. 600 (1994), 38

State v. Gohl, 46 Wash. 408 (1907), 55

Stevens v. United States, 440 F.2d 144 (6th Cir. 1971)

Thomas v. Members of City Council of Portland, 730 F.2d 41 (1st Cir. 1984)

United States v. Cruikshank, 92 U.S. 542 (1876), 32–33, 34, 38, 69, 121, 151, 165–189, 236

United States v. Day, 476 F.2d 562 (6th Cir. 1973)

United States v. Emerson, 46 F.Supp.2d 598 (N.D. Texas 1999), 113

United States v. Finitz, 2000 WL 1171139 (9th Cir. Aug. 17, 2000)

United States v. Graves, 554 F.2d 65 (3d Cir. 1977)

United States v. Hancock, 231 F.3d 557 (9th Cir. 2000)

United States v. Johnson, 441 F.2d 1134 (5th Cir. 1971)

United States v. Johnson, 497 F.2d 548 (4th Cir. 1974)

United States v. Lopez, 54 U.S. 549 (1995), 112, 151

United States v. McCutcheon, 446 F.2d 133 (7th Cir. 1971)

United States v. Metcalf, 221 F.3d 1336 (6th Cir. 2000), cert. denied

United States v. Miller, 307 U.S. 174 (1939), 35–37, 38, 39, 70, 110, 113, 121, 141, 151–152, 200–206, 207, 216, 217, 238

United States v. Napier, 233 F.3d 394 (6th Cir. 2000), 110

United States v. Nelson, 859 F.2d 1318 (8th Cir. 1988), 39, 110

United States v. Oakes, 564 F.2d 384 (10th Cir. 1977), cert. denied, 435 U.S. 926 (1978)

United States v. Tot, 131 F.2d 261 (3d Cir. 1942), reversed on other grounds, 319 U.S. 463 (1943)

United States v. Verdugo-Urquidez, 494 U.S. 259 (1990), 56–57, 120, 152

United States v. Warin, 530 F.2d 103 (6th Cir. 1976), cert. denied, 426 U.S. 948 (1976), 110

United States v. Wright, 117 F.3d 1265 (11th Cir. 1997)

Velazquez v. United States, 319 U.S. 770 (1943)

ANNOTATED BIBLIOGRAPHY

Abraham, Henry J. 1972. *Freedom and the Court.* New York: Oxford University Press. A classic analysis of civil rights and liberties, including careful treatment of the pivotal role of the Fourteenth Amendment and the subject of incorporation.

Alfange, Dean Jr. 2000. **"The Supreme Court and Federalism."** In *Politics and Constitutionalism,* ed. by Robert J. Spitzer. Albany, NY: SUNY Press. A thorough and nuanced treatment of how the boundary of federalism has been defined, and redefined, by the more conservative Supreme Court of the 1990s.

American Law Reports, Federal. 1983. Rochester, NY: The Lawyers Co-Operative Pub. Co. A standard reference work for lawyers summarizing key elements of the law.

Anderson, Jack. 1996. *Inside the NRA.* Beverly Hills, CA: Dove Books. Written by the well-known political columnist and investigator, Anderson argues that the National Rifle Association has alienated itself from most gun owners by its political extremism and its distortions of the nature of gun rights.

Avins, Alfred. 1967. *The Reconstruction Amendments' Debates.* Richmond, VA: Virginia Commission on Constitutional Government. A compilation of all congressional debates, spanning the period from the 1840s through the 1860s, concerning what eventually became the Fourteenth Amendment.

Bellesiles, Michael. 2000. *Arming America: The Origins of a National Gun Culture.* New York: Alfred A. Knopf. A major, groundbreaking piece of historical work that demonstrates the fact that few Americans ever possessed, or were familiar with, firearms, from colonial times up until the Civil War.

Beman, Lamar T., ed. 1926. ***Outlawing the Pistol.*** New York: H. W. Wilson Co. An early book that summarized arguments for and against the then-widely debated proposal to ban possession of pistols. Included reprints and bibliographic citations for dozens of articles from contemporary magazines and newspapers on the subject.

Bogus, Carl T. 1998. **"The Hidden History of the Second Amendment."** *U.C. Davis Law Review* 31(Winter): 309–408. Pathbreaking article arguing that support for the Second Amendment arose from southern representatives desiring to ensure their states' right to organize and use state militias to suppress slave rebellions.

Bonnicksen, Andrea L. 1982. ***Civil Rights and Liberties.*** Palo Alto, CA: Mayfield Pub. An excellent survey treatment of civil rights and liberties, including the concept of incorporation.

Boorstin, Daniel J. 1964. ***The Americans: The Colonial Experience.*** New York: Vintage. A standard book on colonial life and politics.

Brant, Irving. 1965. ***The Bill of Rights.*** Indianapolis, IN: Bobbs-Merrill Co. A standard reference work on the evolution and meaning of the Bill of Rights.

Bruce, John M., and Clyde Wilcox, eds. 1998. ***The Changing Politics of Gun Control.*** Lanham, MD: Rowman and Littlefield. A collection of chapters on various contemporary elements of the gun control debate, including public opinion, interest group behavior, and the Second Amendment.

Burger, Warren. 1990. **"The Right to Bear Arms."** *Parade Magazine,* 14 January, 5–6. The former Supreme Court chief justice's popular essay that underscores the militia-based meaning of the Second Amendment.

Carter, Gregg, ed. 2002. ***Encyclopedia of Guns in American Society.*** 2 vols. Santa Barbara, CA: ABC-CLIO. A comprehensive, interdisciplinary compilation of every major aspect of the gun control issue.

Chase, Harold W., and Craig R. Ducat. 1973. ***Edward S. Corwin's The Constitution and What It Means Today.*** Princeton, NJ: Princeton University Press. A standard reference work on the meaning of the Constitution, Bill of Rights, and amendments.

Cogan, Neil H., ed. 1997. ***The Complete Bill of Rights.*** New York: Oxford University Press. A comprehensive work that compiles all relevant debate from the Congress that formulated and passed the Bill of Rights, including all textual revisions.

"Constitutional Rights in Jeopardy: The Push for 'Gun Control.'" 1998. National Rifle Association. A useful and widely reprinted summary of the NRA's individualist position on the Second Amendment.

Cooley, Thomas M. 1931. *General Principles of Constitutional Law.* Boston: Little, Brown. First pub. 1880. An early constitutional law treatise that links the bearing of arms mentioned in the Second Amendment with militia activity.

Cooper, Jerry. 1997. *The Rise of the National Guard.* Lincoln, NE: University of Nebraska Press. A detailed historical examination of what became the National Guard, tracing its roots to early volunteer militias.

Cornell, Saul, ed. 2000. *Whose Right to Bear Arms Did the Second Amendment Protect?* Boston: Bedford/St. Martin's. Presents several essays that analyze the historical basis of the Second Amendment and the arms bearing tradition.

Cortner, Richard C. 1981. *The Supreme Court and the Second Bill of Rights.* Madison, WI: University of Wisconsin Press. Discusses the evolving nature of civil liberties in the light of the Fourteenth Amendment.

Cottrol, Robert J., ed. 1994. *Gun Control and the Constitution.* New York: Garland Pub. Reprints court cases and previously published articles on the meaning of the Second Amendment.

Cress, Lawrence D. 1982. *Citizens in Arms: The Army and the Militia in American Society to the War of 1812.* Chapel Hill, NC: University of North Carolina Press. A careful historical examination of early American military forces and needs.

Davidson, Osha Gray. 1993. *Under Fire.* New York: Henry Holt. A journalistic inside look at the National Rifle Association.

DeConde, Alexander. 2001. *Gun Violence in America.* Boston: Northeastern University Press. A sweeping examination of gun practices and politics from colonial times to the present.

Dumbauld, Edward. 1957. *The Bill of Rights.* Norman, OK: University of Oklahoma Press. A standard work on the evolution and meaning of the Bill of Rights.

Edel, Wilbur. 1995. *Gun Control: Threat to Liberty or Defense Against Anarchy?* Westport, CT: Praeger. A general examination of most elements of the gun debate, including discussion of the historical evolution of gun laws.

Elliot, Jonathan, ed. 1836. *Debates in the Several State Conventions on the Adoption of the Federal Constitution,* 4 vols. Washington, DC: Clerk's Office of the District Court. A comprehensive compilation of state debates over the ratification of the Constitution.

Emery, Lucilius A. 1915. "**The Constitutional Right to Keep and Bear Arms.**" *Harvard Law Review* 28 (March): 473–477. The first full-blown treatment of the meaning of the Second Amendment in the law journal literature, noting its purpose as tied to citizen service in government militias.

Farrand, Max. 1913. *The Framing of the Constitution of the United States.* New Haven, CT: Yale University Press. An enduringly important book summarizing Farrand's analysis of the intent of the Constitution's framers and the meaning of the document.

Farrand, Max, ed. 1966. *The Records of the Federal Convention of 1787,* 4 vols. New Haven, CT: Yale University Press. A chronological compilation of all written accounts of debate at the Constitutional Convention of 1787, including not only James Madison's notes, but those of others who attended the convention.

Feller, Peter Buck, and Karl L. Gotting. 1966. "**The Second Amendment: A Second Look.**" *Northwestern University Law Review* 61(March/April): 46–70. A thorough early article summarizing historical and constitutional bases of the Second Amendment.

Fischer, David Hackett. 1994. *Paul Revere's Ride.* New York: Oxford University Press. A detailed history of the events surrounding and including the famous ride that lead to the outbreak of the American Revolution. Includes detailed examination of American militias.

Glendon, Mary Ann. 1991. *Rights Talk.* New York: Free Press. Argues that Americans' ever-increasing invocation of rights has resulted in stilted political dialogue that obscures both rights and dialogue.

Gottlieb, Alan M. 1981. *The Rights of Gun Owners.* Ottawa, IL: Green Hill Pubs. Summarizes the gun rights argument from an individualist and revolutionist perspective.

Gun Control. 1992. San Diego, CA: Greenhaven Press. A collection of articles on many aspects of the gun debate, including the Second Amendment.

Gun Control: Restricting Rights or Protecting People? 1999. Wylie, TX: Information Plus. A survey guide to the gun issue, including historical and legal issues.

Halbrook, Stephen P. 1984. *That Every Man Be Armed.* Oakland, CA: The Independent Institute. Book-length treatment by the National Rifle Association's lead lawyer arguing for an individualist view of the Second Amendment.

———. 1998. *Freedmen, the Fourteenth Amendment, and the Right to Bear Arms, 1866–1876.* Westport, CT: Praeger. Argues that the Fourteenth Amendment was meant to bestow an individual right to bear arms.

Hamilton, Alexander, James Madison, and John Jay. 1961. *The Federalist Papers.* New York: New American Library. The collection of eighty-five essays, first printed in newspapers, written by three founders in defense of the Constitution of 1787.

Hays, Stuart R. 1960. **"The Right to Bear Arms, A Study in Judicial Misinterpretation."** *William and Mary Law Review* 2: 381–406. The first article published in a law journal that argued for an individual and revolutionist interpretation of the Second Amendment.

Henderson, Harry. 2000. *Gun Control.* New York: Facts on File, Inc. A thorough reference work that includes cases, laws, bibliographies, and other useful information.

Henigan, Dennis A., et al. 1995. *Guns and the Constitution.* Northampton, MA: Aletheia Press. A collection of pro–gun control essays, including consideration of the role of the Second Amendment.

Herz, Andrew D. 1995. **"Gun Crazy: Constitutional False Consciousness and Dereliction of Dialogic Responsibility."** *Boston University Law Review* 75(January): 57–153. Argues that those in the legal community who defend the individual view of the Second Amendment have abandoned legal and academic tenets and have advanced their arguments to promote the National Rifle Association's political agenda.

Higginbotham, Don. 1998. **"The Federalized Militia Debate."** *William and Mary Quarterly* 55(January): 39–57. Examines the evolution of the American militias as a force for national defense.

Hofstadter, Richard. 1970. **"America as a Gun Culture."** *American Heritage* 21(October): 4–11, 82–85. An often-cited popular article that explains the basis of the American gun culture.

Homsher, Deborah. 2001. *Women and Guns: Politics and the Culture of Firearms in America.* Armonk, NY: M. E. Sharpe. A pathbreaking, wide-ranging examination of women's connections with guns and the gun culture. Includes extensive interviews with women involved in gun politics, as well as female gun owners and women affected by gun violence.

Jenkins, Philip. 1995. **"Home-Grown Terror."** *American Heritage* (September), 38–46. An historical account of politically-inspired, extremist violence in American history.

Jensen, Merrill. 1965. *The New Nation.* New York: Vintage. A classic examination of the formation of America, including military issues.

Karl, Jonathan. 1995. *The Right to Bear Arms.* New York: HarperCollins. A journalistic examination of the self-styled militia movement of the 1990s.

Kates, Don B. 1983. "**Handgun Prohibition and the Original Meaning of the Second Amendment.**" *Michigan Law Review* 82(November): 204–273. An often-cited defense of the individualist view of the Second Amendment.

Kennett, Lee, and James LaVerne Anderson. 1975. ***The Gun in America.*** Westport, CT: Greenwood. A highly regarded, detailed historical treatment of the role of guns and gun control in American development.

Klanwatch Project. 1996. ***False Patriots: The Threat of Antigovernment Extremists.*** Montgomery, AL: Southern Poverty Law Center. A comprehensive chronicle of extremist movements in the United States compiled by a nationally respected organization devoted to tracking domestic terrorist and racist groups.

LaPierre, Wayne. 1994. ***Guns, Crime, and Freedom.*** Washington, DC: Regnery. Authored by a long-time National Rifle Association leader, this book makes the NRA's case against gun control and in behalf of its view of the Second Amendment.

Leff, Carol Skalnik, and Mark H. Leff. 1981. "**The Politics of Ineffectiveness: Federal Firearms Legislation, 1919–38.**" *Annals of the American Academy of Political and Social Science* 455(May): 48–62. A pathbreaking examination of early gun control efforts.

Levinson, Sanford. 1989. "**The Embarrassing Second Amendment.**" *Yale Law Journal* 99(December): 637–659. An oft-cited article arguing for the individualist and revolutionist views of the Second Amendment.

Macaulay, Thomas Babington. 1879. ***The History of England from the Accession of James II,*** 5 vols. New York: T. Y. Crowell. A still widely read work of British history.

Macdonald, Andrew. 1978. ***The Turner Diaries.*** Hillsboro, WV: National Vanguard Books. A novel laced with violence, racism, and anti-Semitism that has inspired many extremist groups, including Oklahoma City bomber Timothy McVeigh.

Mahon, John K. 1960. ***The American Militia: Decade of Decision, 1789–1800.*** Gainesville, FL: University of Florida Press. A careful look at a pivotal period in the evolution of American militias.

Malcolm, Joyce Lee. 1994. ***To Keep and Bear Arms.*** Cambridge, MA: Harvard University Press. A controversial history of the British antecedents of the right to bear arms.

McPherson, James M. 1988. ***Battle Cry of Freedom.*** New York: Oxford University Press. A Pulitzer-Prize–winning history of the Civil War.

Michel, Lou, and Dan Herbeck. 2001. *American Terrorist.* New York: Regan Books. An account of the philosophies and actions of Oklahoma City bomber Timothy McVeigh, including his Second Amendment views.

Millett, Allan R., and Peter Maslowski. 1984. *For the Common Defense.* New York: Free Press. A comprehensive historical examination of the evolution of the American military.

Nisbet, Lee, ed. 1990. *The Gun Control Debate: You Decide.* Buffalo, NY: Prometheus Books. Reprints a variety of articles on the gun issue, including some on the Second Amendment.

Peltason, Jack W. 1988. *Corwin and Peltason's Understanding the Constitution.* New York: Holt, Rinehart, and Winston. A classic reference work on the meaning of the Constitution and its amendments.

Rakove, Jack N. 2000. "**The Second Amendment: The Highest Stage of Originalism.**" *Chicago-Kent Law Review* 76: 103–166. A definitive treatment of the interpretation of the Second Amendment through reliance on original intent or *originalism,* meaning an examination of the purposes and intentions of the drafters of the amendment.

Richardson, James D., ed. 1913. *Messages and Papers of the Presidents,* 11 vols. Washington, DC: Bureau of National Literature. The authoritative compilation of all published presidential documents.

Riker, William. 1979. *Soldiers of the States: The Role of the National Guard in American Democracy.* Salem, NH: Ayer Co. An examination of the militias and their evolution toward the National Guard.

Rossiter, Clinton. 1953. *Seedtime of the Republic.* New York: Harcourt, Brace, and World. The noted political historian's account of the philosophy behind the country's founding.

Rutland, Robert A. 1955. *The Birth of the Bill of Rights.* Chapel Hill, NC: University of North Carolina Press. A detailed analysis of the basis of the modern Bill of Rights.

Samaha, Joel. 1993. *Criminal Law.* Minneapolis/St. Paul: West Pub. Co. A standard text on criminal law that includes treatment of the common law basis of self defense.

Schwartz, Bernard. 1971. *The Bill of Rights: A Documentary History,* 2 vols. New York: Chelsea House. Combines analysis and primary documents to examine the Bill of Rights.

Schwoerer, Lois G. 2000. "**To Hold and Bear Arms: The English Perspective.**" *Chicago-Kent Law Review* 76: 27–60. A definitive account of the

British political and legal disputes concerning militias and the bearing of arms as these issues culminated in the British Bill of Rights.

Sexton, John, and Nat Brandt. 1986. *How Free Are We?* New York: M. Evans and Co. An examination of civil liberties and rights in the light of the bicentennial of the U.S. Constitution.

Shy, John. 1990. *A People Numerous and Armed.* Ann Arbor: University of Michigan Press. Detailed historical examination of early militias, noting that militia service was generally avoided by freedmen and others who enjoyed full political rights, and instead typically fell to those at colonial society's margins.

Skowronek, Stephen. 1982. *Building a New American State.* New York: Cambridge University Press. A sweeping examination of the rise of the modern state, including analysis of evolving military structures.

Snow, Donald M., and Dennis M. Drew. 1994. *From Lexington to Desert Storm.* Armonk, NY: M. E. Sharpe. A comprehensive description of all major American wars and military conflicts.

Spitzer, Robert J. 1998. *The Politics of Gun Control.* New York: Chatham House. A comprehensive political, policy, and legal analysis of all elements of the gun control issue.

———. 2000. **"Lost and Found: Researching the Second Amendment."** *Chicago-Kent Law Review* 76(1): 349–401. Analyzes the mostly-ignored scholarly provenance of writings on the Second Amendment as found in law journals.

Stern, Kenneth S. 1996. *A Force upon the Plain.* New York: Simon and Schuster. A detailed journalistic expose of the modern so-called militia movement.

Story, Joseph. 1987. *Commentaries on the Constitution.* Durham, NC: Carolina Academic Press. First published 1833. An early treatise on the meaning of the Constitution written by a Supreme Court member.

Subcommittee on the Constitution, Federalism, and Property Rights, Judiciary Committee, U.S. Senate. 1998. **"Whose Right to Keep and Bear Arms? The Second Amendment as a Source of Individual Rights."** 105th Cong., 2nd sess., hearing 23 September. Washington, DC: Government Printing Office. Compiled testimony and debate on the meaning of the Second Amendment.

Subcommittee on the Constitution, Judiciary Committee, U.S. Senate. 1982. **"The Right to Keep and Bear Arms."** 97th Cong., 2d sess. Washington, DC: Government Printing Office (February). Essays and selected testimony written in support of the individualist theory of the Second Amendment.

Sugarmann, Josh. 2001. *Every Handgun Is Aimed at You: The Case for Banning Handguns.* New York: The New Press. Argues for banning handguns based on an analysis of their impact on suicide rates, crime, effects on women, minorities, and young people, and includes consideration of constitutional questions.

"**Symposium on the Second Amendment: Fresh Looks.**" 2000. *Chicago-Kent Law Review* 76(1). A contemporary collection of ten articles all devoted to the meaning of the Second Amendment that summarize mainstream thinking and critiques of alternate views of the amendment.

Tatalovich, Raymond, and Byron Daynes, eds. 1998. *Moral Controversies in American Politics.* New York: M. E. Sharpe. An original collection of essays on the similarities found in various social regulatory issues, including gun control.

Utter, Glenn H. 1999. *Encyclopedia of Gun Control and Gun Rights.* Phoenix, AZ: Oryx Press. A single volume reference work composed of over 300 entries arranged alphabetically on all elements of the gun issue.

Veit, Helen E., Kenneth R. Bowling, and Charlene Bangs Bickford, eds. 1991. *Creating the Bill of Rights.* Baltimore: The Johns Hopkins University Press. A compilation of congressional debate in 1789 and 1790 concerning the Bill of Rights.

Vizzard, William J. 1997. *In the Crossfire: A Political History of the Bureau of Alcohol, Tobacco, and Firearms.* Boulder, CO: Lynne Rienner. A definitive examination of the ATF written by a former employee who has since joined the academic world.

———. 2000. *Shots in the Dark: The Policy, Politics, and Symbolism of Gun Control.* Lanham, MD: Rowman and Littlefield. A detailed look at the gun issue, focusing especially on recent legal enactments and the role of the Bureau of Alcohol, Tobacco, and Firearms.

Weatherup, Roy G. 1975. "**Standing Armies and Armed Citizens: An Historical Analysis of the Second Amendment.**" *Hastings Constitutional Law Quarterly* 2(Fall): 961–1001. Analysis linking the Second Amendment with militia activity.

Wiener, Frederick B. 1940. "**The Militia Clause of the Constitution.**" *Harvard Law Review* 54 (December): 181–220. An early, thorough treatment of the meaning of militias in law and history.

Wills, Garry. 1999. *A Necessary Evil.* New York: Simon and Schuster. This noted historian tackles a variety of myths concerning the Constitution, including the individualist and revolutionist views of the Second Amendment.

Windlesham, Lord. 1998. ***Politics, Punishment, and Populism.*** New York: Oxford University Press. A detailed examination of the gun control debate in the 1990s, providing special focus on the assault weapons ban of 1994.

INDEX

Academics for the Second Amendment (ASA), 75, 131, 240
Adams, Samuel, 15
Alcohol, Tobacco, and Firearms, Bureau of (ATF), 95, 96, 104, 108, 131, 237, 238
Alien and Sedition Acts, 29
American Bar Association, 76, 78, 132
American Firearms Association, 132
Anderson, Jack, 74
Antifederalists, 10, 23–28, 49–50, 124, 132
Anti-Semitism, 102, 105
Articles of Confederation, 20, 21, 23, 49, 60, 132
Aryan Nations, 103
Ashcroft, John, 119–122
Assault weapons, 96–100
Assault Weapons Ban of 1994, 11, 81, 84, 96–100, 103, 132–133, 240

Background checks. *See* Brady Handgun Violence Prevention Act of 1993
Baker, James Jay, 119

Bear arms, meaning, 6–7, 53, 55, 147. *See also* Second Amendment
Bell Campaign, The, 133
Bellesiles, Michael, 124–125
Bentsen, Lloyd, 98
Bill of Rights, ix–xi, xiii, xv, xvi, xvii, xix, 8–9, 23, 24–28, 57 81, 133
    opposition to, 25–26
Black, Hugo, xiv, 70
Bonnicksen, Andrea L., 69–70
Booth, John Wilkes, 60
Brady Campaign to Prevent Gun Violence. *See* Handgun Control, Inc.
Brady Handgun Violence Prevention Act of 1993, 11, 81, 84, 90–96, 103, 110–112, 134, 240
Brady, James, 91
Brady, Sarah, 91, 134
Branch Davidian Compound raid. *See* Waco raid
Brant, Irving, 42
British Army, 17–18
British Bill of Rights, xvi, 14–15, 134–135
British heritage, 9, 13–15, 60

Brooks, Jack, 93, 99
Buchanan, Pat, 75
Bullets, armor-piercing, 118
Burger, Warren, 6
Burke, Edmund, xii
Bush, George Herbert Walker, 92–93, 98, 108, 114–115, 127
Bush, George W., 117, 119, 127, 241

Calling Forth Act of 1792, 62, 135, 156–159
Cardozo, Benjamin, 115–116
Cartwright, John, 62, 63
Catholicism, 13–14, 17
Center to Prevent Handgun Violence, 77, 135
Cheney, Dick, 118
Christian Front, 102, 135
Cincinnatus Complex, 16, 135
Citizens Committee for the Right to Keep and Bear Arms, 75, 135
Civil Rights Act of 1866, 68, 174
Civil War, 30, 32, 42, 51, 61, 66, 69, 84, 102, 124, 165
Clinton, Bill, 93, 94, 98, 100, 115, 240
Clymer, George, 26
Coalition to Stop Gun Violence, 136
Collective view. See Second Amendment
Columbine shooting, 1–2, 3, 100–101, 108, 117, 136, 241
Commerce power, 35
Common law, 58–59, 73, 136
Congress, U.S., 2, 4, 7–9, 20–21, 26–28, 32, 62, 63, 66, 79–80, 89, 91–102, 156–165

Constitutional Convention of 1787, ix–x, 13, 20, 54, 63
Constitutional law, 137
Continental Army, 9
Cooley, Thomas, 42
Coolidge, Calvin, 80
Crane, Philip, 89
Crime, 58, 81, 83, 99
Cromwell, Oliver, 14
Cummings, Homer, 121
Cummings, Sam R., 113

Danforth, John, 104
Declaration of Independence of 1776, ix–x, xiv, 17–18, 137
Democratic party. See political parties
Dick Act. See Militia Act of 1903
Dicta, 37–38, 137, 152
Douglas, William O., 37, 70
Dual citizenship, 137

Emerson, Timothy Joe, 112
European history, 13–15

Farrand, Max, 21
Federalism, xv, 23, 28, 112, 138
Federalist Papers, 22, 138
Federalists, 10, 23–28, 49–50, 124, 132, 138
Feighan, Edward, 91
Finkelman, Paul, 54
Firearms Owners Protection Act of 1986, 122, 239
Fletcher, Bob, 106
Foley, Tom, 98
Force Act of 1870, 33, 166
Fortier, Michael, 108

Fourteenth Amendment, xv, 10, 64–71, 120, 138–139, 236. *See also* Incorporation
Frederick, Karl T., 121
Freedman's Bureau Act of 1866, 68, 69

Glendon, Mary Ann, 82–83
Glorious Revolution of 1688, 14
Gore, Al, 119
Gottlieb, Alan, 75
Griswold, Erwin, 50
Gun Control Act of 1968, 38, 81, 116, 238
Gun control bill of 1999, 100–102
Gun culture, 139
Gun deaths, 2
Gun debate of the 1920s, 77–80
Gun Owners of America (GOA), 75, 139
Gun ownership, xx, 5–6
Gun show loophole, 1–2, 95–96, 101, 139
Gun-Free School Zones Act of 1990, 112
Guns, rarity in early times, 30, 124

Halbrook, Stephen, 52–53, 66, 68, 76
Hamilton, Alexander, 22
Handgun ban, 78–79
Handgun Control, Inc. (HCI), 90, 91, 101, 139, 238
Handgun purchase waiting period and background check, 90–96
Handgun sales, 95
Harlan, John M., 70
Hays, Stuart, 51
Henigan, Dennis, 77, 140

Hennard, George J., 97, 239–240
Henry, Patrick, 24, 52
Heston, Charlton, 115, 116, 117, 140, 241
Hitler, Adolph, 107, 236
Hofstadter, Richard, 81
Howard, Jacob M., 66
Hunting, 53–54
  as individual right, 11, 52–56, 66–67
  irony, xix–xx
  legal hunting-sporting tradition, 6
Hyde, Henry, 98–99

Incorporation, xiv–xv, 33, 34, 39, 40, 41–42, 64–72, 140, 166, 171–172, 189, 197, 236, 237. *See also* Fourteenth Amendment
Individualist view, 52–56, 66–67, 75, 112–115, 119–125, 140. *See also* Second Amendment
Insurrection. *See* right of revolution

Jackson, Robert H., xvi
Jacobs, Andrew, 99
James II, 14
Jefferson, Thomas, ix–x, xvi, xvii, 17, 62, 63
Judicial review, xvii
Judiciary Committee, U.S. Senate, 106, 122

Kates, Don, 53
Kennedy, John F., 238
Kennedy, Robert, 238
Killeen, Texas shooting, 97, 98
King, Jr., Martin Luther, 238

King, Rufus, 29
Knox, Neal, 241
Koresh, David, 104
Ku Klux Klan, 60, 102, 141, 152, 165

LaPierre, Wayne, 3, 108, 141, 240
Law journals, 113–115
Lawyer's Second Amendment Society (LSAS), 76, 141, 240
Layton, Frank, 35, 201
Lazare, Daniel, 123, 125
Letters of Marque and Reprisal, 7–8
Levinson, Sanford, 71–73
Lexington and Concord, 18, 107
Liberty, xii, 13–24, 61, 79
Loyalty oaths, 19

Macaulay, Thomas, 14, 15
Macdonald, Andrew, 105
Madison, James, ix–x, xvi, xvii, 21, 22–23, 26, 29, 54, 57, 62, 63
Malcolm, Joyce Lee, 125
Marshall, John, xiii
Marshall, Thurgood, 37
Martin, Luther, 24
Mason, George, 21, 24, 125
McPherson, James, 30
McReynolds, James, 36, 201
McVeigh, Timothy, 60, 107–108, 142, 150, 240, 241
Media, 62–64, 123–125
Metaksa, Tanya, 108
Metzenbaum, Howard, 91
Michigan militia, 108
Militia Act of 1903, 31, 142–143, 160, 237
Militia movement, modern, 74, 75, 101–109, 144, 152
Militias, 5, 9–10, 15–16, 29, 50, 52–53, 55, 56, 69, 143

defined, 16, 28–32, 34, 109, 126
old 28–32
organized or select, 16, 153
purposes, 61–62, 120, 156–159, 193–197, 202–206
slaves, 17
state regulations, 106–107
unorganized or general, 16, 152
Miller, Jack, 35, 201
Million Mom March, 241
Minutemen, 102, 105, 143–144
Montana militia, 106
Morris, Gouverneur, 22

National Alliance, 105
National Defense Act of 1916, 31, 144, 237
National Firearms Act of 1934, 35, 37, 121, 202, 237–238
National Guard, 17, 31–32, 40, 80, 142–143, 153, 194, 237
National Instant Criminal Background Check System (NICS), 92, 95, 111
National Rifle Association (NRA), 3, 7, 51, 73–75, 76, 77, 81, 84, 85, 90, 91, 92, 93, 95, 97, 101, 103, 108, 111, 115, 117–119, 121, 144, 236, 239, 240
Native Americans, 13, 29, 58
Neo-Nazi groups, 102, 105, 108
New York Times, 123
Nichols, Terry, 107–108, 144
Nixon, Richard, 50
NRA. *See* National Rifle Association

Oklahoma City bombing, 107–108, 145, 240
Olson, Joseph, 76

Olson, Norman, 106
Organized militia. *See* National Guard
Oswald, Lee Harvey, 60
Oxford English Dictionary, 6–7

Papism. *See* Catholicism
Paramilitary groups. *See* Militia movement, modern
Peltason, Jack, 42
People, The, meaning, 56–58, 145
Persian Gulf War, 107
Pierce, William. *See* Macdonald, Andrew
Political parties, 83–84, 118–119
  platforms on gun control, 227–234
Pound, Roscoe, 61
Pratt, Larry, 75
Preferred freedoms doctrine, 115–116
Presser, Herman, 33, 189–200
Prohibition, 78
Protocols of the Elders of Zion, The, 102, 105, 146
Purdy, Patrick, 97, 239

Quesnay, Francois, 16

Rakove, Jack, 52
Randolph, Edmund, 22
Rational basis test, 38, 116
Reagan, Ronald, 84, 91, 127, 239
Rehnquist, William, 58
Republican party. *See* political parties
Revolution. *See* right of revolution
Revolutionary War, xii, 9, 18–19, 59–60, 116

Right of revolution, 10–11, 51, 59–62, 71–72, 141, 147, 156–159
Right to bear arms. *See* Bear arms, meaning
Rights talk and rhetoric, 11, 81–84, 101, 115–125, 147
Roosevelt, Franklin D., 80, 102, 121
Rousseau, Jean-Jacques, 16
Ruby Ridge raid, 103, 104, 107, 109, 148, 240
Rutland, Robert A., 42

Safire, William, 123
Schworer, Lois, 15
Second Amendment, x, xix, 3, 40–42, 148
  alternate views, 51–59
  bear arms, meaning, 6–7, 53, 55, 147
  Bill of Rights, 24–28
  British antecedents, 13–15
  chronology, 235–241
  colonial experience, 15–19
  Constitution, 20–23
  Federalist-Antifederalist debate, 23
  Fourteenth Amendment, 64–71
  law journals, 113–115
  legal versus political, 3–4
  liberalism-conservatism, 123–124
  lower court rulings, 38–42, 43, 110–113
  meaning, 4–5, 6–9, 49–50, 62–63, 84
  meaning of the people, 56–58, 120–121
  media, 62–64, 123–125
  old militia system, 28–32
  origins, 13–47

politics, 71–81
rallying right-wing movements, 106, 109
rational basis test, 38
right of revolution, 59–62, 71–72, 106
rights talk and rhetoric, 11, 81–84, 101, 115–125, 147, 148
self-defense, 58–59, 71–72
Southern states, 25
state court rulings, 54–56
Supreme Court rulings, 32–38
symbolism, 31, 126
textbook view, 42
wording, 25–28
Second Amendment Foundation (SAF), 75, 148
Self-defense, 58–59, 71, 78, 148, 207
Shapiro, Walter, 123
Shays's Rebellion, 21, 149
Sherman, Roger, 26
Shields, Pete, 238
Shotgun, sawed-off, 35–37, 200–201
Silver Shirts, 102, 149
Skinheads, 60
Skowronek, Stephen, 31
Slavery, 19, 25, 69
Soldier of Fortune, 105
Staggers, Harley O., 92
Standing armies, 9–10, 15–16, 20, 149
State court rulings, 54–56
State right-to-bear-arms provisions, 55, 65–66, 218–227
Statutory law, 149
Stockton shooting, 97, 239
Story, Joseph, 42
Straw buyer, of guns, 2, 149–150
Sugarmann, Josh, 152

Tenth Amendment, 65, 111, 150

Third Amendment, 50, 64, 150
Thomas, Clarence, 111–112, 113
Treason, 61. *See also* right of revolution
Tribe, Laurence, 123
Trochmann, John E., 106
Turgot, Jacques, 16
Turner Diaries, The, 105, 107, 150

Uniform firearms laws, 80
Uniform Militia Act of 1792, 28–29, 30, 151, 159–165
United Nations, 104–105, 106
United States Revolver Association, 79
USA Today, 125

Vigilantes. *See* Militia movement, modern
Violence Policy Center, 152
Virginia Declaration of Rights, 15–16, 26
Volokh, Eugene, 124–125
Voltaire, Francois-Marie, 16

Waco raid, 60, 103, 104, 107, 109, 134, 152, 240
Waite, Morrison, 33, 166
Wall Street Journal, 123, 124
War of 1812, 30, 152–153
Washington, George, xii, 15, 18, 22
views on militias, 18–19, 153
Weathermen, 102
Weaver, Randy, 103, 153, 240
Whiskey Rebellion, 29
Wills, Garry, 53, 71
Woods, William, 34, 190
World War I, 37

Zachary, Roy, 102

About the Author

Robert J. Spitzer (Ph.D. Cornell, 1980) is Distinguished Service Professor of Political Science at the State University of New York, College at Cortland. His books include *The Presidency and Public Policy* (1983), *The Right to Life Movement and Third Party Politics* (1987), *The Presidential Veto* (1988), *The Bicentennial of the U.S. Constitution* (1990), *President and Congress* (1993), *Media and Public Policy* (1993), *The Politics of Gun Control* (1995; 2nd ed. 1998), *Politics and Constitutionalism* (2000), and *Essentials of American Politics* (coauthored, 2001). He is also Series Editor for the book series "American Constitutionalism" for SUNY Press and is on the Board of Editors for the *Encyclopedia of Guns in American Society* (ABC-CLIO). Spitzer is the author of more than 150 articles and essays appearing in many journals, books, and other publications, on a variety of U.S. political subjects. He currently serves as president of the Presidency Research Group of the American Political Science Association. He also served as a member of the New York State Commission on the Bicentennial of the U.S. Constitution and has testified before Congress on several occasions. Most recently, he testified before the U.S. Senate Judiciary Committee in 1998 on gun control and the meaning of the Second Amendment.